Two Hundred Years of Pushkin

Volume I

'Pushkin's Secret': Russian Writers Reread and Rewrite Pushkin

Studies in Slavic Literature and Poetics

Volume XXXVII

Edited by

J.J. van Baak
R. Grübel
A.G.F. van Holk
W.G. Weststeijn

TWO HUNDRED YEARS OF PUSHKIN

VOLUME I
'PUSHKIN'S SECRET': RUSSIAN WRITERS REREAD AND REWRITE PUSHKIN

Edited by

Joe Andrew
Professor of Russian Literature
Keele University

and

Robert Reid
Reader in Russian
Keele University

Amsterdam - New York, NY 2003

The paper on which this book is printed meets the requirements of "ISO 9706:1994, Information and documentation - Paper for documents - Requirements for permanence".

ISBN: 90-420-0874-1 vols. I-III
ISBN: 90-420-0884-9 vol. I
©Editions Rodopi B.V., Amsterdam – New York, NY 2003
Printed in The Netherlands

Contents

Preface	v
Notes on Contributors	vii

JOE ANDREW
Introduction: Pushkin's Secret — 1

JOE ANDREW
'[She] was brought up on French novels and, consequently, was in love': Russian Writers Reading and Writing Pushkin — 15

LYUBOV KISELEVA
Pushkin in the Mirror of Shakhovskoi — 37

SANDER BROUWER
The Bridegroom Who Did Not Come: Social and Amorous Unproductivity from Pushkin to the Silver Age — 49

BARBARA LÖNNQVIST
The Pushkin Text in *Anna Karenina* — 67

HENRIETTA MONDRY
On the Subjectivism in Pushkin's Universality: The Case of Rozanov — 77

DIANA L. BURGIN
Tsvetaeva's Three Pushkins — 91

CHRISTOPH VELDHUES
Love and Death in Pushkin's *The Stone Guest* and Nabokov's *Death* — 105

JUSTIN DOHERTY
The Pushkin Contexts of Georgii Ivanov's *Disintegration of the Atom*   121

JEKATERINA YOUNG
Dovlatov's *Sanctuary* and Pushkin   135

VALENTINA POLUKHINA
Pushkin and Brodsky: the Art of Self-deprecation   153

STEPHANIE SANDLER
Pushkin among Contemporary Poets: Self and Song in Sedakova   175

HELENA GOSCILO
Casting and Recasting the Caucasian Captive   195

Index   209

Preface

The chapters in the present volume, like those in the companion volumes, *Two Hundred Years of Pushkin. Volume II: Alexander Pushkin. Myth and Monument*, and *Two Hundred Years of Pushkin. Volume III: Pushkin's Legacy*, arise primarily from a conference 'Two Hundred Years of Pushkin: A Bicentennial Conference', held under the auspices of the Neo-Formalist Circle at Mansfield College, Oxford from 13-15 September 1999. The editors of these volumes warmly thank all participants in that conference for their contributions. We are also grateful to those who assisted us at the conference and in the preparation of these three volumes, especially Pearl Aldridge of Mansfield College; Angela Merryweather and David Sherwood of Keele University.

A couple of technical points need to be mentioned. The chapters in this volume are arranged chronologically, by date of the successor authors. Quotations from Pushkin and other writers are mainly given in English; where reference to the original was felt to be necessary (primarily poetry) cyrillic is used. The system of transliteration is that of the Library of Congress, without diacritics.

Joe Andrew and Robert Reid
Keele University   2002

Notes on Contributors

Joe Andrew is Professor of Russian Literature at Keele University, where he has worked since 1972. His main research interests are nineteenth-century Russian literature, feminist approaches to literature, and women writers. He has published numerous articles in these fields, as well as several monographs, the most recent of which are *Narrative & Desire in Russian Literature, 1822-1849. The Feminine & the Masculine* (1993) and *Russian Women's Shorter Fiction. An Anthology, 1835-1860* (1996). He is also co-chair of the Neo-Formalist Circle, as well as co-editor of its journal, *Essays in Poetics*.

Sander Brouwer has been Assistant Professor of Russian Literature at the University of Groningen since 1990. His publications include: *Character in the Short Prose of Ivan Sergeevič Turgenev*, 'Russian Medieval Concepts of Paradise' and 'Problems of Carnivalization and Novelization in Russian Literature'.

Diana L. Burgin is Professor of Russian at the University of Massachussetts in Boston. She is the author of *Richard Burgin, a Life in Verse*, a biographical narrative poem about her relationship with her father and how she came to be a Slavist. She has written articles on Pushkin, Tolstoi, Dostoevskii, Bulgakov, Parnok and Solzhenitsyn. She has also translated Parnok.

Justin Doherty is Lecturer in Russian at Trinity College, Dublin. His principal research interests are in Russian literature and culture of the early twentieth century, and literature of the Russian emigration. Apart from his book on acmeism, *The Acmeist Movement in Russian Poetry* (1995), he has published articles on Gumilev and other acmeists, Pushkin, and Georgii Ivanov.

Helena Goscilo, UCIS Professor of Slavic at the University of Pittsburgh, has authored and edited more than a dozen books, including *Balancing Acts* (1989, 1991), *Skirted Issues: the Discreteness and Indiscretions of Russian Women's Prose* (1992), *Fruits of Her Plume* (1993), *Lives in Transit: Recent Russian Women's Writing* (1995), Russia*Women*Culture,with Beth Holmgren (1996), *Dehexing Sex: Russian Womanhood during and after Glasnost* (1996), *TNT: The Explosive World of T.Tolstaya's Fiction* (1996), and *Russian Culture in the 1990s* (2000). She is currently working on a cultural study of the New Russians (with Nadezhda Azhgikhina) and a volume on Russian book illustrators (with Beth Holmgren).

Lyubov Kiseleva is Professor of Russian Literature and Head of the Department of Russian and Slavic Philology at the University of Tartu, Estonia. Her doctorate was entitled *The Idea of National Identity in Russian Literature between 1807 and 1812* (Tartu, 1982). Her main fields of teaching and research are eighteenth- and nineteenth-century Russian literature and culture, the history of the Russian theatre, the semiotics of Russian culture, and the problems of national identity and multicultural societies. She is the author of 70 publications, and editor-in-chief of the *Trudy po russkoi i slavianskoi filologii, Blokovskii sbornik,* and *Pushkinskie chtenia* (Tartu). Professor Kiseleva is also adviser of the ACLS Humanities Program.

Barbara Lönnqvist is Professor of Russian Language and Literature at Åbo Akademi, the Swedish-language university in Åbo/Turku, Finland. Her main fields of research have been the modernist poets Khlebnikov, Pasternak, Akhmatova, Tsvetaeva, and, more recently, the works of Lev Tolstoi. Professor Lönnqvist is especially interested in the relationship between folklore and literature. Her recent publications include *Mirozdanie v slove. Poetika Velimira Khlebnikova,* and 'A Text within a Text: the Dream in *Anna Karenina*' and 'The English Theme in *Anna Karenina*'.

Henrietta Mondry is Associate Professor in Russian at the University of Canterbury, New Zealand. She received an MA degree from the Latvian State University (1975) and a PhD degree from the University of the Witwatersrand, Johannesburg (1984), where she taught in the department of Russian Studies between 1981 and 1994 prior to New Zealand. She has published books and articles on Dostoevskii, Tolstoi, Gleb Uspenskii, Leontiev and Rozanov among others.

Valentina Polukhina is Emeritus Professor of Russian Literature at Keele University. She specializes in Modern Russian Poetry and is the author of several major studies of Brodsky, including *Joseph Brodsky: A Poet for our Time* (1989), and *Brodsky through the Eyes of His Contemporaries* (1992). She is also the editor of *Brodsky's Genres* (1995), *Brodsky as a Critic* (2000) and *Joseph Brodsky: Selected Interviews* (2000), as well as co-editor, with Lev Loseff, of *Brodsky's Poetics and Aesthetics* (1990) and *Joseph Brodsky: the Art of a Poem* (1999). She is also principal compiler, with Ulle Pärli, of *The Dictionary of Brodsky's Tropes* (1995), and editor of several bilingual collections of poetry by Sedakova, Oleg Prokofiev, Prigov and Rein.

Robert Reid was a lecturer at Queen's University, Belfast before moving to Keele in 1989 where he is now Reader in Russian Studies. His research interests centre on Russian romanticism, particularly Pushkin and Lermontov. His publications in this area include *Problems of Russian Romanticism* and monographs on Pushkin's *Mozart and Salieri* and Lermontov's *A Hero of Our Time*, as well as a number of articles and essays. Since coming to Keele, he has co-edited the journal *Essays in Politics* to which he also regularly contributes translations of Russian poetry.

Stephanie Sandler is Professor of Slavic Languages and Literatures at Harvard University, having taught for nearly twenty years at Amherst College. She has written on Pushkin and on myths of Pushkin in Russian culture, and has recently edited *Rereading Russian Poetry* (1999), and co-edited with Laura Engelstein *Self and Story in Russian History* (2000).

Christoph Veldhues was Assistant Professor in the Department of Slavic Studies at the Ruhr-Universität, Bochum, and now heads the Language Department at the Goethe Institute (German Cultural Centre) in Ankara, Turkey. In Slavistics, he has published widely on theoretical issues, from an enhanced Russian Formalist perspective, using narratology, literary evolution and popular literature. He has applied these theories to, amongst others, Dostoevskii, Leskov, Fet, Makanin and, in particular, Tynianov, who is also the subject of his recently accepted *Habilitation* to be published in 2003 under the title *Formalist Authorial Functionalism: How Tynjanov's Pushkin is Made*.

Jekaterina Young is Senior Lecturer in the Department of Russian Studies, The University of Manchester and editor of the bi-annual academic journal *Slavonica*. Her recent publications include 'Narrativnaia struktura Zony', 'Dovlatov's Compromise: Journalism, Fiction and Documentary', 'Dovlatov's Reception of Salinger', and 'Dovlatov's *Sanctuary* and Pushkin'.

Introduction: Pushkin's Secret

by

JOE ANDREW

Pushkin died when his powers were at their fullest development and he undoubtedly took to his grave some great secret.
And now, in his absence, we are trying to divine this secret.
Fedor Dostoevskii[1]

Pushkin's 'secret' - and the notion does indeed powerfully suggest itself at some stage to all his readers - lies in the very openness of his art, in what Blok called its 'secret freedom': the freedom both to be transformed by the vision of later writers and at the same time totally separated from them.
John Bayley[2]

As these two epigraphs suggest, the relationship between Pushkin and later Russian culture is central to our understanding of him and his works. His impact on the culture was immediate and enormous, and is vital to that culture to the present day. Yet in tracing the development of his significance for Russia so many paradoxes emerge that the answers to the questions 'Who is Pushkin for Russia?' and 'What is Pushkin for Russia?' keep changing fundamentally. Even in his own lifetime he was seen as a Protean figure,[3] and this same epithet may be applied to his posthumous persona and reputation. It is the purpose, then, of this present volume to attempt to answer, *inter alia*, the questions as to who and what Pushkin was for his contemporaries and successors, and, indeed, what he might still become. The primary emphases in the following chapters will be on the specific, even technical ways later writers related to and used Pushkin's works; but there will also be some discussion of the myth and cult of Pushkin in Russian literary culture. In these discussions, therefore, we too will also seek to emulate Dostoevskii, and attempt to divine Pushkin's 'great secret'.

In fact, thanks to the work of Paul Debreczeny and Marcus Levitt,[4] we already have a fairly full picture of the uses (and abuses!) of Pushkin from his contemporary period to the present day. His relationship with the Decembrists, for example, has long been a *locus communis* of Pushkin scholarship, and, not least because of Soviet propagandistic distortions, has been an area infused with as much myth as science, but, thanks to Debreczeny's recent cool re-appraisal of the issue, we are now able to ascertain the extent to which Pushkin's work actually did influence his contemporaries' political thinking.[5] It seems clear now that Pushkin did so influence contemporary readers, but the evidence as it stands 'makes the perception of Pushkin's early political poems extremely complicated'.[6] In a more general way, Pushkin's work came to be used as 'life's guide'. Just as the first chapter proper by Joe Andrew will show that fictional heroines followed Tatiana in seeking to discover the truth about their lives from reading, sometimes with catastrophic effects, so too 'real life' readers used Pushkin's work as a key ingredient in the 'formation of the self'.[7] Memoir literature from the middle of the nineteenth century reveals that more often than not the cherished volume which gave sustenance to the personal development of the memoirist (including the writer Nadezhda Sokhanskaia) was Pushkin, and that the key ingredient was the way in which Pushkin nourished the *inner self*. (As Diana Burgin will show, Tsvetaeva a hundred years later was to use Pushkin for this purpose amongst others: he was the path which led to her self-discovery).

The Protean nature of Pushkin's influence was apparent in other ways even within his own lifetime. As the chapter by Lyubov Kiseleva makes clear, stage adaptations of Pushkin's works began almost as soon as these works appeared. Similarly, they were immediately set to music: *The Caucasian Captive*, for example, was staged as a ballet in 1823, only a year after its first publication, and there are now at least 103 operas based on Pushkin's work.[8] More 'political' adaptations, or interpretations of his work were also soon being made. The century and a half or so since his death has been marked by competing, and utterly contradictory attempts to appropriate Pushkin for a given party (in the broadest sense) position. From the mid-1820s, if not earlier, selective readings of his works have been adduced to present 'my/our' Pushkin. Perhaps the first radical attempt in this direction was the in/famous line developed by Chernyshevskii, Dobroliubov and Pisarev in the 1850s and 1860s, which claimed that Pushkin was now a poet of the past, too much the aristocrat, too much the 'poet' indeed, insufficiently the 'citizen'. Indeed, even within his own lifetime the perception had emerged that his influence was on the wane.[9]

Equally, the state, whether Tsarist or Soviet, began to appropriate Pushkin, not least by virtually flooding the market with his works, especially at the frequent jubilees of his birth or death. Thus, in 1887, fifty years after his demise, between 12 per cent to 18 per cent of all books published were by Pushkin, while 12 years later, at his first centenary, the government distributed free editions to schoolchildren.[10] That is, by the end of the nineteenth century, the battle had been well and truly engaged to determine who would 'own' Pushkin; by this time, indeed, a little earlier, his historical persona had entered the realm of myth.

We cannot be certain when the mythologization of Pushkin began. Even within his life, attempts were made to elevate him to the 'status of poet laureate' by Kireevskii in 1828, a tendency furthered by Gogol in his 1834 article 'A Few Words about Pushkin', in which he declared that Pushkin's 'very life is entirely Russian'.[11] These processes accelerated upon his tragic and premature death in

1837. This event unleashed massive public grief, and a hagiographic lexicon began to be applied to his apparent martyrdom. Already, Pushkin had become a *strastoterpets*, one who had suffered a kind of passion.[12] Significantly, it was at this juncture that Pushkin's life (and now death), and his person began the process of becoming the key elements in the creation of the national myths and cults surrounding the poet. Certainly, they were the factors which were especially important in spreading his fame amongst the lesser educated.[13]

The twin tracks revealed here, that is, the attempt to elevate Pushkin to the position of national poet, and the hagiographic treatment of his life, marriage and death, both of which began in the last decade of his short life, developed apace after 1837. Belinskii's monumental series of articles of the 1840s have clear notes of 'author-worship',[14] and in them Pushkin's works are treated almost as if Holy Writ. By the 1850s, 'author-worship' had become, for Druzhinin at least, 'idolatory',[15] and his article, 'A.S. Pushkin and the Latest Edition of His Works', was only one of the salvoes in the critical war that broke out with the appearance of Pavel Annenkov's new edition of Pushkin's works, starting in 1855. Four years later Apollon Grigorev coined the phrase that has since dominated debates on the culturological significance of both Pushkin's life and works: 'Pushkin is our everything' ('Пушкин - наше все').[16] This phrase and its multifarious implications will be a key *leitmotif* in the present collection.

For the next two decades, however, the dominant voice was to be that of the utilitarian radicals, led by Pisarev, who as already noted, (in)famously 'rubbished' Pushkin. This denigration of the national poet was, of course, all to change in the extraordinary events of June 1880, during the remarkable 'Pushkin Celebrations' surrounding the unveiling of a long-desired monument to him in Moscow, most famous for Dostoevskii's ecstatic appropriation of him in the speech which ends with the words from which we have taken our title. Whether one agrees or disagrees with the later writer's 'prophetic' interpretation, the Pushkin landscape could never be the same again, and we are still experiencing the reverberations from his address.[17]

In 1887 and again in 1899 the deification of Pushkin reached unprecedented levels, and there were even riots at the bookstalls in 1887 when his works came out of copyright.[18] One of the many paradoxes of the Pushkin myth is, of course, revealed in these processes. The more widely disseminated and popular his works were, the less clear his image became, the less was 'his great secret' actually uncovered. Indeed, if the Tsarist authorities had tried to take Pushkin as their own in 1887 and 1899, they were far surpassed by the 'sovietization' of him, especially in the centenary year of 1937. Now it 'was not merely a question of holding a tremendous celebration for Pushkin's anniversary but of establishing, literally, a "Pushkin Year"'.[19] In the many speeches and articles of that year, Pushkin is treated as a quasi-divinity, and these tendencies were to be reinforced in 1949, while even Platonov hailed Pushkin as a unique prophet of the Russian people.[20]

By the 1960s the Pushkin industry was in full spate. Indeed, anyone entering Russian literary scholarship in the 1960s and 1970s, and this includes most contributors to this volume, will be familiar with the Soviet apotheoses of the man who had become much more than a mere national poet. At the same time, however, attempts had begun to strike a more accurate note, to get the balance right, and it is certainly part of the project of this present volume to continue the processes of 'desacralization', by exploring the more purely literary 'secrets' that later writers had sought to unearth in their great predecessor. In this regard, we follow, *inter alia*, Siniavskii's attempt at 'liberating Pushkin from the deadening myth of greatness'.[21] Indeed, Siniavskii's aim, as formulated by one of the contributors to this book, Stephanie Sandler, in an earlier piece, could be adopted as our own. As Sandler puts it, Siniavskii 'rethinks the clichés of the Pushkin cult, invents a new language for reading Pushkin and transforms what has become a nearly predictable topic of Russian literary criticism into a source of surprise and pleasure'.[22]

Part of this search for sources of 'surprise and pleasure' is, precisely, to retrace the pathways by which Russian writers and thinkers have addressed the Pushkin myth. We see this in the chapters by Mondry, Burgin, Doherty, Young and Sandler. In the theoretical opening remarks for her study of Rozanov's radical use of Pushkin's persona, Henrietta Mondry problematizes exactly the issues confronting us in this volume, namely 'the problem of the way he is perceived'. In reviewing recent studies of the perception of Pushkin in Russian culture, Mondry identifies Rozanov as taking a 'consciously subjectivist' approach, and her work results in many illuminating insights into Rozanov's thinking, as well as to some stimulating repositionings of Pushkin's identity. According to Sandler, in an earlier study of the role Pushkin played in Tsvetaeva's life and work, the twentieth-century poet had fought hard against the emerging cult of Pushkin, more so than any of her contemporaries, with the exception of Maiakovskii.[23] In the present collection, Diana Burgin, while not arguing against Sandler's position as such, traces the development of Tsvetaeva's extremely intimate relationship with her predecessor. She begins her chapter: 'Although there is hardly a Russian poet who has not claimed a posthumous creative and personal intimacy with Pushkin, Marina Tsvetaeva's takes second place to none in its fervour, durability and range'. For Burgin, *pace* Sandler, Pushkin did acquire 'mythic-hero status', if only through his marriage to Natalia Goncharova. The myth of Pushkin is also created in Tsvetaeva's *My Pushkin*, in which Pushkin is named 146 times, primarily in the nominative. Consequently, Burgin concludes, Tsvetaeva's relationship is not only the most intimate, but also the most mystical, and mythical.

Justin Doherty reads Georgii Ivanov's *Disintegration of the Atom*, published exactly 100 years after Pushkin's death, primarily along an intertextual route, but the spirit of Pushkin the man and the myth also is seen to imbue Ivanov's work. In Doherty's view, *Disintegration* stands both as 'an anti-commemoration of the Pushkin centenary, and equally a fraught meditation on Pushkin's culturological significance'. Thus, on the one hand, Ivanov may be read as an early exemplar of the tradition of 'desacralization'; at the same time, however, the Pushkinian 'lucidity' which forms the main *leitmotif* of Doherty's discourse, comes to stand as a beacon of life and hope 'in the face of universal negation' which Ivanov, in Doherty's reading, had sought to confront.

By the 1980s the move to counteract the excesses of Tsarist/Soviet deification was beginning to gather momentum, and Jekaterina Young locates Dovlatov's *Sanctuary* within this movement: an element of her reading is to see the work as part of the new irreverent, deflationary counter-balancing of Stalinist excesses. More broadly, her account of Dovlatov problematizes the socio-political and culturological significance of Pushkin in the late twentieth century. Stephanie Sandler, who, as we have seen, had already addressed these issues in her excellent reading of Siniavskii's *Strolls with Pushkin*, returns in part to this subject in her account of Olga Sedakova's relationship with Pushkin.

In 1996 Sedakova had already encapsulated many of the issues we are currently considering: 'Russian thought tries to find itself and its future in its love for Pushkin, as if standing before a fortune-teller's mirror'.[24] Are we here any further on than Dostoevskii's 'great secret' which is buried with the national poet? Well, yes and no. David Bethea has addressed these issues in both *Puškin Today* and his more recent *Realizing Metaphors*. Pushkin, Bethea suggests, is 'an ever-emerging cultural myth and point of reference to which other writers have had to return, almost hypnotically, in order to resolve the "anxiety of [his] influence"'.[25] Again, Pushkin 'has become in the context of Russian/Soviet Pushkin studies what Apollon Grigoriev first identified as "our everything" (*nashe vse*) - the father figure ... [the] culture's "origin without origins"'.[26] At the same time, however, many writers have approached Pushkin not so much 'hypnotically', but through rather more rational, conscious reading strategies. These strategies form the main basis for most of the following chapters, and, for the remainder of this *Introduction*, I will focus on what these strategies were and are.

Once more we need to start with Grigorev, although here with a very different emphasis. In assessing the varying reading/re-writing strategies adopted by his successors, 'Pushkin is our everything' verges perilously on 'Pushkin is anything you want to make him into'! He becomes, in other words, a kind of blank screen on to which any image may be projected, or, to switch metaphors, a gold-mine to be plundered almost at will, and to suit the later writer's own very different agenda. What might Pushkin become? For Tsvetaeva, for example, he acted as a kind of spiritual guide, a Virgil to her Dante, even as a protector: 'nothing is frightening with Pushkin as company', she exclaimed in 1921. As Diana Burgin shows, Tsvetaeva's reading of Pushkin was essentially a process of self-discovery, of self-revelation: Pushkin's secret, in other words, becomes *her* secret. In turn, he becomes her object of desire, and, in the end, her 'intimacy' with him becomes self-identification. In truth, this leads to Pushkin appearing in some very strange guises: he is 'Her Black Rebel Pushkin' which, as Burgin allows, fades into 'a Pushkin in blackface, rampaging in "white infuriate rage"'.

Later, Burgin recalls that Tsvetaeva had also written to Pasternak of Pushkin's putative Jewishness, and this leads us back to Mondry's reading of Rozanov's Pushkin. To begin with, Mondry too goes back to Grigorev: 'From Grigorev's "Pushkin is our everything" Pushkin becomes *Pushkin as everything*' (Mondry's emphasis). In essence, Mondry argues, Rozanov very clearly, in his 'consciously subjectivist' interpretation, used Pushkin to corroborate his own ideas. As Mondry puts it, 'Rozanov as an individual in his interpretation of Pushkin expressed two *idées fixes* of his world-view - the theme of Jewry and Judaism and the theory of sex'.

Yet, we should be careful not to assign Rozanov and his (ab)use of Pushkin to the dustbin of historical curiosities. Mondry has shown us that there is a creativity in Rozanov's approach, which may still lead to fruitful applications. She concludes her chapter:

> Rozanov looked at the world through the prism of the 'gaze' described by Lacan, in which the gaze carries a charge of self-expression and recognition of oneself in others. Between object and subject a single continuum is created. Rozanov's recognition of Pushkin came from his recognition of Pushkin in himself, and of himself in Pushkin. It is in this new, phenomenological sense that finally Pushkin actually does become 'our everything'.

Indeed so: the *selective interest* which is the hallmark of Rozanov's Pushkin may be the key ingredient, *mutatis mutandis*, of all readings of Pushkin. Similarly, we see at both ends of our present historical continuum how inheritors used Pushkin for polemical purposes. As Joe Andrew notes, Elena Gan's treatment of the motif of 'the heroine's reading' polemicizes with Pushkin's own version of the same theme, while Young argues that Dovlatov's *Sanctuary*, set as it is in Pushkin's Mikhailovskoe, allows the Soviet writer to seek parallels between the state's treatment of the writer in both periods. Equally, Dovlatov, Young argues, uses Pushkin in his polemic against the *derevenshchiki*. From this position it is but a short step to the more structural and literary rereadings/rewritings of Pushkin, and this step we now take.

As we saw earlier, John Bayley has reminded us that Pushkin was seen as a Protean figure even within his lifetime. Bayley develops the point: 'he modelled for his successors a wide range of literary forms'. Like Shakespeare 'he too was a fertilising influence'.[27] A particular instance of this, as Emerson has recently reminded us, is the case of Tatiana 'the most richly inspirational source for Russian literary heroines well into the [twentieth] century'.[28] The influence may be of a fairly general kind. In the present volume, Barbara Lönnqvist recalls Tolstoi's famous 'discovery' of Pushkin's prose style in 1873, while Young will speak of 'Dovlatov's conscious continuation of Pushkin's style.' Such imitation may not always be an act of explicit homage, of course: as Valentina Polukhina notes, Brodsky's borrowings and even (partial) quotations from Pushkin are sometimes parodic and shocking.

In fact, from fairly early on, as Debreczeny and Layton for example have shown,[29] Pushkin's works, especially his 'Southern Poems', began to spawn a whole host of imitations. As Helena Goscilo demonstrates in the last chapter of this collection, Pushkin emerged as a kind of early superstar with a swarm of epigones in his wake. 'Pushkin's *Caucasian Captive* precipitated a veritable Caucasian epidemic', Goscilo notes, before going on to show how this 'epidemic' has much more recently re-appeared in a rather healthier strain, in the work of Makanin. Goscilo's work allows us to see clearly the mechanics of literary adaptation, while Lyubov Kiseleva's contribution, 'Pushkin in the Mirror of Shakhovskoi' enables us to see the same processes within Pushkin's own lifetime. Kiseleva sums up what mechanisms are at work: 'The theatrical "rewriting" (stage versions) - the interpretation of the text into the language of another form of art and the system of another author - is like a double mirror where the poetics of both the interpreter and the interpreted original are reflected'. As she goes on to show, Shakhovskoi's 'versions' of *Ruslan and Liudmila* and *The Fountain of Bakhchisarai* raise questions of fidelity to the original, as well as illustrating how imitators will replicate, replace or omit motifs from the original to suit their own artistic agendas. In effect, we must talk of a *transformation* of Pushkin. Such mechanisms seem to have been most effective when the imitator was able to develop 'the inner potential of the original text'.

This discovery of the 'inner potential' of the Pushkin text is, it seems to me, a more purely literary version of 'Pushkin's secret'. Certainly, from as early as the 1820s Russian writers have indeed attempted to unearth this 'inner potential', effectively to rewrite Pushkin's works to bring out what the successor writer had discovered. Thus, Andrew suggests that many of the 'society tales' of the 1830s and 1840s are versions of *Evgenii Onegin*, while, elsewhere, Alexander Zholkovsky has described the different writerly strategies used to 'mine' Pushkin's texts, giving us such engaging phrases as 'Winking at Pushkin', 'The Helping Hand' and 'On Loan from Pushkin'.[30]

The literary secrets of Pushkin are also used *in combination* with those of other writers. In the present collection, for example, Kiseleva reveals the way in which Shakhovskoi fuses Pushkin and Shakespeare to produce a new synthesis. This not only tells us about the working methods of the successor writer, but enables us to see Pushkin himself in a new light, to discover, that is, the 'inner potential'. Similarly, Doherty provides convincing evidence of the fascinating, dialectical clash produced when Ivanov uses Kruchenykh with (and against!) Pushkin. In a different way, Sandler's analysis of Sedakova's *Ballad of Continuation* focuses on the manner in which Sedakova's three epigraphs, from Lermontov and Pasternak as well as Pushkin, engage in a kind of polylogue in the later text, while Zabolotskii is also introduced as yet another subtext. Finally, Goscilo argues that Makanin's reworking and updating of Pushkin's *Caucasian Captive* is enhanced by the introduction of Dostoevskii, especially his concept of beauty.

Other chapters in the present volume focus on the way in which later writers take a particular Pushkinian motif to replay it, rework it and re-interpret it, thereby, in their own way, realizing its 'inner potential', and disclosing his literary 'secret'. This was happening even within Pushkin's own lifetime. Indeed, as Andrew shows in the opening chapter, in his study of the motif of the 'heroine's reading', it was even happening within Pushkin's own œuvre, in the sense that *The Tales of Belkin*, especially *The Blizzard*, offers a parodic account of Tatiana's modelling of her life on literature. More broadly, Andrew demonstrates both how influential this motif was in the 20 years following the completion of *Onegin*, as well as the way it shifted in 'value'. If reading may be said to deceive the heroine in the master text, gradually, reading accrues other meanings, before shifting completely to be a means of awakening the heroine, both to life and to creativity.

The heroine's reading was, then, a highly productive motif, as the examples of Odoevskii, Gan, Zhukova and Dostoevskii demonstrate: in effect, it leaves Pushkin to take on a life of its own. Sander Brouwer's study, 'The Bridegroom Who Did Not Come: Social and Amorous Unproductivity from Pushkin to the Silver Age', takes this approach yet further, coining the terms 'motifeme' and 'mythologeme' to denote text elements which can be found in Pushkin's *Evgenii Onegin* and which spawn a whole series of later texts, especially the works of Turgenev, but, as Brouwer's title suggests, spanning the whole century. In essence, Brouwer's approach is structuralist, explicitly influenced by the work of Iurii Lotman. In this sense, *Onegin* is seen as the master text for the whole century, and the hero's amorous failure in Pushkin, Goncharov, Turgenev and others is inextricably linked with his social inadequacy.

What differentiates Brouwer's approach from Andrew's, however, is that *Onegin* is also seen as a kind of 'junction box': the motifs which are so central to Pushkin's work, and which were to become so generative in his successors can, in turn, be traced back both to Russian folklore and Western sources. Having traced the lineage of these generative motifs, Brouwer sums up Pushkin's *pivotal* position:

> One of the things Russian Romanticism inherited from Western Europe was the theme of impossible and unfulfilled love as the only true love. There it had developed in a long tradition going back to the twelfth and

thirteenth century, to the time of the troubadours and more specifically to the Romance of Tristan and Iseult. It would require much investigation to establish whether Russian culture had, by the nineteenth century, retained enough of its medieval Manicheanism to connect this theme with a world-denying worldview, as had been the case, according to Denis de Rougemont, in Western European literature. The subjective reasons for seeing real love as unrealizable in this world may have been different for each author. For instance, as Agnes Dukkon has argued, the hidden drive behind the Turgenevian hero's failure to realize his love in some amorous relationship is the secret wish to keep his essentially aesthetic ideal at an elegiac distance and to 'prove' this ideal by earthly suffering and eternal longing. That wish can hardly be ascribed to Pushkin. It was Pushkin, however, who made the connection between the Romantic theme of unhappy love and that of social estrangement, thus shaping the image that appeared to be so successful in Russian literature.

Andrew and Brouwer are not alone in following this route to Pushkin's secret. Lönnqvist follows Eikhenbaum in finding 'similarities and echoes' of Pushkin's work in Tolstoi, noting *The Tales of Belkin* as an especially generative text. The names of *Peasant-Lady* find a new modulation in *Anna Karenina*, while the ethos of the 'Englishness' motif of Pushkin's tale is radically reworked in Tolstoi's version of it. Indeed, Lönnqvist's study of this motif reveals precisely the power of this kind of approach, in the sense that the same motif comes to represent a key element in the essential spirit (if there is such a thing!) of the two writers. As Lönnqvist has it, 'If the "English way of life" at Muromskii's estate is depicted with Pushkinian irony', then Englishness in Tolstoy becomes associated with 'modernity', 'machinery' and 'an aura of "foreignness" ("not ours")'. These processes continue to the present day, as Sandler shows in her study of Sedakova: 'One might say that, in *Ballad of Continuation*, she effectively returns this kind of poem to one of its Pushkinian premises, this despite her having reversed many of the other motifs, like the desert landscape or the thirst it would engender'. This statement seems to sum up this use of Pushkin. Later writers discover a key motif cluster, a motifeme/mythologeme which has great 'inner potential'. The motifs may be replayed with their same value, may be extended, or reversed. In the end, however, writers from Pushkin's contemporaries, like Gan and Odoevskii, to those still living today have gone back to culture's 'origins without origins' to find both *his* secret, but also to uncover their own paths.

On occasion, a successor will be more focused in their use of Pushkin, in the sense that an individual later work will play against an individual Pushkin text. This more precise version of intertextuality is seen especially in the chapters by Veldhues, Doherty, Sandler and Goscilo. In one sense, the insights arising in these chapters are an extension of those adduced so far. For example, Veldhues traces the way Nabokov's *Death* displays very exact semantic, syntactic and prosodic echoes of Pushkin's *Stone Guest*, with similar triangles centred on the motif of 'forbidden love'. Pushkinian motifs are thus replayed, but this time, across the whole text. And it is a two-way process: Pushkin illuminates Nabokov, but Nabokov's treatment of the textual material from his predecessor also allows us to read *Stone Guest* in a new way. Similarly, Doherty sees that Ivanov's *Disintegration of the Atom* has 'underlying structural and thematic dependence on Pushkin', especially the latter's 'On the Hills of Georgia ...' from which Doherty derives his title. In Doherty we find a new approach, in that the key borrowing Ivanov makes is *structural*: both texts are organized around the principle of oxymoron. This principle can be extended beyond Ivanov himself. In Doherty's view, 'Pushkin's own ability to create harmony out of contradiction can serve as a model for resolution of the fissuring of the modern psyche which Ivanov's prose poem so effectively articulates'. As in Veldhues' reading, the later writer here too reflects back to the original: the Pushkin work stands re-illuminated after Ivanov's treatment of it. Sedakova also borrows Pushkin's formal properties to structure her work, while Makanin may seem the most 'slavish' adherent of the master, even cribbing his title, but, in his radical reworking of the original, especially in terms of gender orientation, he goes at least as far as earlier borrowers and intertextualists.

For some writers Pushkin's influence is more general, more all-pervasive. We see this to some extent in Young's reading of Dovlatov, in whom she detects the same general ethos. We find something similar in Sandler's account of Sedakova, who models her whole poetic approach on Pushkin: 'Sedakova emulates the fine balance in his work between engagement with contemporary cultural politics and commitment to transcendent aesthetic values'. But it is in Polukhina's treatment of Brodsky that we find the most broad-ranging generalist influence. Polukhina begins her chapter thus: 'Pushkin had a far larger influence, intellectually and emotionally, on Brodsky than has generally been recognized or than Brodsky himself would like us to think'. For Polukhina Pushkin can be found in Brodsky in all manner of ways, in 'numerous borrowings, citations, reminiscences, allusions, echoes of Pushkinian texts, dissolved as it were, in Brodsky's poetry'. Moreover, Brodsky's pursuit of Pushkin's secret, of his inner potential, was the matter of his lifelong dialogue with the writer he called simply 'Alexander Sergeevich'. Polukhina's exhaustive approach could perhaps be termed 'archaeological', an attempt to uncover the whole range and gamut of the borrowings, citations and so on. The end result is a full account of the multi-faceted relationship which existed between the two poets, which Polukhina sums up as follows:

> In conclusion, I will say that in his relationship to Pushkin Brodsky remained true to himself: on the one hand he followed in his steps, just

as he, in general, followed the tradition but, on the other hand, he made a decisive break with tradition and, in many ways, departed from Pushkin's course but only, by doing so, to continue his work. He could have been describing his own work when he said about Pushkin, 'he is, to a certain degree, a sort of lens into which the past goes and out of which the future emerges'. At the end of his life Brodsky thought and sometimes sounded like Pushkin, departing from him and looking back at him.

'A sort of lens into which the past goes and out of which the future emerges': this indeed is one metaphor for summing up what Pushkin has been for Russian culture for nearly the last two centuries. He is a lens, a filter, the 'origin without origins', whose 'inner potential' is still being revealed, whose 'great secret' has been partially divined, but surely not in its entirety. As we enter the twenty-first century, however, is Pushkin still 'our everything' for Russian culture? Ten years after the end of 'official culture' with the collapse of the Soviet Union, are modern writers now at last able to complete Siniavskii's project of 'liberating Pushkin from the deadening myth of greatness'? These are the questions which Stephanie Sandler has returned to in the opening remarks of her chapter in the present volume as she traces the irreverent, even dismissive approach to Pushkin to be found in the likes of Kibirov and Prigov. Paradoxically, indeed, with the end of the deadening mythologizing of the Soviet period, which succeeded similar tendencies in late Tsarist culture, will Pushkin now begin finally to slip from centre stage, to cease to be 'our everything'? If this were to happen, it would perhaps be no bad thing, and Russians, as well as non-Russian readers of Pushkin might at last be able to see him as he really is. Perhaps Olga Sedakova, both poet and scholar (as well as Christian) has pointed the way forward. Her use of Pushkin's more obscure works reveals her scholarly side but also, in Sandler's formulation, is 'her way of circumnavigating the massive myth of Pushkin, indeed of finding her way through the myth back toward the poetic legacy of language, rhythms, and meanings'. In the end, maybe Sedakova has best understood the true nature of Pushkin's 'great secret'.

NOTES

1. Dostoevskii, F.M., *Polnoe sobranie sochinenii v tridsati tomakh*, Nauka, Leningrad, 1972-90, XXVI (1984), pp. 136-49 (149).
2. John Bayley, *Pushkin. A Comparative Commentary*, Cambridge University Press, Cambridge, 1971, p. 16.
3. Ibid., p. 5.
4. See Paul Debreczeny, *Social Functions of Literature. Alexander Pushkin and Russian Culture*, Stanford University Press, Stanford, 1997, and Marcus C. Levitt, *Russian Literary Politics and the Pushkin Celebrations of 1880*, Cornell University Press, Ithaca and London, 1989. I am indebted to these authors for factual material in the ensuing discussion.
5. Op. cit., pp. 5ff.
6. Ibid., p. 11.
7. See ibid., pp. 21-42 for a fascinating discussion of this process in the decades following Pushkin's death.
8. See ibid., pp. 173 and 175; see also the chapter 'Gilding the Lily: Pushkin's Lyrics in the Hands of Russian Composers' by Arnold Mcmillin in Joe Andrew and Robert Reid, eds, *Pushkin's Legacy* (forthcoming).
9. See Debreczeny, pp. 15-16, as well as Richard Freeborn 'Belinskii and Pushkin' in Andrew and Reid (forthcoming).
10. See Debreczeny, pp. 163-4.
11. Ibid., p. 226. John Bayley, however, argues that, while 'Mickiewicz gave the Poles their national poem and became the focus of their cultural identity - a god-like figure to his fellow-countrymen', Pushkin 'is not like this.' (Op. cit., p. 4). The weight of evidence would seem to be against Bayley.
12. See Debreczeny, pp. 223-9, as well as Stephanie Sandler, 'Sex, Death and Nation in the *Strolls with Pushkin* Controversy', in *Slavic Review*, LX, 2, Summer, 1992, pp. 294-308 (298).
13. See Debreczeny, p. 229. In these processes his ill-fated marriage took on a particular resonance: for an illuminating exploration of this, see Stephanie Sandler, 'Pushkin's Last Love - Natal'ya Nikolaevna in Russian Culture' in Marianne Liljeström, Eila Mäntysaari and Arja Rosenholm, eds, *Gender Restructuring in Russian Studies*, Slavica Tamperensia II, Tampere, 1993, pp. 209-20, as well as the recent and very popular Serena Vitale, *Pushkin's Button*, Fourth Estate, London, 1999.
14. John Bayley's phrase, op. cit., p. 17.
15. Marcus Levitt's word, p. 27: see his very helpful account of all these processes.
16. Ibid., p. 30. For a very recent discussion of the continuing importance of this phrase, see David Bethea, *Realizing Metaphors. Alexander Pushkin and the Life of the Poet*, The University of Wisconsin Press, Madison, Wisconsin, 1998, especially pp. 37-8. Alexander Zholkovsky begins his even more recent, and very lively account of Pushkin's culturological significance, 'Pushkin Under Our Skin', thus: '"Pushkin is our everything," goes the ever quotable formulation by a nineteenth-century critic. In Russian culture, Pushkin is all-important, omnipresent, taken for granted'.: in A.D.P. Briggs, ed., *Alexander Pushkin. A Celebration of Russia's Best-loved Writer*, Hazar Publishing, London, 1999, pp. 189-96 (189).
17. His remarks are too well known to need any discussion here. Suffice it to mention Shestov's elaboration of his views in 1897, where he speculates on what *precisely* might have been the 'great secret' Pushkin carried to his grave, by wondering 'What *Hamlet*, what *Macbeth* did he take with him to the grave, and how would Russian literature have developed if Pushkin had lived as long as Shakespeare?' Quoted from Lev Shestov, 'A.S. Pushkin' in D.J. Richards and

C.R.S. Cockrell, eds and transl., *Russian Views of Pushkin*, Willem A. Meeuws, Oxford, 1976, pp. 107-19 (108).
18. See Levitt, pp. 154-5.
19. Ibid., p. 163.
20. See Debreczeny, p. 238.
21. See Sandler, 'Sex, Death and Nation', p. 296.
22. Ibid., p. 308.
23. See Stephanie Sandler, 'Embodied Words: Gender in Cvetaeva's Reading of Puškin', in *Slavic and East European Journal*, XXXIV, 2, 1990, pp. 139-57 (139).
24. See Olga Sedakova, 'Pushkin Akhmatovoi i Tsvetaevoi' (paper presented at the Moscow Tsvetaeva Museum, May, 1996).
25. See David M. Bethea, ed., *Puškin Today*, Indiana University Press, Bloomington and Indianapolis, 1993, p. 1.
26. See Bethea, *Realizing Metaphors*, pp. 37-8.
27. Op. cit., p. 5.
28. See Caryl Emerson, 'Tatiana' in Sona Stephan Hoisington, ed., *A Plot of Her Own. The Female Protagonist in Russian Literature*, Northwestern University Press, Evanston, Illinois, 1995, pp. 6-20 (6).
29. See Debreczeny, p. 80, and Susan Layton, *Russian Literature and Empire. Conquest of the Caucasus from Pushkin to Tolstoy*, Cambridge University Press, Cambridge, 1994, pp. 36-54.
30. See Zholkovsky, op. cit.

'[She] was brought up on French novels
and, consequently, was in love':
Russian Writers Reading and Writing Pushkin

by

JOE ANDREW

1. PREAMBLE

That reading plays a very important role in character definition, and character formation, in *Evgenii Onegin* has long been a commonplace in the literature.[1] The first purpose of this chapter is to review Pushkin's 'novel in verse' from this perspective, as well as recent criticism on the subject, and to reassess the role that Tatiana's reading in particular plays in her character, and in the broader thematics of the work. I will then seek to trace how this *topos*, the heroine's reading, developed and expanded in the two decades following the completion of *Onegin*. This survey will begin with Pushkin's own parody of it in *The Tales of Belkin*, especially *The Blizzard*, before a consideration of works by Odoevskii, Gan, Dostoevskii and Zhukova. Implicit in all this will be a re-affirmation of the part played by Pushkin and this work in particular in the formation of Russian literature in the period immediately after his death. Indeed, my research suggests that many of the central works, by both male and female authors, in the 1830s and 1840s are fairly explicit re-writings of, or polemics with, *Onegin*. In all this I will also seek to focus especially on the force of one word in my title quotation, namely, 'consequently' ('следственно').

2. READING DECEIVES

2.1 *Evgenii Onegin*

As George Gibian notes, 'The influence of literature on human conduct has been a matter of concern throughout the ages', as the examples he gives, including *The Æneid* and Plato's *Republic*, illustrate.[2] As Gibian further notes, in nineteenth-century literature we commonly come across novels in which 'the reading of books *molds* the characters' concept of love and their feelings and behaviour in affairs of the heart' (my emphasis).[3] And the process was self-reinforcing, in the sense that, in Russia especially, perhaps, 'real life' people used literature as a guide to life. As Paul Debreczeny has put it recently: 'Using works of literature to model one's behavior was a common practice in early nineteenth-century Russia'.[4] This inter-relationship 'literature-life-literature' is undoubtedly one of capital importance in nineteenth-century Russian literary culture, and, as in so many regards, *Evgenii Onegin* is the *fons et origo* of the theme. As we know, Pushkin was one of the most self-consciously literary of writers and so, as we might expect, this work is profoundly self-reflexive in that the relationship between literature and life, and the impact reading has on character are amongst the central themes of the novel. We see this in the way each of the three main characters, Onegin, Tatiana and Lenskii are defined by what they have read, to a greater or lesser extent: as Todd has it, 'they become what they read, to alter Feuerbach's formula, not merely what they eat'.[5] Undoubtedly, the primary site of this theme is the heroine, Tatiana, and it is to her I now turn.

Even before we read about what she reads, she is deliberately characterized, not perhaps as a realistic personage, but as if a literary heroine. As Debreczeny has noted, 'All the characteristics the author gives her - her taciturn shyness, melancholy withdrawal from human contact, and solitary communion with nature - mark her as the heroine of a sentimental novel'.[6] Once these traits are laid before us, we enter her literary world. The narrator begins this section (2, xxix) 'She liked novels early on'.[7] The most significant aspect of this prefatory remark is perhaps the age at which Tatiana had begun imbibing these sentimental novels. She is thought to be seventeen[8] at this point in the novel, so must have begun reading Rousseau and Richardson, and the others, in her early teens. That is, although still fairly young, even by the norms of the day, she has already been formed by the books she found in her mother's 'library'. That Tatiana has, indeed, been formed (or a similar near synonym) by sentimental novels is, of course, a commonplace of *Onegin* criticism.[9] The narrator himself makes this apparent: 'They [novels] replaced everything for her; She fell in love with the deceptions[10] / Of both Richardson and Rousseau' (2, xxix). We note the 'everything' and 'fell in love'. Novels, and their deceptions, are, for the young woman, hardly more than a girl in reality, an all-consuming, all-encompassing passion; we might even say an addiction.

But what *exactly* have these novels done to or for Tatiana, and is their effect good or bad? Although the emphases vary somewhat, most of the recent criticism suggests that Tatiana has derived her view of life from literature; moreover, the general opinion is that she believes that life is *like* literature. (As Miss K.I.T., the narratress of the later *Peasant-Lady* will say 'Provincial misses! ... they derive their knowledge of the world and of life from books!') Thus Luc de Beaudoin has claimed that Tatiana's 'entire conception of life and her love for Onegin is modelled on the Sentimental and epistolary novels she reads';[11] Debreczeny makes the same point: 'she modelled herself on the fictional characters she read about'.[12]

Emerson shares this now common view that Tatiana had been quite active, even self-conscious in her relationship with literature: for Emerson too, Tatiana had 'modelled her life'[13] on Rousseau's Julie, Richardson's Clarissa and de Staël's Delphine. For Todd the process is perhaps slightly less dynamic, or character-centred: for him Tatiana's 'understanding of life is shaped by literary' conventions.[14] I would see this perhaps a little differently. As noted above, literature for Tatiana is absorbed, at a fairly young age, in a rather unmediated way, and takes over everything in her life ('replaced everything for her'). Such a reading is, I believe, corroborated by the way this theme and related themes are developed. Thus the epigraph to Chapter 3 (the chapter in which Pushkin will discuss the changing morality of literature, leading on to his 'introduction' to Tatiana's letter), 'Elle était fille, elle était amoureuse' seems to me to anticipate the 'consequently' of *The Blizzard*. This reading is reinforced, I would argue, by the line (3, vii) 'The time had arrived, she fell in love'. It is a semi-automatic, almost mechanistic process.[15] That is, Tatiana acts on an almost unconscious level on the imperatives derived from the novels from which she has derived her world-view. At the same time, we should also note that, in the diegetic present, Tatiana *is* a self-conscious reader. Having met Onegin in Chapter 2, she returns to literature with redoubled passion to find corroboration for her view of Onegin as the one she is destined to love: 'Now with what attention / She reads the sweet novel' (3, ix).

In any event, and particularly as regards her misperception of Onegin, it seems certain that her reading has deceived Tatiana; moreover, as the novel unfolds, she realizes that life is not the same as in books. There are a number of aspects to the theme of '(self-)deception' by literature. From the outset, as de Beaudoin among many others has noted, Tatiana 'entertains fantasies inspired by books ... [she] is fond of the "deceptions" of these Sentimental epistolary works'.[16] Debreczeny takes a similar, if rather blunter view: 'Tatiana's reading in fact misleads her: inflaming her imagination, literature persuades her that a stranger she has fleetingly met is the hero of her dreams'.[17]

When we examine the text, the narrator, whether ironically or not, seems unequivocal in his view of the nature of his heroine's relationship with the fictional world: we recall that 'She fell in love with the deceptions / Of both Richardson and Rousseau'. Famously, the word for 'deceptions', *'obmany'*, rhymes with *'romany'*, 'novels' (or 'romances', of course). In other words, because of her reading, and too credulous ingestion of it, Tatiana has become engaged in a false view of life, or, at least, of the relationship between literature and life. The imbrication of 'novel "means" deception' is reinforced by repetition of the rhyme when Tatiana returns to reading in Chapter 3, as already noted, to corroborate her fantasy about Onegin. We read that 'Now with what attention / She reads the sweet novel, / With what lively attention / She drinks the seductive deception!' (3,ix). By the next stanza she has taken the next, short step to imagine herself to be the heroine of a novel, like Julie, Clarissa or Delphine.[18]

What are the implications of this? Both before[19] and after Pushkin, writers suggest that such an (ab)use of literature is actually dangerous, as we shall see later in this chapter. Does *Evgenii Onegin* suggest this? Up to a point, the answer would seem to be 'yes'. There are a number of indications of this. Thus, we are told that Tatiana's father, Dmitrii, took no interest in his daughter's reading, not being a reader himself, and 'did not see any harm in books' (2, xxix). A commonplace of the language, perhaps, but the narrator immediately suggests that there *is* something at least clandestine about Tatiana's consumption of literature, noting that Dmitrii 'did not bother about / What secret tome of his daughter's / Slumbered under her pillow till morning' (ibid.). (The nocturnal devouring of literature in secret will become a key topos for the followers of Pushkin, and will accrue decidedly erotic, taboo-breaking connotations, as we shall see.)

Now, all this is no doubt playfully ironic, but seeds of ambiguity are sown, to be more fully developed in the next chapter of the novel. Indeed, the quasi-erotic nature of Tatiana's passion for literature soon emerges quite clearly as she ponders on the significance of Onegin's arrival in her life: 'For a long time her imagination, / Burning with languor and longing, / Had craved the fateful food' (3,vii). In other words, her devouring of the 'seductive deception' of novels had made her *already ready* to give herself to the hero. And now, returning once more to these favourite primers, 'She wanders alone[20] with a *dangerous* book' (3, x: my emphasis). Irony, I feel, is abandoned here. The book is dangerous because it makes Tatiana's experience of life, of love and of the 'hero', at this point at least, *inauthentic*: 'She sighs and, appropriating to herself / Another's rapture, another's sorrow'[21] (ibid.). Moreover, as the narrator soon further emphasizes, and as much of the rest of the novel will demonstrate, she has made a big mistake in entrusting her fate to the 'modish tyrant' (3, xv). The naming of this error lays the ground for the narrator's more general attack on Romanticism: 'You will perish, my dear' he claims, before deploying some strong, and deliberately 'high-style' rhetoric to demolish these 'fantasies'. Before 'perishing', he claims, she will be visited by such things as 'blind hope', 'dark bliss', 'the magical poison of desires', 'your fateful tempter' (ibid.).

Now, all this should not be overstated. Neither Pushkin, nor his narrator-persona was a tragic moralizer in the manner of his follower, Elena Gan. Moreover, we should also remember that Tatiana is a product not merely of her reading of Sentimental novels, but is shaped by a number of forces. While it is true, as Debreczeny has noted, that the familial and social environment cannot satisfy all her needs,[22] and this is why she has turned to literature in such a big way, these other determinants are important from the first, and, as some at least argue, will ultimately be more important. Thus, as Ryan and Wigzell have convincingly demonstrated,[23] we cannot understand her dream,[24] nor her psyche more generally, without a deep awareness of Pushkin's use of folk sources in the work. Katz has shown us equally convincingly that 'real life', in the shape of the pattern of life and, especially, of marriage of her mother and nanny will, in the end, be the path that Tatiana will follow.[25]

More generally, the tension between a life mediated through literature and 'real life' will form one of the central dialectics of the whole work, as is well known, as well as shaping many post-Pushkin works, as we shall see. For the moment, there are still a number of other aspects of the theme of the heroine's reading to be considered. Perhaps the area where she is most deceived by novels is her misapprehension concerning the man with whom she falls - and remains - in love.[26] Again, the view that Tatiana has mistakenly interpreted Onegin is a commonplace of the criticism. For Clayton, for example, the figure she believes him to be is entirely a figment of her imagination: for him, her 'letter does not have a "real" addressee. The Onegin to whom she directs the letter is unknown, a phantom'.[27]

Todd has made a very similar point, while locating Tatiana's action in sending him the letter in a broader context: 'Tatiana, who also ignores social conventions, but whose understanding of life is shaped by literary ones, views this silent newcomer as a hero like those in her sentimentalist novels and acts upon this assumption'.[28] And, indeed, when we turn to the text, the narrator again makes this point quite apparent. Having reviewed Tatiana's longing for 'the fateful food', he announces: 'Her waiting was over ... Her eyes were opened: She said: it is he!' (3, viii) In other words, she merely projects on to Onegin the characteristics of the novelistic heroes who seethe in her imagination. Moreover, as Nabokov amongst others has noted,[29] she manages to fuse in her feverish fantasies heroes who are, in fact, quite dissimilar.

Pushkin is making a twofold point by dwelling on his heroine's mistake. Firstly, there is the fact that she confuses illusion and reality. Secondly - a point made by a number of commentators - she is basing her interpretation (or fantasy) *on the wrong books*. While Richardson and Rousseau were all the rage for her mother's generation, and perhaps appropriate to their needs, Onegin has been shaped by an altogether different set of models.[30]

These books probably formed part of her mother's trousseau.[31] In fact, the role of Tatiana's mother (and, to a much lesser extent, her father) in determining the daughter's fixations has exercised a number of commentators. Indeed, the parental presence (or lack of it) at the heroine's education will be a significant theme in the literature of the 1830s and 1840s. For de Beaudoin, Praskovia Larina is a 'precedent' for her daughter's reading habits;[32] while Diana Burgin suggests that she 'inherited' her taste for sentimental novels from her mother.[33] However, as I have argued elsewhere,[34] there is a lack of clarity about whether the mother had even read Richardson and the others;[35] furthermore, the text does not make clear whether she had played any role in encouraging Tatiana to read, or not. And, as we have already seen, her father certainly does not concern himself with the issue, one way or another. No, for me the key points here are that, most probably, Tatiana, like many of her fictional 'daughters' was left *unsupervised* in her literary education, 'alone with a dangerous book'; and that this lack of guidance played its own significant part in nurturing her misguided fantasies. The climax of the theme of Tatiana's reading is, in fact, her own writing of the self[36] in her letter to Onegin. Extensive, even exhaustive work now exists which has traced Tatiana's borrowing of lines, ideas, stylistic devices and tropes from her favourite authors, most especially from Rousseau's *Julie*, adjudged to be the single largest influence on the young heroine.[37] Diana Burgin has summed up the impact of her reading at this point particularly trenchantly: 'Tatiana Larina's "Letter" is thus born in her reading, her desire *to be* her favorite authors' creation, and her aspiration to emulate and create her beloved heroines' love letters' (my emphasis).[38]

Although much pored over, this letter still strikes us as an extraordinary document, which reveals in almost every syllable that Tatiana, at this stage, is living in a state of complete - and, in a number of senses - dangerous fantasy, induced by her mistaken reading of literature.[39] Iurii Lotman has done well to remind us how shocking her behaviour could be construed to be:

> In sending her letter to Onegin, Tatiana behaves in conformity with the norms of behaviour of a heroine of a novel; however, the real, quotidian norms of behaviour of a Russian gentry young woman of the beginning of the nineteenth century make such an action unthinkable: and the fact that, unbeknownst to her mother, she enters into correspondence with a man she hardly knows, places her action on the farther side of all the norms of decency.[40]

It is salutary to inject a dose of reality at this stage, as this is precisely what the novel itself now does. Indeed, even within the letter itself, Tatiana shows that she is dimly aware of the enormity of what she is doing, albeit in a somewhat derivative and melodramatic way: 'I finish! I'm afraid to read it through ... / I'm dying of shame and fear ...'

Increasingly, indeed, as the novel develops, and as Pushkin matures as a man and as a writer, 'real life' overcomes the power of literature, and Tatiana comes to a new, and better understanding of the interrelationship between literature and life. In fact, of course, it was never quite as simple as I may have suggested. Even from her reading, as Gregg has suggested,[41] Tatiana would have known that, if she were not able to marry the man she loves, she would have to marry the man chosen for her. And, as Katz has shown us so compellingly,[42] the examples of her mother, known to her before the novel begins, and of her nanny, revealed to her as she ponders writing to Onegin, show her what is the normal pattern for young Russian women of her time, irrespective of which class they emanate from. This is the model she will ultimately follow, of course.

At the same time, as Todd in particular has shown us,[43] Tatiana comes to an important new awareness of the relationship between life and literature, especially in her reading of Onegin's reading during her visit to his home, following Onegin's murder of Lenskii and his subsequent disappearance from the area. Here she not only becomes aware that he might be just a 'parody' of his own reading; she also acquires new, more contemporary models by which to assess him; finally she becomes able to see that life is, in the end, quite different from literature.[44] And so, by the end of the novel, it is commonly argued, Tatiana has escaped from her reading, has broken free of the 'deceptions' of novels, and has found, if not happiness, then certainly tranquillity and serenity. As Carolyn Ayers has suggested, echoing Todd, the heroine 'needs to learn to read in order to learn from reading'.[45] Moreover, Tatiana has outgrown her reading in another sense. To quote de Beaudoin: 'It would seem that Tat'jana has herself broken away from the Romantic mould imposed on women as objects of male completion. She has literally stepped out of the confines of the text to join the metatextual narrator in a rejection of Romantic idealism'.[46]

And yet, as others have shown, even in her final speech to Onegin, she is playing a part, and sources identified for this speech include, yet again, Julie[47] and a folk song.[48] The truth of the situation might actually be somewhere in the middle ground, a third way which combines life and literature, so that 'Life's Novel' shows that literature is not life, nor that life is an imitation of literature, but rather that one should use one's mature understanding of literature to understand one's own life. In this sense, as in so many others, Pushkin's 'true ideal' is valorized. As Katz has it: 'Pushkin's heroine synthesizes the experience of her favourite fictional characters with the models of behaviour provided by her nearest and dearest to make the "right" decision - the only true Pushkinian choice'.[49]

Yet, even as Pushkin was finishing *Evgenii Onegin* he was moving on to provide a similar, but also subtly different reading of the theme of the heroine's reading in *The Tales of Belkin*, especially *The Blizzard*, to a consideration of which I now turn.

2.2 *The Blizzard*

In this, the second of the tales, the interpenetration of literature and life is an even more central theme than in *Onegin*: the whole story could, indeed, be said to be focused on this theme. As Bethea and Davydov have shown in their seminal article on the collection, the opening of the story in particular is driven by a huge weight of literary convention.[50] The scope for metatextual games, and for literary parody is enormous, occasioned in part by the fact that there are, in a sense, *four* levels of 'authorship': Pushkin, Belkin, Miss K.I.T, who allegedly told the story to Belkin, and *the central characters themselves*. (We should also note, *en passant*, that the role of Miss K.I.T in creating the seemingly incredible events has been the subject of some scrutiny - and criticism: she is, for example, called to account by Debreczeny.[51]) Centrally, however, for our present purposes we might say that the exposition is created by the characters' own fantasies, which to an even greater extent than in the case of Tatiana, are based on their reading of Sentimentalist fiction: as Wolf Schmid has suggested, it is an almost paradigmatic instance.[52] In other terms, Maria Gavrilovna (and Vladimir) are utterly convinced of the veracity of the 'deceptions' of novels, and *seek to organize their lives as if they were fictional characters*.

Equally, Maria Gavrilovna, again, even more so than in the case of Tatiana, is a purely literary heroine: she appears 'inseparable from the sentimental novels she reads'.[53] As with her predecessor, the key question is whether she is able to outgrow her literature-fuelled fantasies. Even more important for our purposes here are the obvious, and, we assume, deliberate links between her and Tatiana, as Debreczeny amongst others has noted.[54] Like her literary sister she is seventeen, slender, pale, and, of course, brought up on French novels, and 'was, consequently, in love'. At this stage we are not given any details about her reading (although there is an explicit reference at the end to, inevitably, Rousseau's *Julie*). However, as the story begins in late 1811, in the deep provinces, we may assume that her reading is also of the Sentimental, epistolary kind, and that she too is one of the provincial misses who, according to Miss K.I.T. in her second story, 'derive their knowledge of the world and of life from books!' What happens here, as well as later, it seems to me, is that the core situation of *On*egin is re-presented without all the subtlety and fine nuancing. Remembering Shklovskii's celebrated dictum, that is, *The Blizzard* is a parody of a parody.

The parodic echoes of *Onegin* are apparent from the outset. We learn that Maria is in love *as a consequence* of her reading. This simply makes explicit what chapters two and three of the novel in verse had suggested. Just as Tatiana had chosen *Onegin* because he seemed to fit the bill, the narrator of *The Blizzard* makes this implication explicit: 'The object, chosen by her was a poor army warrant officer' (p. 63)[55]: that is, she 'falls in love' not with Vladimir, but with Vladimir as 'an object', he, as Onegin had been, is '*he*'. The fact that his name is Vladimir, as was Lenskii's, makes the link with the novel even more apparent. Later we discover that Maria's mother has the same Christian name as Tatiana's mother, Praskovia. The parodic nature of the plot is further enhanced by recurrent linguistic devices, 'It stands to reason', 'of course' and so on, which reinforce the almost mechanistic nature of the plot development. It all seems to fit a pre-ordained plan, pre-ordained, that is, by the fantasies of Maria, Vladimir, and, behind them, Miss K.I.T.

So, then, like Tatiana, Maria has too literally entered the world of fiction, and believes that her life will turn out to be like that of one of her favourite literary heroines. But, as in the case of Tatiana, life conspires against literature, as Bethea and Davydov, amongst others have noted. As they have it: 'What has been promised by the *loci communes* of the sentimental novel undergoes step-by-step frustration'.[56] The prose of life enters, almost from the outset, to defeat the sentimentalist expectations of Maria, along with Vladimir and Miss K.I.T. According to Schmid the entire tale may be read 'as a prosaic antidote to the sentimental idyll of Karamzin'.[57] And it is not only in the outrageous denouement that we see this; it is present almost from the outset. That is, there is, actually, no 'consequently' at all, and the expectations of Maria and her doomed beloved are soon comically thwarted. Thus, their secret trysts have to be stopped as winter sets in; Maria's parents are not at all 'cruel', and give their usual blessing before Maria retires for the night of her elopement. Indeed, Pushkin has clearly moved his agenda on from Tatiana, in the sense that Maria is not at all a spiritual orphan as the earlier heroine had been, and as many of her successors were to be.[58] Moreover, after the fateful night of the blizzard, when Maria falls ill and in her delirium gives her secret love away, they decide that she should marry Vladimir. In other words, if Maria had not believed in the 'deceptions' of literature, none of this silly rigmarole need have happened.

In any event, because of the bizarre set of events of the night of the blizzard, chance or fate intervene to frustrate all expectations. In another way, as David Bethea has recently commented, '"Life" emerges triumphant, but it is a life uniquely aware of literary role-playing and conventions'.[59] Now, in *Evgenii Onegin*, Tatiana has to learn some painful lessons before she too, and through her, real, Russian life emerge triumphant. She changes and grows, through her reinterpretation of the interrelationship between literature and life. What happens to Maria in these regards? In this kind of area, it seems to me that, although *The Blizzard* is a parodic reworking of the novel, which was being completed at exactly the same time as the tale was written, the shorter work operates utterly differently. Certainly, Maria is spared the separation from the man she still claims to love, as Tatiana was not spared, nor does she suffer the agonies that some of the 'daughters of Tatiana' were to undergo. But, equally, I find it highly debatable as to whether she has really changed at the end. As Ann Shukman noted, she is still prepared to play the role of a literary heroine even at the end of the story.[60]

Indeed, the narrator makes this explicit in a number of metatextual remarks. As Maria awaits the final scene with Burmin, 'She prepared a most unexpected *denouement* and impatiently awaited the moment of *romantic explanation*' (p. 72, my emphases). Burmin is sent to the garden by Praskovia, to find Maria 'by the pond, under a willow, *with a book* in her hand and wearing a white dress, a *real heroine from a novel*' (ibid., my emphases). Pushkin makes his cross-reference to *Onegin* even more apparent as Burmin begins his speech: 'Maria Gavrilovna remembered St-Preux's first letter' (p. 73). In other words, exactly echoing Tatiana in chapters two and three, and even in her final speech, Maria is still imagining that she is like Rousseau's Julie, that is, she still 'imagines herself to be a heroine' of the French novels on which she had been brought up. It is, in fact, only in the very last line that Maria, having discovered that she and Burmin are already married, and so can 'live happily ever after', behaves 'not as the "literary" heroine would have done, i.e. fainted or cried out, but with the reaction of a normal girl'.[61] In other words, the heroine's reading remains deeply embedded in her consciousness almost to the very end, and her escape from 'the confines of the text to join the metatextual narrator in a rejection of Romantic idealism', as de Beaudoin has it, is far from entirely convincing.

Either way, in this work, written, as we know, while Pushkin himself awaited the 'romantic denouement' of his own marriage, he was able to be relaxed and full of parodic bonhomie about the deceptions of literature and the tragic consequences that might befall those who took novels too literally. Maria and Burmin are spared not, perhaps, because they are able to escape their literary masks, as Bethea and Davydov suggest,[62] but because Pushkin simply chose to spare them, for reasons of autobiographical wish-fulfilment. His followers, however, saw things rather more darkly. At the same time, the topos of the heroine reading was transmogrified into an epiphanic moment of awakening, although by no means necessarily to a better life.

3. READING DECEIVES; READING AWAKENS

3.1 *Princess Zizi*

As Carolyn Ayers has suggested, in the post-Pushkinian society tale, education in general, including reading, became an important ingredient to explain the heroine's character.[63] On the whole, she suggests, the society tale would seem to advocate independent reading for the heroine, which is then viewed as a positive marker, specifically of her aspirations to step beyond her pre-ordained sphere. At the same time, unsupervised reading may well be unbalanced, arbitrary, and possibly, therefore, an ambiguous factor in the heroine's development. Odoevskii's *Princess Zizi* reflects many of these tendencies, as well as continuing in part the theme of the deceptions of reading.

The format of much of the story seeks deliberately to recreate the fictional world in which Tatiana and Maria had been so engrossed, comprised as it is of letters between Zizi and her confidante Maria Ivanovna. Moreover, the preamble to this correspondence has another, rather sly allusion to *Onegin*, in that we are told that Zizi's first letter, composed somewhere around 1815, 'was written in fairly correct Russian' (p. 262),[64] unlike Tatiana's which the narrator has to translate from the French original. Already, in one sense, we have moved on from Tatiana. Zizi's reading is then foregrounded, in the sense that within twenty lines of her first letter we are told of her reading habits. Again, there are subtle references back to Tatiana, as well as new motifs. The first work she refers to is *Clarissa*, so that we at once know that Zizi too is enamoured of Richardson. But it is the new notes, I feel, that are particularly significant.

As soon as Zizi mentions her reading, she adds 'I continue to steal books from papa's library, as before' (p. 263). Clearly, then, the reading of this heroine is unsupervised, and highly arbitrary; so arbitrary, in fact, that she is unable to complete *Clarissa*, as the final volume is missing! Moreover, Odoevskii also seeks to develop the motif of nocturnal secrecy which was really only latent in Tatiana's case. Not only does Zizi break the taboo of parental prohibition in stealing the books, but the whole situation is loaded with a more general erotic *frisson*. Whereas Tatiana had read her mother's books, these are specifically her father's books: the disobedient daughter invades the patriarchal library, which is locked, to steal the father's secret. The primal, fairy-tale resonances are further enhanced when Zizi scratches herself pulling Richardson's novel from behind the restraining wire.

At first, there is no real suggestion that Zizi will follow Tatiana to imitate the fate of Clarissa, or Julie or Delphine. Indeed, reading is seen more as an emblem of the woman striving to educate herself above and beyond her restricted provincial station. Thus, when the villainous male protagonist begins to visit, Zizi is afraid to talk to him of her reading, though she longs to, for fear of appearing a 'pedant'. Like Tatiana, she does indeed fall in love with him, precisely because he is the first man she has met, but, at this stage, there is no suggestion that this is *because of* her reading proclivities. However, we are not to be disappointed. Later in the tale, Gorodkov, although now married to her sister, will come to visit Zizi. As she, in a scene that also echoes *The Blizzard*, awaits her fate, Zizi recalls her whole life. In particular, she remembers the impact the books she had read in secret had had on her, how the 'forbidden book' had lain beneath her pillow, as Tatiana's had as well, and how reading had widened 'her sphere of ideas' (p. 284), had changed her whole view of life. In this regard she follows Tatiana very closely. Moreover, when she remembers the seducer Gorodkov, she reflects that 'in his conversation she had heard the cherished, beloved words which, before he came along, she had encountered only in books' (p. 285). Retrospectively, at least, we are led to surmise that Zizi had fallen in love with this 'perfidious tempter' precisely because she had been made ready for this by her illicit reading.

In fact, Zizi escapes Gorodkov's evil designs, which were anyway pecuniary. Odoevskii's rereading of the Tatiana plot has, however, added some new important notes. Reading valorizes the heroine, and is emblematic of her desire to escape the claustrophobic confines of the provinces. At the same time, he has darkened the dangers facing the gullible heroine (neither Tatiana nor Maria Gavrilovna faces actual seduction), and these twin tracks were to be further developed by both male and female writers over the next decade.

3.2 *The Ideal* and *Society's Judgement*

Elena Gan, the daughter of Princess Elena Dolgorukaia, received, for a woman of her day, an unusually high level of education, primarily from her mother.[65] In many of her works we see that education, through prescribed reading, is of paramount importance for the formation of her heroine. As a brief account of two of her best works, *The Ideal* (*Идеал*) and *Society's Judgement* (*Суд света*) will reveal, education to a high level was a decidedly mixed blessing, and could also once more have dangerous consequences for the idealistic young woman who believes in the deceptions of fiction.

Like her creator, the heroine of *The Ideal*, Olga, together with her friend and confidante, Vera, has been educated by her mother. This scene, recalled when the two childhood friends meet after a number of years is deeply valorized. There are several key ingredients which render their education virtually an ideal exemplar of what an education for a young woman should be like. The whole scene is presented as an idyll, in an Edenic Crimea. More significantly, what and how the girls had learned is in very marked contrast to their fictional predecessors: 'during the short southern winters they would devote themselves even more avidly to *study under the careful guidance of the mother*' (p. 8, my emphasis).[66] Polemically, then, Gan in her first work, sets out a new agenda for female reading. These young women do not steal books from mama's or papa's library, but follow a specific course of study ('учение' in the original), under careful guidance.[67] From the age of thirteen (that is, as they begin to grow from girls to women), the mother's library, which contains hundreds of books is made available to them. Olga's mother, herself 'an intelligent, almost learned woman, was something of a free-thinker' (pp. 8-9) and inculcates in the two girls a very thorough, systematic *classical* education: 'Self-sacrifice, magnanimous actions were what stirred their youthful hearts, and from earliest times they grew used to thinking and feeling on the model of the ancients' (p. 9). What they read is also exemplary, a purposeful blend of the ancient and modern, the rational and emotional, the male and female: in the lap of nature 'sitting on the edge of a precipice ... with enormous pleasure they read at first Plutarch and then the inventions of Countess Genlis and Baroness de Staël' (p. 10).

Gan was in some ways an idealist, but she was no fool. Sadly, that is, this exemplary approach to the heroine's reading does not bring happiness. Throughout her work there is, in fact, a very strong intimation that, wonderful though such an education may be in and for itself, it may even be counterproductive. As Carolyn Ayers has written recently: the 'heroines' enhanced sensibilities only bring them increased pain when they face the banalities of a life that falls far short of the ideal they have discovered through learning'.[68] Indeed, in this story Olga's heightened intellectual capacity and sensibilities bring her much grief and suffering, in several ways. We see this from the opening scene, the society ball.[69] Olga is the target of much hostility from the crowd of women, because she reads books, and, even worse, may actually write them herself![70] Moreover, in fact, at least according to her hard-bitten confidante Vera, the values they had learned are effectively, *damaging*: 'I came to see how irrelevant in our society are lofty ideas, magnanimity, nobility' (p. 10).[71] For Olga herself her 'ideal' education will also prove actually dangerous, in a way that will bring Gan close to a rereading of Tatiana's situation. Like Tatiana she is married off to a military man, Colonel Goltsberg, with whom she has nothing in common. She still lives in the world of books, in a way that is akin to the young Tatiana: 'sometimes, when she read some moralistic novel, an ideal appeared before her' (pp. 11-12). As the true nature of the life of an army wife emerges, Olga seeks escape: 'Olga understood her situation and only talked to her husband about the most trivial things. And this disharmony, this spiritual loneliness reinforced her tendency to solitude and reverie ... She gave herself up to her books, her poetry, her *fantasies*' (p. 14 - my emphasis).

And so, 'books' only intensify 'fantasies', a clear echo of Pushkin's 'romany' leading to 'obmany'. So far, so unfulfilled and unhappy. Things will deteriorate significantly, however, because, following Tatiana, Maria Gavrilovna and Zizi, Olga will let these 'fantasies' lead her into falling in love with a man she does not know, although she believes that she does. This is the poet, Anatolii, Olga's ideal. She has read his poetry, and believed that its ardent sentiments reflect the man. When she meets him in the 'northern Babylon' of St Petersburg, she all but enters into an adulterous liaison with him, even though, in reality, he is a worthless, vain 'perfidious tempter'. Throughout this sorry second half of the tale, Gan makes it apparent that it is precisely Olga's book-induced fantasies which lead to this near- tragic outcome, and there are many allusions to *Onegin* to reinforce the point. Thus, when we first encounter Anatolii, in the metonymic guise of a package of his books which Olga receives, she ejaculates 'It's he! He!' as Tatiana had done when deciding that Onegin would be her true love. (This exclamation will be repeated when she later actually meets him at a dacha on the edge of town.) When she first sees him she is at the theatre, the visit to which is heralded by a (slightly incorrect) quotation, a disguised epigraph, in fact, from chapter one of *Onegin*: 'The theatre's full, the boxes glitter'. The narrator leaves us in no doubt what kind of man Anatolii really is, terming him a 'Lovelace towards women' (p. 31). In other words, like Onegin, he is 'certainly no Grandison'. Tatiana discovers the true Onegin when she reads his reading during her visit to his house. So too, Olga uncovers the real side of her ideal, when she reads Anatolii's venal letter to a friend, also on a visit to his empty home. In the end, again following Tatiana in a different, religious key, Olga finds redemption, but the problem of what and how the heroine should read has been left unresolved. This remained of great concern to Elena Gan throughout her short life, and she returned to it on several occasions, including in perhaps her finest work, *Society's Judgement*. The reading and education of the heroine Zenaida are treated in a very similar way to *The Ideal*.

Society's Judgement is an even darker work, and opens with a very bitter prologue about the reception of the woman of intellect in provincial society, where she will be 'exhibited like a dancing monkey, like a snake in a flannel blanket',[72] in other words, like a fair-ground freak. The story as a whole is a complex one, but one of the resonances of the title is the way in which Zenaida too is treated as 'a degenerate of the female gender' (p.54) by society's judgement. At the end of the story, like Olga in *The Ideal*, and, *mutatis mutandis*, following in the steps of Tatiana, Maria and Zizi, Zenaida takes to the pen to explain her conduct, and this testament (she is dead by the time its recipient receives it) gives a brief account of her life, including her education. Like Olga, Zenaida reveres the memory of her mother, who among many other things, was her 'teacher' ('наставница') (p. 106). Sadly, she had died when Zenaida was at the critical age of 13. Her father is crushed by grief, and so Zenaida is left much to her own devices. Despite the lack of maternal supervision, however, she does acquire as rigorous and broad-ranging an education as Olga, by virtue of attending her brother's lessons, and by reading omnivorously in the family library. Thereafter, although this is now less of a central theme, the consequences of this reading are similar to those for Olga. She is married to another military man with whom she has nothing in common, and is shunned by female society for her cleverness. But Zenaida is made of sterner stuff than Olga, and she does not make the same mistake as earlier heroines. When she does meet a man who could fulfil her, the main narrator Vlodinskii, she eschews all but the most platonic of relationships. Admittedly, this does not save her, or him for that matter, from the story's tragedies, but there is some kind of advance, in that this heroine does not seem to believe in the 'fantasies' or 'deceptions' of books, whether novels or not.

Generally, Elena Gan followed on where Pushkin had left off, and certainly added important new aspects to the theme of the heroine's reading. For the most part, however, she did not develop the motif of the 'purloined book', which we see in *Princess Zizi*, except in her final, testamentary work, *A Futile Gift* (*Напрасный дар*), in which the teenage poetess, Aniuta begins to discover her own 'gift' by stealing and immersing herself in the 'forbidden fruit' of library books. (As I have written in detail on this work and this theme elsewhere, I will say no more on this work here.[73]) This topos was to remain important in the rest of the 1840s, as we will see from a brief consideration of two early works by Dostoevskii.

4. READING AWAKENS

4.1 *Poor Folk* and *Netochka Nezvanova*

In both these works, the adolescent heroines, Varenka and Netochka, follow almost exactly in Princess Zizi's footsteps by stealing books from a man's library. In both cases, and the treatment is indeed very similar, the theft and the secret reading of the purloined volumes give the adolescent girls coded erotic pleasure, and the scene is a marker of their entry into the adult, patriarchal world.[74]

In *Poor Folk*, Varenka's tale is an interpolation in the main, epistolary novel. Amongst many painful episodes she recounts her feelings for the tutor, Pokrovskii. He is in his twenties, while Varenka is about 15. As her feelings for him deepen, she increasingly wants him to stop treating her like a child, that is, she wants him to treat her as a woman. To this end, she decides she needs to be better educated, and so, one day, she sneaks into his room, full of trepidation: 'my heart was beating so hard, so hard that it seemed to want to leap out of my chest' (p. 35). She steals one of his books, and the illicit, quasi-sexual nature of the purloining of these letters is made obvious by her breathless recreation of the scene: 'Blushing, turning pale, trembling with excitement and fear, I took the stolen book back to my room, resolved to read it all the way through at night, by my night-light, while mummy was sleeping' (p. 36). We note several details: the bodily sensations; the nocturnal scene, the reading in bed, the desire to keep her secret from her mother. All of these moments return us to chapters two and three of *Onegin*, but in a very different key.

Bathetically, her captured treasure turns out to be a worm-eaten, incomprehensible Latin tome, but she perseveres, and returns for more. She is discovered, and Pokrovskii's anger produces a reaction in her which both again points up the covert sexual connotations of the scene, and also echoes Tatiana's letter: 'I didn't know what I could do, where I could put myself *from shame*' (p. 37 - my emphasis). Soon, however, he forgives her, and willingly lends her books for her to read during the long night watches as her mother draws closer to death. This lending of books brings them closer together. But when her mother makes a temporary recovery their meetings must come to an end ... A coda to the episode comes shortly afterwards. It is Pokrovskii's birthday, and Varenka decides that she must prove herself a true grown-up, by giving him books, and hits on - a complete set of Pushkin! And so we have described a metatextual full circle. The heroine's reading is now a mark of her maturation: the sign of complete maturity is the ability to buy the complete Pushkin!

Netochka Nezvanova treats these motifs in a very similar vein. In the second section of the ultimately incomplete novel, Netochka, having escaped the clutches of her evil and abusive step-father, Efimov, is now living as a ward in the house of Petr Aleksandrovich. She reaches the age of 13, and begins to feel that she is entering a new phase of her life. She prefaces this episode in language which again only very thinly disguises the link between reading and sexual maturation: 'And at this time fate suddenly and unexpectedly turned my life in an extremely strange way ... and I myself, without noticing it, was entirely transported into a new world; there was no time for me to turn round, to look round, to think; I could perish, I even felt that: but the allure was stronger than fear' (p. 232). This new forbidden, but enticing world is not some illicit vice, but the locked library of her guardians. Developing the motif from *Princess Zizi* and his own earlier work, Dostoevskii emphasizes the fairy-tale, mythic, rites of passage elements of Netochka's initiation into the patriarchal world. There are *three* doors leading out of the dining-room, the *third* of which leads into the library. The bookcases here, as in Zizi's house, are usually locked, but one day Netochka finds the key on the floor. Most of the books belong to the paternal figure of Petr, who had inherited them: the word of many fathers down through the generations. Netochka had been allowed some reading: 'but up to now I had been given things to read with great circumspection, so that I had guessed without difficulty that there was much forbidden to me, and much was a secret for me' (p. 233). Now, like Zizi, Aniuta and Varenka she decides to break this prohibition, and takes a novel. For her too this action produces a vivid bodily response: 'I carried the book off to my room with such a pounding and faltering heart, that I felt that a major revolution was taking place in my life' (ibid.). She doesn't yet read the book, but makes safe the key to ensure later access. Despite the fact that, in the earlier episode of the novel, she had shown great treachery and lack of filial feeling for her poor, abused mother, - and indeed, had colluded in this abuse! - Netochka now makes the following extraordinary declaration: 'I hid it [the key], and - this was the first bad thing I had done in my life' (ibid.).

Clearly, then, Dostoevskii has developed this motif of the stealing of the forbidden fruit from the (Fathers') tree of knowledge, to bring out the primal moment. For the following three years Netochka is able to read without restraint and, indeed, it effects a revolution in her life. Reading has become the heroine's door to the patriarchal world, but she must still literally steal the key to this sanctum.

For both of the young Dostoevskii's young heroines reading is initially fraught with danger, although it ultimately might liberate them. In this sense, he has moved beyond the Pushkinian notion of the 'dangerous book'. For one of the fullest, and final treatments of this topos we must return to the year before Dostoevskii had *Poor Folk* published, 1845. It is with a consideration of Maria Zhukova's *The Dacha on the Peterhof Road* (*Дача на петергoвскoй дороге*) that I will conclude.

4.2 *The Dacha on The Peterhof Road*

As in *The Ideal*, one of the main dynamics here is provided by the differences between two deeply contrastive heroines, the worldly-wise Mary, and the utterly Romantic Zoia. It is the latter's life and death which is to prove the most dysphoric version of the tale of the heroine's reading. As again in Gan, we learn of this only later in the story. Zoia had grown up as one of Miss K.I.T.'s 'provincial misses who derive their knowledge of the world and of life from books'. The daughter of a Swiss governess and yet another decent but boring military man, Zoia had been orphaned young, and was raised by one of the several valorized older women in the story, Vera Iakovlevna.[75] In an unsupervised way, Zoia is able to read all the small library left by her mother. Soon she knows virtually by heart 'Chateaubriand, and Lessing, and Iffland, and

Madame Cottin, and even Byron - in the original, but the poor girl understood little of this' (p. 277).[76] Carolyn Ayers sees this in a positive light: 'For Zoia, this is a "blessed time", when she is allowed to discover moral ideas unencumbered by any attached expectations. Lacking intellectual guidance after the death of her mother, Zoia nevertheless benefits from a protective and nurturing home environment that does not actively *discourage* learning.'[77] Certainly, at this stage, there are no warnings against this kind of reading - but the consequences are, I believe, to be literally fatal.

Indeed, although willingly and apparently happily engaged to a dull but worthy local man, Zoia 'falls in love', not, this time with the first man she sees, but with the first romantic stranger, namely the visiting and significantly named Prince Evgenii. She breaks off her engagement, only to discover that Evgenii has been toying with her feelings. Zoia is driven to a nervous collapse by the treachery of this latest 'perfidious tempter', although she had fallen all too willingly. In fact, we already know the long-term consequences of her collapse, and this knowledge deprives the reader of any real hope that she will recover. Moreover, knowing the consequences, we can see how dreadful will be the result of her insane actions.

The implications and resonances of Zoia's actions and beliefs had already emerged in a long conversation with Mary. Here as elsewhere in the story, Zhukova makes very apparent that she is continuing the discourse of *Evgenii Onegin* and taking it to one of its possible conclusions. Thus, as we are introduced to the still half insane young woman, we are told that her true love is for music. When she sings, for hours on end, 'she said that *he* is listening to her, that *he* is talking to her in the music. Who this *he* was, she didn't say; what's more, no-one knew whether he was a real being or the creation of her deranged imagination' (p. 263 - italics in original).

Clearly, I believe, Zhukova echoes Tatiana, to lay bare one interpretation of her story. Again we have the whispered 'he', while to 'imagine oneself a heroine' is to be 'deranged'. Zoia and thoroughly modern Mary discuss love and marriage: Mary dismisses the romantic notions of 'antediluvian' Zoia, who believes that one should only marry for love, as 'straight out of a novel' (p. 272). In other words, Zoia believes in the 'deceptions' of novels, which are later equated with 'ravings'. Fearing for her mental state, Mary tries to be gentle with her wild friend, but eventually declares: 'Get to know life, Zoia, and you'll stop saying this' (p. 273).

Zhukova, then, takes this theme further than any of the other writers considered here. But are we to think that the heroine's reading is to blame for her 'ravings'? I think we should. Towards the end of the interpolated section detailing poor Zoia's fall, the three older women gather together to consider the state of modern morals. One declares that nowadays 'there is a different education, everything foreign ... Eternal love is only found in novels' (p. 303).

By the end of the story, Zoia, who believes that this kind of love is found in real life as well as in novels, pays the ultimate price of death.

Bethea and Davydov in their article on *The Tales of Belkin* argue for the central role of *The Undertaker*, and that Pushkin in that story, as it were, 'buries' Romanticism. So too here: in the death of Zoia Zhukova takes the topos of the 'deceptions' of novels, the 'fantasies' of books to its ultimate conclusion. Tatiana, Maria, Zizi, Olga and the others have escaped more or less from the 'dangerous book'. In the *Tales of Belkin* Pushkin had in some sense also suggested that Romanticism can kill, in the cases of Vladimir, and Silvio in *The Shot*. Zhukova takes up this theme to develop it in a much darker vein. For the Russian heroine, then, as we have seen in several different variations, what and how she reads in the first half of the nineteenth century was a very serious matter indeed: what you read could change your life for good or ill, or even kill you!

NOTES

1. See the following works, for example, Luc J.Beaudoin, *Resetting the Margins. Russian Romantic Verse Tales and the Idealized Woman*, Peter Lang, New York, 1997, pp. 157-212; Diana L.Burgin, 'Tatiana Larina's *Letter to Onegin*, or *La plume Criminelle*', *Essays in Poetics*, XVI, 2, 1991, pp. 12-23; J. Douglas Clayton, *Ice and Flame. Aleksandr Pushkin's 'Eugene Onegin'*, University of Toronto Press, Toronto, Buffalo, London, 1985; Paul Debreczeny, *Social Functions of Literature. Alexander Pushkin and Russian Culture*, Stanford University Press, Stanford, California, 1997, pp. 21-8; Caryl Emerson, 'Tatiana' in Sona Stephan Hoisington, ed., *A Plot of Her Own. The Female Protagonist in Russian Literature*, Northwestern University Press, Evanston, Illinois, 1995, pp. 6-20; George Gibian, 'Love by the Book: Pushkin, Stendhal, Flaubert', *Comparative Literature*, VIII, 2, 1956, pp. 97-109; Michael R.Katz, 'Love and Marriage in Pushkin's *Evgeny Onegin*', *Oxford Slavonic Papers*, XVII, 1984, pp. 77-89; Iurii Lotman, *Roman A.S. Pushkina 'Evgenii Onegin.' Kommentarii*, Prosveshchenie, Leningrad, 1980; Stanley Mitchell, 'Tatiana's Reading', *Forum for Modern Language Studies*, IV, part 1, 1968, pp. 1-21; Vladimir Nabokov, *'Eugene Onegin'. A Novel in Verse by Alexandr Pushkin*, Routledge and Kegan Paul, London, II and III, 1964; William Mills Todd III, *Fiction and Society in the Age of Pushkin. Ideology, Institutions, and Narrative*, Harvard University Press, Cambridge, Mass. and London, 1986, pp. 106-36. See also the chapter by Marguerite Palmer in *Alexander Pushkin. Myth and Monument*.

2. Gibian, op. cit., p. 97.

3. Ibid., p. 98. The other novels Gibian discusses are Stendhal's *Le Rouge et le Noir* and Flaubert's *Madame Bovary*.

4. Debreczeny, op. cit., p. 21. This was a phenomenon which was not only to be found in Russia, of course, as Gibian has illustrated, and as a reading of Jane Austen would show, especially *Sense and Sensibility* and *Northanger Abbey*.

5. Todd, op. cit., pp. 110-11.

6. Debreczeny, op. cit., p. 22.

7. Here and throughout all translations are my own, unless otherwise stated.

8. For this suggestion, see Lotman, op. cit., p. 19.

9. Of course, the other characters are similarly formed, especially Onegin and Lenskii. For discussions of this see de Beaudoin, who comments (op. cit., p. 176): 'Each character has his/her reality shaped by literature, even the metatextual narrator'; Todd, op. cit., pp. 110-11 and Debreczeny, op. cit., p. 24. The last critic also has an interesting discussion of whether those characters who are not particularly influenced by their reading fare any better.

10. This word can be translated as 'deceits', 'deceptions', 'illusions', and otherwise. *Pace* Nabokov who comments (op. cit.II, pp. 287-8) 'This might be rendered also: "she fell in love with the deceptions," but I am certain that "fictions" or "illusions" comes closer to Pushkin's meaning ...' I feel that 'deceptions' fits Pushkin's theme best.

11. de Beaudoin, op. cit., p. 176.

12. Debreczeny, op. cit., p. 22.

13. Emerson, op. cit., pp. 8-9.

14. Todd, op. cit., p. 125. See especially Nabokov, Lotman and Burgin for the precise influences on Tatiana. Rousseau's *Julie* would seem to have been the most important influence, and indeed the most enduring: see Katz, op. cit., pp. 79-80.

15. Debreczeny, op. cit., p. 25, offers a different interpretation of this line, seeing it as a reflection of the power of both biological time and societal pressures.

16. de Beaudoin, op. cit., p. 175.

17. Debreczeny, op. cit., p. 24.
18. See Nabokov, op. cit., II, pp. 338-48 for details of these heroines: we should note that they are all victims in one way or another.
19. Lotman, op. cit., p. 55, notes the following: 'Even in the 1770s the reading of books, especially novels, was regarded as a dangerous occupation and a not entirely decent one for women'.
20. The theme of the lack of supervision of the woman's reading, both in Tatiana's case, and especially in other writers will be discussed later in this chapter. See also Carolyn Jursa Ayers, 'L'Education Sentimentale or the School of Hard Knocks? The Heroine's Education in the Society Tale' in Neil Cornwell, ed., *The Society Tale in Russian Literature. From Odoevskii to Tolstoi*, Rodopi, Amsterdam and Atlanta, 1998, pp. 153-68, especially, pp. 159-60.
21. See Lotman, op. cit., p. 229 for an interesting discussion of Tatiana's sincerity at this point.
22. Debreczeny, op. cit., p. 23.
23. See W.F. Ryan and Faith Wigzell, 'Gullible Girls and Dreadful Dreams. Zhukovsky, Pushkin and Popular Divination', *Slavonic and East European Review*, LXX, 4, 1992, October, pp. 647-69.
24. There have been many analyses of Tatiana's dream as, amongst other things, a 'royal road to her unconscious'. For two of the most recent (and controversial!), see J.Douglas Clayton, 'Towards a Feminist Reading of Tatiana's Dream', *Canadian Slavonic Papers*, XXIX, 2-3, 1987, pp. 255-65 and Daniel Rancour-Laferriere, 'Puškin's Still Unravished Bride: A Psychoanalytic Study of Tat'jana's Dream', *Russian Literature* XXV (15 February 1989), pp. 215-58.
25. See Katz, op. cit., passim.
26. If mistake it be, we should also note how powerfully productive for the culture this mistake has proven to be!
27. Clayton, op. cit., 1985, p. 126.
28. Todd, op. cit., p. 125.
29. See Nabokov, op. cit., II, pp. 338-47.
30. See for example Debreczeny, op. cit., p. 25, and Gibian, op. cit., especially pp. 99-100.
31. This is Debreczeny's suggestion: see op. cit., p. 25.
32. de Beaudoin, op. cit., p. 175.
33. Burgin, op. cit., p. 13.
34. See Joe Andrew, 'Mothers and Daughters in Russian Literature of the First Half of the Nineteenth Century', *Slavonic and East European Review*, LXXIII, 1, Jan. 1995, pp. 37-60, especially pp. 42-50.
35. Todd, for example, notes, (op. cit.,p. 123): 'Richardson's novels were once so popular that Tatiana's mother did not have to read them to feel their influence; now Tatiana must pore over them, but they still retain their power to impose their patterns upon the willing reader'.
36. See Burgin's delightful article on Tatiana the writer.
37. For this, see especially the work of Nabokov, Lotman and Burgin.
38. See Burgin, op. cit., pp. 16-17.
39. How dangerous this mistake might be, Zhukova will show; Jane Austen *mutatis mutandis* had already done this.
40. Lotman, op. cit., p. 230.
41. R.A. Gregg, 'Tat'yana's Two Dreams: The Unwanted Spouse and the Demon Lover', *Slavonic and East European Review*, XLVIII, 1970, October, pp. 492-505, especially, p. 494.
42. Katz, op. cit.

43. See especially p. 127.
44. See ibid., p.128. See also Lotman, op. cit., pp. 314-21 for the way in which Pushkin radically altered the contents of Onegin's library in the process of working on the novel, changes which markedly diminished him.
45. Ayers, op. cit., p. 166.
46. de Beaudoin, op. cit., p. 207.
47. See Katz, op. cit., p. 88 and Nabokov, op. cit., III, p. 240.
48. See Todd, op. cit., p. 131.
49. Katz, op. cit., pp. 88-9. In the light of my own work on the role of mothers in their daughters' lives, I am not convinced that 'nearest and dearest' is really the right phrase!
50. See David M. Bethea and Sergei Davydov, 'Pushkin's Saturnine Cupid: The Poetics of Parody in *The Tales of Belkin*', *PMLA*, XCVI, 1, 1981, pp. 8-21.
51. See Paul Debreczeny, *The Other Pushkin.A Study of Alexander Pushkin's Prose Fiction*, Stanford University Press, Stanford, 1983, pp. 85-91.
52. See Wolf Schmid, 'Nevesučij zenich i vetrenye suzenye.Podteksty i razvertyvajuščiesja rečevye kliše v povesti Puškina "Metel"' in Eric de Haard, Thomas Langerak and Willem G.Weststeijn eds, *Semantic Analysis of Literary Texts. To Honour Jan van der Eng on the Occasion of his 65th Birthday*, pp. 443-66, especially pp. 443-4.
53. Bethea and Davydov, op. cit., p. 10.
54. Debreczeny, op. cit., 1983, p. 86.
55. All references to this story will be to the following edition: A.S.Pushkin, *Sobranie sochineii v desiati tomakh*, Khudozhestvennaia Literatura, Moscow, 1959-62, V (1960), pp. 63-76.
56. Op. cit., p. 11.
57. Schmid, op. cit., p. 446.
58. For discussions of this type see Joe Andrew, *Women in Russian Literature, 1780-1863*, Macmillan, Houndmills, 1988 and Joe Andrew, *Narrative and Desire in Russian Literature, 1822-49*, Macmillan, Houndmills, 1993.
59. See David M.Bethea, *Realizing Metaphors.Alexander Pushkin and the Life of the Poet*, The University of Wisconsin Press, Wisconsin, 1998, p. 132.
60. See Ann Shukman, 'The Short Story, Theory, Analysis, Interpretation', *Essays in Poetics*, II, 2, 1977, pp. 27-95, p. 62.
61. Ibid., p. 83.
62. Bethea and Davydov, op. cit., pp. 11-13.
63. Ayers, op. cit., p. 155.
64. All references to this work will be to the following edition: V.F.Odoevskii, *Sobranie sochinenii v dvukh tomakh*, Khudozhestvennaia literatura, Moscow, 1981, ed. V.I. Sakharov, II, pp. 258-303.
65. For an account of Gan's life and work see H.A.Aplin, *M.S.Zhukova and E.A.Gan. Women Writers and Female Protagonists, 1837-1843*, Unpublished Ph.D Dissertation, University of East Anglia, 1988.
66. This and subsequent translations from this work are from *The Ideal* in Joe Andrew, *Russian Women's Shorter Fiction. An Anthology, 1835-1860*, Oxford University Press, Oxford, 1996, pp. 1-49.
67. See also Ayers, op. cit., pp. 159-60.
68. Ibid., p.160.

69. For discussions of this topos, see Joe Andrew, 'Le grand monde est un bal masqué': The Function of the Ball in the Russian Society Tale' in E. Egerberg, A.J. Mørch, O.M. Selberg, eds, *Life and Text. Essays in Honour of Geir Kjetsaa on the Occasion of his 60th Birthday,* in *Meddelelser* 79, Oslo, 1997, pp. 45-57, and Joe Andrew, 'Another Time, Another Place: Gender and the Chronotope in the Society Tale' in Neil Cornwell, ed., *The Society Tale in Russian Literature. From Odoevskii to Tolstoi*, Rodopi, Amsterdam and Atlanta, GA., 1998, pp. 127-52.
70. For a discussion of this theme, see Joe Andrew, '"A Dancing Monkey or a Snake in a Flannel Blanket": The Image of the Female Writer in Russian Literature in the First Half of the Nineteenth Century' in Linda Edmonson, ed., *Gender in Russian History and Culture*, Palgrave, Houndmills, 2001, pp. 52-72.
71. This was a common enough situation in real life Russia at the time. As Debreczeny, 1997, p. 49 observed about the writer Sokhanskaia: 'Although the schooling Sokhanskaia had received at the Kharkov Institute left much to be desired, she had been "educated beyond her station"'.
72. For this work, see *Society's Judgement* in Joe Andrew, *Russian Women's Shorter Fiction. An Anthology, 1835-1860*, pp. 50-121. For a broader discussion of this theme see the reference in note 70 above.
73. For a discussion of this work, see Joe Andrew, *Narrative and Desire*, pp. 131-8.
74. For a discussion of *Netochka Nezvanova* in these terms, see ibid., pp. 214-26, and for *Poor Folk*, see Joe Andrew, 'The Seduction of the Daughter: Sexuality in the Early Dostoevsky and the Case of Бедные Люди *[Poor Folk]* ' in Joe Andrew and Robert Reid, eds, *Neo-Formalist Papers,* Rodopi, Amsterdam and Atlanta, 1998, pp. 123-41. All references to the texts will be to the following edition: F.M.Dostoevskii, *Polnoe Sobranie Sochinenii v tridsati tomakh*, Nauka, Leningrad, 1972; *Netochka Nezvanova* in II (1972), p. 142-267 and *Poor Folk* in I (1972), pp. 13-108.
75. For a discussion of these and other matriarchs, see Joe Andrew, 'The Benevolent Matriarch in Elena Gan and Mar'ia Zhukova' in Rosalind Marsh, ed., *Women and Russian Culture. Projections and Self-Perceptions,* Berghahn Books, New York, Oxford, 1998, pp. 60-77.
76. All references to this work are to the following edition: V. Uchenova, ed., *Dacha na petergovskoi doroge: Proza russkikh pisatel'nits pervoi poloviny XIX veka* , Sovremennik, Moscow, 1986, pp. 245-322.
77. See Ayers, op. cit., p. 160 (her italics).

Pushkin in the Mirror of Shakhovskoi

by

LYUBOV KISELEVA

The literary-historical and theoretical issue of Pushkin's contacts with 'archaists', and in particular, with Shakhovskoi in 1818 was raised by Iurii Tynianov[1] who showed that Pushkin in the years after graduation from the Lyceum was undergoing an evolutionary development in the direction of overcoming literary group interests. The young Pushkin was a follower of the school of Karamzin-Zhukovskii because of his family traditions and connections. Pushkin's Lyceum epigrams devoted to 'the evil trinity' of Shishkov, Shikhmatov and Shakhovskoi served as a contribution to the epoch of the establishment of 'Arzamas', a proud feeling of belonging to the corporation of the best men of letters of the period, and also as an expression of youthful polemic energy.

Together with the recognition of his poetic vocation Pushkin experienced an urge to liberate himself from the group framework, to embrace the whole spectrum of contemporary literature. Tynianov has shown the importance of Pushkin's literary contacts with the 'junior archaists'.

The interest in the 'senior archaist' Shakhovskoi developed in the same direction but it was also enhanced by another factor. As an active playwright, producer and a theatre figure Shakhovskoi personified the theatre in the literary circles of St Petersburg at the end of the 1810s. This was the facet of literary life and customs which was of utmost interest to Pushkin in his post-Lyceum years.[2]

It is well known that Katenin introduced Pushkin to Shakhovskoi.[3] His visits to the theatrical salon of Shakhovskoi, better known as an 'attic', helped Pushkin to enter the world of the *coulisses* not only with the purpose of becoming acquainted with the life of the theatrical Bohemia (which was so well liked by young noblemen[4]), but also in order to have an inside look at the problems of the craft of scenic and dramatic composition, and to obtain the basic knowledge of straightforward theatre criticism (which was later expressed in the article 'My vision of the Russian theatre' ['Мои замечания об русском театре']).[5]

As for the personal relations between the younger and older contemporaries, we may say that the period of the late 1810s was the time of the most intensive relationships. The leading position, without any doubt, was occupied by Shakhovskoi who was 22 years older than Pushkin and was enjoying the prime of his talent and literary influence. Later on Pushkin and Shakhovskoi met again but then the roles were reversed. When speaking about creative work and literary texts, we should mention a unilateral contact which was, on the whole, characteristic of their relations even later on. Until then Pushkin would be related to the texts of Shakhovskoi,[6] although later Shakhovskoi would work with Pushkin's texts.

However, in the present chapter we cannot deal with all aspects of the extensive problem of the creative contacts between Pushkin and Shakhovskoi. It is not our aim to analyse Pushkin's opinions about Shakhovskoi (these are relatively well known) or his references to the works of his elder contemporary. For us Pushkin is important when seen through the prism of Shakhovskoi. This is why we shall be discussing the stage versions, to be more exact, the dramatized versions of two poems - *Ruslan and Liudmila* and *The Fountain of Bakhchisarai* which were made by Shakhovskoi in the 1820s. The theatre version of *The Queen of Spades* and an original Shakhovskoi tragedy, *Smoliane [the people of Smolensk] in 1611* written by him in the tradition of *Boris Godunov* in 1829-30 have been discussed in our other papers.[7]

Theatrical 'rewriting' (stage versions) - the interpretation of a text into the language of another form of art and the system of another author - is like a double mirror where the poetics of both the interpreter and the interpreted original are reflected. The study of 'rewritings' and their stage life gives us an indicator of the reception of the artistic text by contemporaries. They must not be neglected when analysing Pushkin's creative work even when the scopes of the 'original' and the 'interpretation' are not on the same level.

Ruslan and Liudmila was in fact the first of Pushkin's works to be rewritten as a play. In 1824 Shakhovskoi wrote *Fin*, a comedy.[8] By that time Pushkin had become popular as an author of 'Southern Poems' which were recognized as romantic in Russia. In this connection it is characteristic of Shakhovskoi, a strong opponent of Sentimentalism, that he selected an elegiac episode - the story of Fin and Naina, which in Pushkin's poem is a travesty of the elegy. We could expect as much from Shakhovskoi, but such expectations would not be realized.

Shakhovskoi's stage version was created, in part by expanding speeches, and by inserting situations which enrich the plot, as well as by the introduction of new personalities and the transformation of the protagonists' characters. Although Shakhovskoi tries to preserve Pushkin's irony (especially in the episode of the declaration of love made by an old sorceress to her rejected adorer), the piece on the whole achieves a new meaning - the genre of comedy demanded *a happy ending*. As a result the sorcerer Buduntai - the 'teacher' of Fin (Tavals in Shakhovskoi's piece) in a decisive moment gives back their youth to the unsuccessful lovers. The hero's faithfulness and constant loyalty triumphs over the pride and frivolity of Naina, who, in Shakhovskoi's version, in her youth fell under the influence of 'foreign customs'. Everybody is happy, and virtue is not disgraced.

In our view, Shakhovskoi must have noticed the intertextual play of words with Batiushkov's elegy *The Song of Harald the Brave* (*Песнь Гаральда Смелого*). As Proskurin has noted: 'In the story about Fin Pushkin "deconstructs" the elegiac model (that is, the Batiushkov model: L.K.) by including it in the comic discourse and revealing it as if it were a literary character ... The dénouement of the love story of Fin and Naina is a venomous mockery of elegiac "*Petrarchism*"'.[9] At the same time, we should not forget that Batiushkov himself parodied the elevated image of his hero in a letter to Viazemskii of February 1816, and made him a 'чухонец' (which is almost Fin[n]!).[10]

In brief, we have a situation in which the noble love of a hero from antiquity for a cruel beauty, with colouration derived from Ossian, was simultaneously attracting poets and provoking parodies. On the one hand, Shakhovskoi in his comedy stressed the elegiac mode; but, on the other hand, with his didactic development of the story and its *happy ending*, he took the story, so to speak, to its logical conclusion. To his initiated audience, this could only have seemed a parody. The attempt to unite the travesty of the elegy with a didactic comedy of the eighteenth century was unsuccessful. For us the performance of *Fin* lacked real theatrical success not because of the impact of unfortunate extraneous circumstances (the first-night performance took place just before the St Petersburg flood of 1824[11]), but because of the work's eclecticism and its all too obvious literary idea.

Even within the literary-historical perspective Shakhovskoi's attention to Pushkin's provocative poem, which is both highly polemical and ambivalent, is worthy of note. We should emphasize the fact that Russian audiences in the 1820s (who, it should be remembered, did not protest against the didacticism in Shakhovskoi's own, original comedies), proved themselves to be fairly sensitive to the unintentional parody in the stage version of Pushkin's poem. This happened because this *unintentional* parody excluded the *intentional* parody on which Pushkin had based the entire poetic structure of his *Ruslan and Liudmila*. In the complicated history of the reception of *Ruslan and Liudmila* the theatre episode under discussion here acquires the character of indirect proof of the receptivity of his contemporaries to the literary games which were so characteristic of Pushkin throughout his creative life.[12] Shakhovskoi with his version certainly attempted to be 'a friend of Liudmila and Ruslan' but he was unable to understand the constructional principle of the poem.

The next step, made by Shakhovskoi in the field of dramatizing Pushkin's poetry is *Kerim-Girei*. A romantic trilogy in five parts after *The Fountain of Bakhchisarai*,[13] it was first staged in 1825 and had a longer stage life, still being performed in the 1840s. The role of Zarema was played by the famous Ekaterina Semionova which definitely added to the success of the first-night performance. The staging of *The Fountain of Bakhchisarai*, to a certain extent, was a simpler task. In this case an increase in the 'bulk of the text' was the primary task. To create a full-length performance, it was necessary to increase the amount of the text, which in its turn created the need for new characters to be introduced.

In our view, Shakhovskoi grasped the dual character of *The Fountain of Bakhchisarai*, in which the lyrical element prevails over the narrative. This contradiction can be clearly perceived, and is one which ultimately led Pushkin to abandon further attempts to 'enlarge' the elegy into a *poema*. This is why Shakhovskoi's efforts, when staging the poem, were concentrated on increasing the role of the plot and dramatic moments.

In his development Shakhovskoi follows Pushkin almost exactly[14] but in staging *Kerim-Girei* he was able to create a more interesting and more original play than *Fin*. The playwright has fully used, and deepened in his own manner, the principle of ethnographic and confessional motifs which Pushkin used for building up his plot[15] and which he himself valued the most in his 'Southern Poems'.

In naming *Kerim-Girei* a 'romantic trilogy' Shakhovskoi does not define his play's genre which might be called a tragedy, or even a religious-political tragedy. Even the work's compositional structure: Part One - 'The Tartar Camp', Part Two - 'The Polish Castle', Part Three - 'The Fountain of Bakhchisarai' - shows how Shakhovskoi utilizes the confessional-ethnographic material. In Pushkin's work the religious motif of the opposition between Christianity and Islam is reduced. In reality, the fact that most of the protagonists follow the 'laws of the Prophet' is essentially only a motivation for the plot and the context in which it develops. It is merely exotic *couleur locale* in the tradition of Byron's 'Eastern Poems'. In the case of Shakhovskoi it becomes the core of the whole action.

Mariia in *Kerim-Girei* from the very beginning sees her mission as devoting her whole life to praying for the sinners and non-Christians (see p. 20). When she is captured by Girei, she prays to God that he will be converted to Christianity:

    Когдаж Твоим предназначеньем
    Мария для того жива
    Чтоб, как Эсфирь, своим смиреньем,
    Смирила яростного льва;
    Когда повелено Тобою
    На то в плену ей слезы лить,
    Чтоб верою твоей живою
    Неверных души оживить ... (p. 34)[16]

(When by Thy Predestination / Mariia lives / So that, like Esther, by her submission, / She might subdue the ferocious lion; / When it is decreed by Thee / That she should then shed tears in captivity, / So that, by Thy living faith / She might bring life to the souls of infidels ...)

Shakhovskoi's Girei has serious religious doubts, but he refuses to break the 'covenant of the fathers'.[17] This is what decides his fate, causes his spiritual catastrophe and deepens his feeling of disillusionment with life which, in Pushkin's treatment, was caused by unhappy love:

Мария! Ах! в душе твоей
Был свет, но он с тобою скрылся,
Погас, исчез, на век затмился ...
Затмился ... (p. 49).

(Mariia! Ah! in your soul / There was light, but it was hidden with you, / It went out, vanished, was eclipsed forever ... / Was eclipsed ...)

The contradictions between the Islamic and Christian faiths (the intolerance of Islam, which refuses to recognize the love of enemies; the forgiveness and the forbearance of Christianity) leads to a political conflict in *Kerim-Girei*. The leader of the Moslems, mullah Khamid, intrigues against Mariia, incites Zarema to murder, and plots against Girei, because he is afraid that the Khan might adopt Christianity and cause the 'fall' of the Crimea.

As we can see, the characters of Pushkin's main protagonists were quite radically transformed by Shakhovskoi.[18] The scope of the chapter does not allow for a detailed analysis of this issue. It should only be mentioned that the character of Zarema was transformed the least, because it was more profoundly developed by Pushkin. We shall continue by following the ethnographic line which was treated more thoroughly by Shakhovskoi than by Pushkin. In the poem *The Fountain of Bakhchisarai* the Polish (Western, Christian) world was only sketched in, the main emphasis being laid on the exotic Orient - the world of the harems, the world of love and limitless passions, as well as oriental despotism. The third ethnographic component in Pushkin's poem - the Georgian - is also reduced. We can see it in the peculiar way Pushkin intertwines the two worlds: Christian tolerance and ardent passions ('a sword I have / Born as I was close to the Caucasus', Zarema tells Mariia).

Shakhovskoi, in reverse, gives a Walter Scott-like panorama of different peoples with their customs and national features. In the first part of the trilogy *Kerim-Girei* the traditions of the Tartar warriors are given a thorough treatment. Shakhovskoi brings to the stage six quite separate protagonists with deliberately oriental and conventional-literary names (Iusuf, Mahmet, Uzbek,

Pasvan, etc.). These protagonists seem purely functional: although each of them has his role in the plot, the overall purpose is to demonstrate the negative features of an Oriental character (they are supercilious, benevolent, greedy, servile, insidious, cruel) against the background of which Girei is to appear more vivid - a personality who is not idealized, but still a wise and noble man in spite of his despotism.

The Polish camp is also depicted in more detail than in Pushkin's poem. Shakhovskoi has introduced the idealized characters of the Polish peasants, Jan and Juzefa, as well as the stable-boy Arthur who are ready to sacrifice their lives to save the old prince and his daughter Mariia. Some kind of dissonance is brought into this ideal picture by the hint of some serious sin, which the master of the castle committed in his younger days, and which makes his daughter refuse marriage and devote all her life to prayer. However, these circumstances merely emphasize Mariia's virtues. On the whole, the Poles in the play suggest a nation which is worthy of representing Christianity as opposed to Islam.

An unexpected innovation in Shakhovskoi's romantic trilogy is the introduction of the Jewish character, Haim. In the play he is constantly called 'жид' (a derogatory name for a Jew), and this has a clearly expressed negative connotation. He is a traitor who shows the Tartars a safe way to the castle, and he leads to the situation which results in Maria's captivity. In general, he is characterized by several negative features which have been traditionally associated with the anti-semitic image of Jews. Jan says of him: 'An innkeeper, a robber and a rich man', which fully coincides with the image of a usurer in the European tradition. Indeed, all the protagonists of the play, although so different from each other, equally consider him contemptible.[19] At the same time, precisely thanks to Jan who saves his life[20] we learn details which serve to humanize his image (his wife and 'a throng of children'). From Haim's own words it becomes clear that his betrayal was not inspired by personal but *national* vengeance. He acts in accordance with orders from the Jewish community which regards the Muslims as a tool for retaliation against Christians who humiliate and suppress Jews. The following remark in part explains the behaviour of Haim and shows the Polish nobility in a new light:

> ... польский пан,
> когда потешиться захочет:
> "Повесь жида!" - Еврей висит, а он хохочет.

> (the Polish landlord / when making a joke: /
> 'Hang the Jew!' - The Jew hangs, and he laughs.)

The character of Haim has too significant a role in the play to be considered merely a secondary character. One of the reasons for introducing him into a play based on *The Fountain of Bakhchisarai* might have been Pushkin's poem *The Black Shawl* (1820) in which the 'despised Jew' is an engine of the plot, although this seems a rather insufficient basis.

Even in the 1800s Shakhovskoi displayed an interest in the Jewish theme, an interest which was occasioned by contacts with L. Nevakhovich, a Jewish literary figure from St Petersburg. With Nevakhovich Shakhovskoi wrote a religious tragedy *Deborah* (1810), a subject derived from the Old Testament.[21] In this work, however, his interest was limited to a biblical plot. In the new context it has developed under the influence of Scott's novel *Ivanhoe*, a work renowned as the stimulus for interest in the Jewish theme in European literature. The novel was published in 1820 and was immediately translated into Russian. As early as 1821 it was staged in St Petersburg, in Shakhovskoi's version.[22] The complicated character of Isaac, the usurer, is not without the author's sympathy in Scott's novel although he is far from being a positive hero. In Shakhovskoi's *Kerim-Girei* the Jew becomes a negative character, although he is but not as one-sided as Haim.

But the themes of Jewish protest against oppression, and vengeance for this humiliation, are missing in Scott's novel. It seems to us that Shakhovskoi took the theme from the same literary source as Scott had used in his approach to the problem, namely Shakespeare's *The Merchant of Venice*.

As is well known the character of Shylock also attracted Pushkin by its complexity. Shakespeare's Shylock is disgusting because of his greed and violence, but, at the same time, he attracts our sympathy and respect because of his determination to protect his self-esteem. His hatred of those Christians who insult him and the sentiment of vengeance have been treated in an especially ambivalent way in Shakespeare's play. Shakhovskoi, who knew English, was most probably aware of Shakespeare's play even before it was staged in Russia in 1835. In our view, he attempted to combine the principles of Scott and Shakespeare. His Haim, like Shylock, strives after wealth and is prepared to fight anybody who stands in his way. At the same time, the motif of social damage and the national humiliation of Jews is also relatively strong in Shakhovskoi's play as it was in both Scott and Shakespeare.

But there is yet another motif in Shakhovskoi, an important one for him and one which safeguards the ideological framework of *Kerim-Girei*, and which leads on to the next play he was to base on Pushkin - *Khrisomania or the Love of Money* (*Хризомания, или страсть к деньгам*, 1836), after the short story *The Queen of Spades*. In *Khrisomania* Hermann, a Russian German in Pushkin's story, is transformed into the Jew Irmus.[23] In *Kerim-Girei* Haim, like the later Irmus, is called 'a man of the world' and he himself says about his people: 'We are poor hermits roaming across the earth' (p. 8, cf. also p. 12). The fact that Jews are cosmopolitans, even if forced to be so, causes and explains their negative features for Shakhovskoi, as it equally does their state of oppression. Shakhovskoi is prone to sympathize with all his protagonists when they try to protect the customs of their homeland, even if this leads them into criminal activity. Paradoxically, therefore, in *Kerim-Girei* the enemies, the Tartars and the Poles, come closer to each other, because they are loyal to their land and religion. For Shakhovskoi the character of Haim is necessary as a contrastive background to preserve his idea of patriotism as the norm of human existence. It is precisely here that Shakhovskoi's 'archaism' is best expressed.

In conclusion, we would wish to emphasize that Shakhovskoi, in rewriting Pushkin's *The Fountain of Bakhchisarai* as the original play *Kerim-Girei*, in our view has very wisely followed a tendency which conformed with the direction of the development of Pushkin's interests, as well as the general development of Russian literature: from Byron to Walter Scott and Shakespeare. Equally, he was able to do this within the framework of his own artistic abilities, and his own artistic system. Thus we may speak of a 'selective' Pushkin, as read through the eyes of Shakhovskoi, because Shakhovskoi's texts are not only the products of adaptation to the laws of the stage, but stand as translations into a different author's system. His plot innovations as such are not important, but their direction is significant. We have tried to show that the playwright was successful only when he was able to catch new tendencies; and succeeded in understanding and developing the inner potential of the original text.

NOTES

1. See Iu.N. Tynianov, *Arkhaisty I Pushkin* in Iu.N. Tynianov, *Pushkin I ego sovremenniki*, Nauka, Moscow 1969, pp. 55-6. Here it is strongly emphasized that Pushkin's departure from orthodox Karamzinism coincided in time with the crisis inside the circle: 'The characteristic deviation of Batiushkov and Zhukovskii and the anxiety of the more orthodox Viazemskii and A. Turgenev belong to the year 1818' (see p. 58).
2. See L. Grossman, *Pushkin v teatral'nykh kreslakh. Kartiny russkoi stseny 1817-1820 godov* in Leonid Grossman, *Zapiski d'Arshiaka. Pushkin v teatral'nykh kreslakh*, Khudozhestvennaia literatura, Moscow, 1990.
3. Tynianov quoted the words of Annenkov which later gained general importance in the literature about Pushkin: 'In 1818 Pushkin simply came to Katenin and gave him his walking-stick saying "I came to you as Diogenes to Antithsenes. Beat me - but teach me!" - "To teach the master is to spoil him!", - answered the author of *Olga*' (Ibid., pp. 58-9). For Pushkin's references to Shakhovskoi in the Lyceum, see: S.M. Shavrygin, *Tvorchestvo A.A. Shakhovskogo v istoriko-literaturnom protsesse 1800-1840-kh godov*, Dmitrii Bulanın, St Petersburg, 1996, pp. 36-7.
4. See Iu.M. Lotman, *Teatr I teatral'nost' v stroe kul'tury nachala XIX veka* in Iu.M. Lotman, *Izbrannye statii v 3 tomakh*, Aleksandra, Tallinn, 1992, vol. 1, pp. 277-8.
5. This article was written in 1820, but was not published until 1895.
6. In the course of his work on *Ruslan and Liudmila* Pushkin made use of Shakhovskoi's 'fairy-opera' *The Mermaid* which belonged to the series of well-known 'Mermaids' in the 1800s which had a long stage life in the Russian theatre. The elements of the textual links between Pushkin's poem and Shakhovskoi's fairy-opera were carefully analyzed by Iakubovich in his commentaries and there is no need for us to repeat these things; however, the functions of these borrowings still need to be discussed. Pushkin's jokey poem which is based on parody and travesty incorporates elements of a fairy-opera - a genre which is also comic and parodical. Regarding *Ruslan and Liudmila* see the recent interesting work by Oleg Proskurin, *Poezia Pushkina, ili podvizhnyi palimpsest*, Novoe literaturnoe obozrenie, Moscow, 1999, Chapter I. This author, however, does not write about the fairy-opera as one of the preliminary texts of the Pushkin poem.
7. See my '"Pikovye damy" Pushkina I Shakhovskogo' in *Pushkinskie chteniia v Tartu, 2. Materialy mezhdunarodnoi nauchnoi konferentsii, 18-20 sentiabria 1998g* ., Tartu University Press, Tartu, 2000, pp. 183-203.
8. In the research literature this comedy as well as the other stage versions of Pushkin made by Shakhovskoi have been referred to many times, but as yet it has not been analyzed in a detailed way. The most important discussions are: S. N. Durylin, *Pushkin na stsene*, Izdatel'stvo Akademii Nauk SSSR, Moscow, 1951, pp. 9-13, 22-8 and 33-7; L. Grossman, *Pushkin v teatral'nykh kreslakh*, p. 408; A.A. Gozenpud, ed., A.A. Shakhovskoi, *Komedii. Stikhotvorenia*, Sovetskii pisatel', Leningrad, 1961, p. 65. The only analytical article about *Fin* was written by my student: M. Reppo-Shabarova, 'Komedia A.A. Shakhovskogo "Fin" kak perelozhenie poemy A.S. Pushkina *Ruslan I Liudmila', Russkaia Filologia. Sbornik nauchnykh rabot molodykh filologov*, Tartu University Press, Tartu, 1998, pp. 23-9.
9. Proskurin, op. cit, pp. 32 and 33.
10. See K. Batiushkov, *Sochinenia*, St Petersburg, 1886, III, pp. 371-2; see also the commentaries of Semenko to *The Song of Harald the Brave* in K.N. Batiushkov, *Opyty v stikhakh I proze*, Nauka, Moscow, 1978, p. 558. Shakhovskoi may well not have known about this joke of Batiushkov's, but it certainly could have reached Pushkin.

11. Shakhovskoi's comedy was staged in St Petersburg seven times in the 1824-29 period (including four times in 1827) and in Moscow six times between 1825 and 1834. In our view, Durylin's talk (op. cit., p. 13) of the success of *Fin* is exaggerated.
12. In this connection the ironical words of N.N. Raevskii, who said in a letter to Pushkin on 10 May 1825 that Shakhovskoi should not turn the first chapter of *Evgenii Onegin* into an 'octology', take on an additional meaning. On the one hand, it is clear that the experiment of a playwright who tried to use the material of a comedy for revitalizing the compositional principle of an ancient drama (the comedy *Fin* had the author's subtitle 'In the style of a Greek trilogy') was noticed. This principle is followed by Shakhovskoi in his other stage versions of Pushkin. On the other hand, it is significant that *Onegin* is connected with the earlier poem, a fact which was also emphasized by Pushkin himself. It is possible that the definition 'octology' by Raevskii is an ironical play of words based on the four-part structure of *The Mermaid* in the creation of which Shakhovskoi participated.
13. See *Kerim-Girei. Romanticheskaia trilogia v piati deistvijakh, v stikhakh. Soch. Kniazia A.A. Shakhovskogo. Soderzhanie vziato iz Bakhchisaraiskogo Fontana poemy A.A.(sic!) Pushkina, I mnogie ego stikhi sokhraneny tselikom* in *Panteon russkogo I vsekh evropeiskikh teatrov*, 1841, Part 4. Book 11.
14. Because of the rules of the theatre Shakhovskoi was unable to use the motif of 'secret love', that is, of realizing the game on stage with a (pseudo-)biographical 'subtext' which was brought to the attention of the readers of *The Fountain of Bakhchisarai* by its epilogue.
15. See Proskurin, op. cit., p.137.
16. It is important to mention that Shakhovskoi's Mariia is depicted one-sidely as a positive heroine - a Christian who opposes Muslims. The fact that she is a Catholic, not Orthodox, does not seem to bother the playwright. In one part, indeed, the 'Catholic' motif is especially stressed. Mariia promises Girei that the Catholic world will protect him when the Crimea is inevitably invaded by Russia: 'И западной святыни знамя / Спеши воздвигнуть сам: пока / России мощная рука / В Тавриде вновь не водрузила / Взятаго от нея креста' (p.37). ('And the standard of the western shrine / Hasten to erect yourself: before / The mighty hand of Russia / Once more erects in Tauride / The cross stolen from it').
17. The following words of Girei might serve as some sort of proof of the presence of a mild anti-Catholic motif: 'Быть может, сам я вижу, / Что наш закон не чист и ложен, / .... / Но я люблю моих татар,- / И храбрых *падшей власти римской*/ Рабами сделать не хочу.'(p. 37. Emphasis added). ('Perhaps, I see myself, / That our law is not pure, is false, / .... / But I love my Tartars, - / And the brave ones *of the fallen Roman power* / I do not wish to make slaves.')
18. This has been in part discussed by Reppo-Shabarova in her article 'Kerim-Girei, Krymskii khan' A.A. Shakhovskogo I *Bakhchisaraiskii fontan* A.S. Pushkina (transformatsiia obrazov glavnykh personazhei)', *Russkaia Filologia*, X. *Sbornik statei molodykh filologov*, Tartu University Press, Tartu, 1999, pp. 44-50. Here the Biblical *Book of Esther* as one of the prior texts of the third part of Shakhovskoi's play is also discussed.
19. Equally, the Muslims refuse to regard the Jews as brothers and almost kill Haim when he dares to remind them that Mohammed is from Izmail, which means that 'he is to a small degree a Jew' (p. 7).
20. His commentary here is typical: 'A good deed! Yes, I saved a Jew, but he is also a human being' (p. 7).
21. This was mentioned by Shakhovskoi himself in the preface to the tragedy. About L.N. Nevakhovich and, in particular, about his contacts with Shakhovskoi, see the article by A.L. Zorin, K.Y. Rogov and A.I. Reitblat in *Russkie pisateli 1800-1917. Biograficheskii slovar'*, Nauchnoe izdatel'stvo 'Bol'shaia Rossiiskaia Entsiklopediia', Moscow, 1999, IV, pp. 244-5.
22. See: *Ivanoi, or the Return of Richard the Lion Heart. A Romantic Comedy in Five Parts with a Tournament, Ballads, Singing and Dancing* by A.A. Shakhovskoi, taken from the novel

Ivanhoe by Walter Scott. (The Russian title is *Ivanoi, ili Vozvrashchenie Richarda L'vinago serdtsa*. This play has not been published: the manuscript may be found in the St Petersburg State Theatrical Library, I.XV.4.38). The first-night performance took place on 21 January 1821. The play had some success, with seven performances in 1821.

23. For further discussion of this work, see, in the first place, our publication of the text: *'Khrisomania, ili Strast' k den'gam' A.A. Shakhovskogo, Trudy po russkoi I slavyanskoi filologii. Literaturovedenie. III: K 40-letiu 'Tartuskikh izdanii'*, Tartu University Press, Tartu, 1999, pp. 179-254.

The Bridegroom Who Did Not Come: Social and Amorous Unproductivity from Pushkin to the Silver Age

by

SANDER BROUWER

1. THE SILVER AGE

One of the recurrent images of the Russian Silver Age was that of the femininity of Russia and the Russian people, expressed in such traits as passivity, receptiveness, submissiveness and formlessness; and the masculinity of the West, especially Germanic culture, that was seen as active, aggressive-expansive, individualistic to the point of egocentricity, rationalistic and form-giving.

Ideas about the femininity of the Russian soul and of the Slavs in general were not new.[1] In fact, nations are quite often personified as women (we need only to think of the French Marianne; Rozanov wrote of the Jewish people, and Nietzsche of the French, as feminine - and, to be sure, of the German people as masculine). But in the Silver Age, these ideas were reshaped under the influence of 'sophiological' philosophy, in which the 'eternally female' principle of affirmation of the created world, conceived of as an essentially harmonious unity, was seen to be embodied in the Russian mentality. On the other hand, Ivanov, in 1917, connected the feminine Slav soul with the orgiastic, with dionysian immoderation (as did Berdiaev[2]), and the 'Germano-Romanic brothers' with the apollinian principle.[3]

As Georgii Fedotov noted in his 1927 essay on Blok's *On the Field of Kulikovo*, what was new in the conception of Russia's womanhood in this period was the image of Russia not as a mother – a tradition leaning on the age-old identification of Russia with 'mother-moist-earth,'[4] - but as a beloved woman or a wife. Russian poets of the nineteenth century, like Nekrasov, spoke of Russia as a mother,[5] but beginning with Solovev they began to address her as a 'beloved' or a 'wife'. The best known example is, of course, Blok's 'Oh my Russia, my wife' from his 1909 'The river widely streams. It flows and grieves lazily',[6] but already in 1905, Belyi had written of Russia as a 'sleeping Beauty' and had compared her to Katerina from Gogol's *Terrible Vengeance*, who has 'consciously to decide whether she will give her soul to her beloved husband, the cossack Danila, who is fighting against foreign intrusion ... or to the wizard from the foreign land'.[7] From the outset, this image of Russia as a beloved woman was thus accompanied by the motif of rivalry for her favours with strong forces from the outside.

On the other hand, in the historiosophy of the sophiologists, an eschatological marriage of this feminine Russia with the masculine West was foreseen. A fertilization by Western masculinity should take place to set loose Russia's energy, which would bring about the coming of the 'new word', the 'new Christ', and an age of harmony. Boris Groys has reconstructed this myth in Solovev's thought:

> Sophia is the mystical name for Russia; she is engaged for a mystical wedding with the Antichrist - the West (that, to be sure, will thus become conscious of its Christian roots and be saved), whereby for 'the West' we should really read the Russian westernised intelligentsia including Solovev himself, rather than the real geographical West.[8]

Thus, the relation between Russia and the West, and between the Russian people and the intelligentsia was conceived of in terms of gender. Solovev's idea was taken up by many poets and thinkers, such as Blok, Belyi, Ivanov, Rozanov and especially Berdiaev. They all conceived of the male stimulus for the Russian nation as something coming from the outside. Berdiaev wrote: 'everything that was masculine, liberating and form-giving always existed in Russia as something not-Russian, foreign, Western European, French or German or Greek in the days of old'.[9] The little amount of form that Russia had developed it had received passively: 'The Russian people does not feel that it is a man, it is always posing as a bride, it feels itself a woman in front of the colossus of the state'.[10] That is why, according to Berdiaev, a stern autocratic and bureaucratic state form had developed in Russia,[11] that had employed only the brutal and negative masculine potential of its foreign models. In 1917 he wrote: 'The Germanic spirit, masculine and sexually predatory had enslaved the Russian soul earlier than it started to enslave the Russian body'.[12] In themselves, the Slavs, according to Ivanov, are 'incapable of building a society based on force, [they] foster in their soul ... the secret of harmony and ... identification with the community'.[13] Feminine Russia may, however, rebel against its oppressive husband, the state. For Rozanov, in the revolution of 1905, 'The woman-Revolution stood up against the man-state'.[14]

What is needed, therefore, is a positive masculine infusion. Many thinkers expected this from the intelligentsia, which thus may in a way be seen to play the role of amorous rival of the state. Berdiaev thought that what the Russian people needed from the educated classes was an 'act of the will',[15] 'masculine conquering and forming'; the intellectuals should infuse the popular 'element' with 'Logos', 'light' and 'sense'.[16] This masculine principle had been taken over by the intelligentsia from that same Western Europe - again, from the outside. However, the way it had developed, the Russian intelligentsia had never been capable of fulfilling its task as a man, because 'it had not learned from Europe, which would have saved it, but had slavishly subordinated itself to it'.[17] Berdiaev constantly chides the intelligentsia for remaining too close to Russian femininity, however far it had been alienated from the Russian soil. It had always shown insufficient spiritual masculinity,[18] the 'Russian boys' had always remained too feminine. That is why Berdiaev calls upon them to 'be men'.

Those attempts the intelligentsia had made to infuse Russia with a masculine spirit remained half-hearted and often took on the form of demonic vogues - superficial flirtations with fashionable imported trends. This half-heartedness Berdiaev and Ivanov see reflected in the Byronism of the thirties, in Ivan Karamazov and, very explicitly, in Stavrogin:

> Stavrogin's powerlessness before his crippled wife is the powerlessness of metaphysical squiredom before the Russian soil, the soil that is the eternally female principle, eagerly awaiting the bridegroom. Liza too is waiting for her bridegroom, but meets with him only for an hour. The image of the bridegroom is doubled. Stavrogin is incapable of marrying, incapable of uniting with a woman, of fertilizing the soil.[19]

In the same vein contemporary works are interpreted, like Belyi's *Silver Dove*:

> The theme of the Silver Dove is the meeting of a cultured member of the Russian intelligentsia ... with the mystical sect of the Doves. ... Darialskii's union with Matriona is the union of the intelligentsia with the people, from which the New Russia should be born.[20]

For the poets and philosophers of the Silver Age, the marriage of the westernized intelligentsia with the Russian nation thus remained a matter for the future. What I am proposing here is that this complex image itself can already be discerned in nineteenth-century Russian literature and thought, and that it was introduced there by Pushkin. Although it had not yet been formulated explicitly and did not exist as an independent image, it was present in the form of a certain plot-scheme, a motifeme or mythologeme if you will. It may be designated as one of the typical 'motifs' or 'plots' of Russian literature.[21] Let us see how this plot functions there.

2.   PUSHKIN AND THE NINETEENTH CENTURY

As Iurii Lotman has argued,[22] the unpredictability of the plot of the nineteenth-century Russian novel is greatly enhanced by its readiness to retain within the text the semiotic charge of extratextual elements that are included in it (in Bakhtinian terms, by its openness to unfinished contemporary reality). On the other hand, this unpredictability is compensated for by a tendency to construct the plot along a limited number of plot lines, which leads to the re-activization of archaic plot-schemes that are stored in the cultural memory. This brings about a 'Russianization' of plot stereotypes which may themselves be inherited from European Romanticism.

One of these 'Russian plots', described by Lotman as central in the range of what he dubs the 'plot space' of the nineteenth-century Russian novel, is that of the active male protagonist who has estranged himself from the socium to which he originally belongs, acting simultaneously as a potential 'saviour' and 'tempter', or 'undoer'. It is here that a parallel modelling of the relationship between the male protagonist and the woman, on the one hand, and his social position as an outsider, on the other, comes to the surface.

The work in which this parallelism is first realized is *Evgenii Onegin*, and it is also in this work that the motif is first traceable of depicting the heroine as a representative of the Russian national spirit from which the intelligentsia had estranged itself: Tatiana 'has a Russian soul' ('русская душою': 5, IV).[23] Tatiana, in her letter, imagines Onegin as either her 'guardian angel' ('ангел хран*итель*') or her 'perfidious tempter' ('коварный искус*итель*'). This way of imagining love is obviously connected with her literary background, at first Sentimentalist, especially her reading of Richardson, Rousseau, Goethe's *Werther*, and others, as well as later, more contemporary Romantics, including Byron, Maturin, Lewis, Nodier:

> And now her idol has become
> either the pensive Vampyre,
> or Melmoth, gloomy vagabond,
> or the Wandering Jew, or the Corsair,
> or the mysterious Sbogar (3, XII).[24]

This is confirmed by the almost equal terms (stressed by the similar rhyme) in which Lenskii, the arch-Romantic, conceives of his love:

> 'I' he reflects, 'shall be her savior (спас*итель*).
> I shall not suffer a depraver (разврат*итель*)
> With the fire of both sighs and compliments
> to tempt a youthful heart' (6, XVII).

Still, this is only half the picture: Tatiana's combination of idealization and demonization can with equal success be explained by her half-folkloric background (witnessed best in her behaviour during Yuletide, but attested in various places in the novel). In Russian wedding folklore, the traditional metaphors for the bridegroom show the same antithetical characteristics: on the one hand he is a prince (князь), a falcon (сокол), a brave young man (удалой добрый молодец), a beloved guest (гость возлюбленный) and indeed a saviour (избавитель) for his bride who sits waiting for him by the window, which is also Tatiana's typical pose;[25] on the other hand he is a stranger (чуженин; чужд господин; чуж отецкий сын), a bandit and evildoer (ворзлодей), a repulsive fellow (остудник), an oppressor (супостат), an undoer and bringer of destruction (погуб*итель*, разор*итель*; cf. Pushkin's rhymes mentioned above); the members of his company are cannibals and robbers (людоеды-разбойники).[26]

In the image system of *Evgenii Onegin*, antithetical qualities are sustained throughout the novel, and cannot be restricted to the hero's amorous behaviour, nor to Tatiana's perspective. Markovich has pointed out that qualifications of Onegin as a saintly hermit, however ironical they may be, recur in the author text:

> В своей глуши *мудрец пустынный* (In his backwoods an *eremitic sage*; 2, IV)
> Умы *пустынников* моих (the minds of my two *eremites*; 2, XVII)
> Онегин жил *анахоретом* (Onegin *anachoretically* lived; 4, XXXVII)
> Вот жизнь Онегина *святая* (this was Onegin's *saintly* life; 4, XXXIX)
> Татьяна долго в *келье* модной / Как очарована стоит
> (Long does Tatiana in the modish *cell* / as one enchanted stand; 7, XX)
> От света вновь *отрекся* он (the *monde* he once again *renounced*; 8, XXXIV)

The same is true of his demonic traits, mainly through associations with demonic literary heroes: The Vampire, Melmoth, the Wandering Jew, Jean Sbogar. Both lines converge in Tatiana's dream, in which Onegin, being surrounded by devilish monsters, recalls Faust at the Brocken as well as St Anthony.[27]

In the article mentioned above, Lotman shows that from Pushkin onwards these antitheses in the image of the (male) hero who has transgressed society's moral boundaries remain a remarkably constant factor in one of the main plot lines of Russian plot space: as an outsider, he is expected fundamentally to reform that society, either by introducing positive new moral standards (as, for example, Kostanzhoglo, Myshkin, but also practical 'doers' like Bazarov, Stolz, Chernyshevskii's heroes and others) or by bringing destruction, in which case Antichrist-like associations may easily appear (as in the usurer in Gogol's *Portrait*, the Napoleonic heroes Hermann, Chichikov and Raskolnikov, or Stavrogin).[28] The persistent association of these two antithetical roles with the outsider-hero in nineteenth-century Russian literature itself witnesses a process of re-mythologization: one recognizes the archaic role stereotypes described in 1982 by Lotman and Uspenskii in the figure of the outsider or outcast (изгой) in the pre-Petrine period. This 'stranger of one's own' (наш чужой, свой чужой) was on the one hand the object of enmity and defence, and on the other of superstitious respect.[29]

In Russian literature after Pushkin, the demonic and sacral connotations of the male protagonist gradually disappear, although elements of amoralism, criminality and demonic spiritual emptiness remain strong in the work of Gogol and Dostoevskii. However, the parallel modelling of the hero's social and amorous position remains an outspoken feature. One may recall here Chatskii (Griboedov's *Woe from Wit*), Beltov (Herzen's *Who is to Blame?*), Oblomov and Raiskii (Goncharov's *The Precipice*), and many others. The phenomenon is especially noticeable in the superfluous heroes of Turgenev. Although Turgenev's works witness a strong denial of any sacral or demonic potential of these outsiders - Lotman speaks of their 'de-mythologizing' role in nineteenth-century Russian literature[30] - they also show a clear tendency to construct social and amorous unproductivity in a parallel way. Dale Peterson has called attention to a 'recurrent formulaic structure within the basic fable that constitutes the central symbolic action in Turgenev's six novels'.[31] This 'basic scenario' Peterson describes as 'the injection, or more commonly the return, of an ex-provincial protagonist into the heartland of what Turgenev labels, in the last words of his last novel, Bezymiannaia Rus', 'Anonymous Russia';[32] this appearance, in what is for the protagonist a new milieu, results in a clash with the environment, which 'coincides with his meeting a heroine who emerges from that same milieu';[33] both the protagonist and the 'indigenous heroine who is an overreacher in her environment (...) usually prove to be totally incompatible once suspended in the resident culture surrounding them'.[34]

Indeed, in Turgenev's novels, but also in Herzen's and Goncharov's, we observe the impossibility for the male protagonist, often the carrier of imported values, to engage in some practical activity, to develop into a useful member of society or further the interests of his native culture in the widest sense, along with his failure to marry the young woman, who, as a rule, is a representative of that native culture. In this light it is highly significant that Chernyshevskii, in his famous review of *Asia*: 'The Russian man at a rendezvous' without any reservations treats its hero's indecisiveness in establishing an amorous relation as the expression of his social superfluity. Annenkov, who objected to Chernyshevskii's analysis of the superfluity of Russia's aristocratic intelligentsia, nonetheless adopts this identification as a matter of course. This may serve as a strong indication that the noted parallelism was indeed deeply rooted in the hidden layer of unconscious images or myths of Russian literature of the time. Chernyshevskii's own *What Is To Be Done?*, by the way, while on the one hand a novel about woman's liberation, may on the other hand be read as a positive, happy-ending variant of our parallel plot: Vera Pavlovna's emancipation, made possible by Lopukhov's unselfish help, is a model for Russia's own development. For Chernyshevskii, as Irina Paperno writes, 'the role of liberator and teacher of a woman was a projection of his wish to become a savior and teacher of mankind'.[35]

The same line of thought may be found with Herzen. In 1863, in a period in which he was looking for a figure who might act as a redeemer, he writes:

> Only he who is called to activity and understands the way of the people without forgetting what science has taught him; who harmonises his actions with its strivings and on this foundation works for the common national cause, only that man will be the bridegroom who cometh ... Who then will that longed-for lover be?[36]

Here we note the possible sacral connotations of the figure of the bridegroom, a connotation that may have existed all along in the image of the nocturnal lover (Christ the bridegroom comes at midnight) which entered Russian literature from Zhukovskii's translations of Bürger's *Lenore*, and which, as is well known, influenced Onegin's image in Tatiana's dream.

Thus the idea of the male Russian *intelligent* relating to his native culture as a lover to his beloved is expressed in the nineteenth century mainly through parallel plot construction. Aspects of this idea may be found, however, in more direct images. Thus, Gogol clearly writes of Russia's feminine nature in contrast with male Western Europe: 'She (Moscow - SB) is still to this day a Russian beard, but he (Petersburg - SB) is already a tidy and punctual German ... Moscow is feminine, Petersburg is masculine. In Moscow you have brides everywhere, in Petersburg suitors'.[37] Herzen and Kavelin spoke of the femininity of the Slavs in the fifties and sixties.[38] Riabov is right[39] if he sees in the following passage from Herzen's *Prolegomena* an attempt to genderize the opposition 'people-government'; moreover, the intelligentsia is put into opposition to the people by the same terms, so that government and intelligentsia may here be seen to act as rivals:

> At the base we have the *rural commune*, pacific as it waits ...; keeping safe like a mother who guards her child at her breast ... The feminine element and cornerstone of the whole building, its monad, the alveolus of the enormous tissue which one calls Russia. At the summit, at the side of the State which crushes, of the government which *pacifies - free thought* becomes a force, a power recognized by its enemies ... as nihilism.[40]

The genderization is even carried further in the terms Herzen uses to reproach Russian tsarism for its unpredictable shifting of position: now it acts against the people's interests, now it tries to further it:

[From the time of Peter the Great] the emperor is changeable like Proteus: he is woman as well as man ... Today he is the first among the *nobility*, tomorrow among the *people*; today the fancy may take him to continue the insane reign of Paul I, tomorrow to proclaim himself Pugachev II. I have always admired the hermaphrodite adjective which Voltaire used in saying *Catherine le Grand*: confusion of sex, of function, accumulation, absorption, promiscuity.[41]

3. THE HISTORICAL BACKGROUND

The purpose of this chapter is merely to sketch the bare outlines of a certain complex of images. I will not attempt to explain why that complex became prominent in our period, though I can agree with Riabov's proposition that the emergence of Russia's image as a woman was part of the tendency among Russian intellectuals in the nineteenth century (with important forerunners in the eighteenth) to shape Russia as the 'Other' with regard to Western Europe. Its femininity, contrasted with Western masculinity, may thus be seen as a variant of the East - West opposition of Nature and Culture, Village and Town, and Heart and Reason.[42]

But if we broaden our scope a little, we recognize elements of this image in other areas and periods; it did not just appear out of the blue. The parallel modelling of social and amorous characteristics of the male hero is not new for nineteenth-century Russian literature. In the classical Russian wonder-tale, the hero is rewarded in the end by his marriage to the princess and by the same act receives half of the kingdom, thus rising socially from being the last fool in the land to its ruler. In the French novel of the latter half of the eighteenth and first half of the nineteenth century, the hero, from St Preux to Julien Sorel, may realize his social ascension through a series of well-chosen amorous liaisons.

But the most relevant backgound is formed by the image of the ruler as the mystical husband of the land.[43] It was known in late Muscovite political imagery: from the late fifteenth century onwards;[44] the image can there be recognized of the ruler marrying the land, and of Russia as the bride of the ruler. We find earthly power personified as the widow Vasiliia in one of Maksim Grek's works in the 1540's.[45] Ivan Timofeev writes in his *Vremennik* (1617) that the true tsar was the bridegroom of Russia, just as Christ was the Bridegroom of the Church.[46] Almost a century later, in 1704, Iosif Turoboiskii writes that 'every tsar is the bridegroom of his empire'.[47] Joanna Hubbs describes how during one of the weddings of Mikhail Romanov, in 1623 or 1624, his bride wore a garland inscribed with the name of each Russian city, which she explains as an identification of the bride with the land.[48] The image of Russia as a bride we find in the *Lament on the Captivation and Final Ruin of the Muscovite State* (1612), in which the Muscovite state is described 'as a bride prepared for her bridegroom and a beautiful wedding'.[49] From the sixteenth century onwards, the image of the ruler as dragon-slayer can be reconstructed – that is, as defender of the realm against its heathen enemies –, marrying Wisdom (Премудрость) as the female image of the well-organized theocratic Russian state. This complex forms the background of the *Tale of Petr and Fevroniia*.[50] On the other hand, the image of Wisdom-Sophia was consciously used during Sophia Alekseevna's regency (1681-89) 'to change the focus of the integrating myth of Muscovy, to superimpose the image of Divine Wisdom over the tradition of Christocentric iconography of the monarchy, and through this creative act to tap into a source of emotional sympathy and support for the regent's cause'.[51]

To be sure, the metaphor of the ruler's marriage to his realm was well known in Western Europe as well. It was

> not unknown in Antiquity ... but will not be easily found in the earlier Middle Ages. ... The secular marriage metaphor, however, became rather popular in the later Middle Ages when ... the image of the Prince's marriage to his *corpus mysticum* - that is, to the *corpus mysticum* of his state - appeared to be constitutionally meaningful.[52]

Kantorowicz describes how even Aristophanes calls the 'basileia' the bride of Alcibiades.[53] Lucanus in his *Pharsalia* writes of Cato as 'urbi pater urbique maritus' ('the father of the city and husband of the city': the qualification 'urbi maritus' is taken over by Servius and Priscianus). In the first half of the fourteenth century the Prince is called 'husband of the republic' by Lucas de Penna ('princeps ... est maritus reipublicae iuxta illud Lucani'), Cynus of Pistoia, Albericus de Rosate, and others. In this period, this was clearly an aspect of the transference of imagery from the ecclesiastical sphere (the bishop as the 'mysticus coniunx' ['mystical spouse'] of his bishopric) into the political, and of the emergence of a 'mystical monarchy'. Lucas de Penna also calls the Prince the 'sponsus' of the state, explicitly drawing the parallel with Christ the 'sponsus' of the Church. The image of the king as 'mysticus coniunx' of the land became well known in France in the fifteenth and sixteenth centuries. Thus, at the coronation of Henry II of France in 1547, it was said that 'le roy espousa solemnellement le royaume'.[54] In mediaeval England, it was hardly known, but it was important for the Tudor lawyers with their christological interpretation of the King's body politic and its relation to his subjects. James I said in his speech to the first Parliament in 1603: 'I am the husband, and all the whole island is my lawful wife'.[55] And in 1607 Francis Bacon wrote: 'Reges enim regnis suis, ut Iupiter Iunoni, veluti Matrimonii vinculo iuncti recte censentur' (in Arthur Gorges' translation of 1619: 'For Princes may well be said to be married to their dominions, as Iupiter was to Iuno').[56]

Whereas in Western Europe, the image of the king as husband of the land had a strong fiscal-juridical background,[57] such a background seems to be missing in Russia. There, the transfer of ecclesiastical imagery[58] to the secular sphere probably owes more to the process of sacralization of the figure of the tsar in the period named.[59] In any event, the metaphorization of ruler and ruled as husband and wife need not have been invented in the nineteenth century. It is interesting to follow its lines of development in the eighteenth century. One may, for instance, point to Sumarokov's tragedy *Dimitrii the Impostor* (1771), in which the Russian heroine Kseniia, who is harrassed by Dimitrii, the representative of foreign (Polish) intervention, is so emphatically associated with Moscow that she becomes a symbol of it.[60] If Joe Andrew is right in seeing, in the arrangement of characters in Fonvizin's *The Minor* an 'allegorical discussion of the 'unnatural' order within Russia whereby a woman has usurped the rightfully male crown', with Starodum as the Wise Father restoring natural patriarchal order,[61] then surely Sophia, the marriageable girl around whose fate the dramatic plot is built, must allegorically represent Russia. Her name is unlikely to be accidentally chosen, bearing in mind the association Sophia / Премудрость / Russia.[62] In this light, the name Sophia for Chatskii's beloved in *Woe from Wit* may well form an ironic commentary to Fonvizin's comedy.

What characterizes the situation in our period, however, apart from the fact that the image complex was so widespread, is that the social and amorous position of the hero is invariably one of failure: the hero does not overcome his estrangement or superfluousness, and he does not get the young woman - or the young woman him. We should therefore perhaps speak not of the image of Russia as beloved woman, but rather as unattainable beloved. Indeed, one of the things Russian Romanticism inherited from Western Europe was the theme of impossible and unfulfilled love as the only true love. There it had developed in a long tradition going back to the twelfth and thirteenth century, to the time of the troubadours and more specifically to the Romance of Tristan and Iseult. It would require much investigation to establish whether Russian culture had, by the nineteenth century, retained enough of its mediaeval Manicheanism to connect this theme with a world-denying worldview, as had been the case, according to Denis de Rougemont, in Western European literature.[63] The subjective reasons for seeing real love as unrealizable in this world may have been different for each author. For instance, as Agnes Dukkon has argued, the hidden drive behind the Turgenevan hero's failure to realize his love in some amorous relationship is the secret wish to keep his essentially aesthetic ideal at an elegiac distance and to 'prove' this ideal by earthly suffering and eternal longing.[64] That wish can hardly be ascribed to Pushkin. It was Pushkin, however, who made the connection between the Romantic theme of unhappy love and that of social estrangement, thus shaping the image that appeared to be so successful in Russian literature.

REFERENCES

Andrew, Joe, *Women in Russian Literature, 1780-1863*, St Martin's Press, New York, 1988.

Annenkov, P.V., 'Literaturnii tip slabogo cheloveka. Po povodu Turgenevskoi "Asi"', in Annenkov, P.V., *Vospominaniia i kriticheskie ocherki*, II, M. Stasiulevich, St Petersburg,1879, pp. 145-72. (Originally, in *Atenei*, XXXII, 1858).

Bacon, Francis, *De sapientia veterum*, R.Barker, London, 1609. (*The Wisedome of the Ancients*, done into English by Sir Arthur Gorges, J. Bill, London, 1619. Reprinted Garland, New York and London, 1976.)

Belyi, Andrei 'Lug zelenyi. Kniga statei' in *Simvolizm kak miroponimanie*, Izdatel'stvo 'Respublika', Moscow, 1994, pp. 328-417.

Bem, A.L., 'Lichnye imena u Dostoevskogo', in *O Dostojevském: sborník statí a materiálů*, Edice Slovanské knihovny, Prague, 1972, pp. 244-86.

Berdiaev, N.A., *Sobranie sochinenii v 5-i tomakh*, YMCA-Press, Paris 1989-97.

Berkov, P.N., *Istoriia russkoi komedii XVIII v.*, Nauka, Leningrad, 1977.

Billington, James, H., *The Icon and the Axe: An Interpretive History of Russian Culture*, Weidenfeld and Nicolson, London, 1966.

Bocharov, S.G., *Siuzhety russkoi literatury,* Shkola 'Iazyki russkoi literatury', Moscow, 1999.

Dostoevskii, F.M., *Polnoe sobranie sochinenii v 30-i tomakh,* Nauka, Leningrad, 1972-1990.

Dukkon, A., 'Problema "literaturnosti" i "original'nosti" v proizvedeniiakh Turgeneva 1850- kh gg.', forthcoming.

Dunham, V.S., 'The Strong-Woman Motif' in Black, Cyril E., ed., *The Transformation of Russian Society. Aspects of Social Change since 1861,* Harvard University Press, Cambridge, Mass., 1960, pp. 459-83.

Fedotov, G.P., 'Na pole Kulikovom', *Sovremennye zapiski*, XXXII, 1927, pp. 418-35.

Freidenberg, O.M., 'V"ezd v Ierusalim na osle (Iz evangel'skoi mifologii)', in Freidenberg, O.M., *Mif i literatura drevnosti,* ed. N. V. Braginskoi, Nauka, Moscow, 1978, pp. 491-531.

Gasparov, B.M., *Literaturnye leitmotivy. Ocherki russkoi literatury XX veka*, Nauka, Izd. firma 'Vostochnaia literatura', Moscow, 1993.

Herzen, A.I., *Sobranie sochinenii v 30-i tomakh*, Nauka, Moscow, 1954-65.

Gippius, V.V., 'On the Composition of Turgenev's Novels (excerpted and translated version of 'O kompozitsii turgenevskikh romanakh' by David Lowe), in Lowe, David, ed., *Critical Essays on Ivan Turgenev*, Hall, Boston, Mass., 1989, pp. 144-54.

Gogol, N. V., *Sobranie sochinenii v 7-i tomakh*, Moscow, Khudozhestvennaia literatura, 1984-6.

Grechina, O.N., 'O folklorizme "Evgeniia Onegina", *Russkii fol'klor*, XVIII, 1978 (Slavianskie literatury i fol'klor), pp. 18-41.

Groys, Boris, 'Weisheit als weibliches Weltprinzip: die Sophiologie von Wladimir Solowjow', in *Die Erfindung Rußlands*, Carl Hanser Verlag, München, 1995 pp., 37-49.

Gura, A.V., 'Poeticheskaia terminologiia severorusskogo svadebnogo obriada' in Putilov, B.N., ed., *Fol'klor i etnografiia. Obriady i obriadovyi fol'klor*, Nauka, Leningrad, 1974, pp. 171-80.

Hubbs, Joanna, *Mother Russia. The Feminine Myth in Russian Culture*, Indiana University Press, Bloomington and Indianapolis, 1993.

Ivanov, V., *Sobranie sochinenii v 4-i tomakh*, Foyer Oriental Chrétien, Bruxelles, 1971-87.

Kagan-Kans, E., *Hamlet and Don Quixote: Turgenev's Ambivalent Vision,* Mouton, The Hague-Paris, 1975 (Slavistic Printings and Reprintings, 288).

Kantorowicz, E.H., *The King's Two Bodies. A Study in Medieval Political Theology*, Princeton University Press, Princeton NJ, 1957.

Kleiman, R.Ia., *Skvoznye motivy tvorchestva Dostoevskogo v istoriko-kul'turnoi perspektive*, Stiintsa, Kishinev, 1985.

Krivonos, V.Sh., *Motivy khudozhestvennoi prozy Gogolia*, Izdatel'stvo RGPU im. A. I. Gertsena, St Petersburg, 1999.

Levinton G.A. and Smirnov, I.P., '"Na pole Kulikovom" Bloka i pamiatniki Kulikovskogo tsikla', *Trudy otdela drevnerusskoi literatury*, XXXIV, 1979, pp. 72-95.

Likhachev, D.S., 'Kontseptosfera russkogo iazyka', *Izvestiia RAN*, seriia literatury i iazyka, I, 1993, pp. 3-9.

Lotman, Yury M., *Universe of the Mind: a Semiotic Theory of Culture*, Translated by Ann Shukman, Introduction by Umberto Eco, I. B. Tauris & Co, London, 1990.

Lotman, Iu.M., 'Siuzhetnoe prostranstvo russkogo romana XIX stoletiia' in *Izbrannye stat'i v trekh tomakh*, 'Alexandra', Tallinn, 1991-3, III, pp. 91-106.

Lotman, Iu.M., *Besedy o russkoi kul'ture. Byt i traditsii russkogo dvorianstva (XVIII - nachalo XIX veka)*, Iskusstvo, St Petersburg, 1994.

Lotman, Iu.M. and Uspenskii, B.A., '"Izgoi" i "izgoinichestvo" kak sotsial'no-psikhologicheskaia pozitsiia v russkoi kul'ture preimushchestvenno dopetrovskogo perioda ("svoe" i "chuzhoe" v istorii russkoi kul'tury)', *Trudy po znakovym sistemam*, XV, 1982 (*UZ Tartuskogo GU*, 576), pp. 110-22.

Mann, Iu.V., *V poiskakh zhivoi dushi. 'Mertvye dushi': pisatel'-kritika-chitatel'*, Kniga, Moscow, 1984.

Markovich, V.M., *I.S. Turgenev i russkii realisticheskii roman XIX veka (30-50-e gody)*, Izdatel'stvo Leningradskogo universiteta, Leningrad, 1982.

Pamiatniki literatury Drevnei Rusi, konets XVI-nachalo XVII veka, Khudozhestvennaia literatura, Moscow, 1987.

Materialy k 'Slovariu siuzhetov i motivov russkoi literatury': ot siuzheta k motivu, Tiupy, V.I., ed., Institut filologii RAN, Novosibirsk, 1996.

Meletinskii, E.M., *Poetika mifa*, 2-e izd., 'Vostochnaia literatura', RAN/Shkola 'Iazyki russkoi literatury', Moscow, 1995.

Nabokov, V., *Eugene Onegin: A Novel in Verse by Aleksandr Pushkin*. I. *Translator's Introduction*. *Eugene Onegin: The Translation*. Revized edition, Princeton University Press, Princeton NJ, 1975 (Bollingen Series, 72).

Odesskii, M.P., 'Ob "otkrovennom" i "prikrovennom": Sofiia v komediiakh V.I. Lukina', *Literaturnoe Obozrenie* 1994, No. 3-4, pp. 82-7.

Paperno, Irina, *Chernyshevsky and the Age of Realism*, Stanford University Press, Stanford, California, 1988.

Peterson, Dale E., *The Clement Vision. Poetic Realism in Turgenev and James*, National University Publications, Kennikat Press, Port Washington, New York and London, 1975.

Pliukhanova, M.B., *Siuzhety i simvoly moskovskogo tsarstva*, Akropol', St Peterburg, 1995.

Riabov, O.V., *Zhenshchina i zhestvennost' v filosofii serebriannogo veka*, Ivanovskii GU, Ivanovo, 1997.

Riabov, O.V., *Russkaia filosofia zhenstvennosti (XI-XX veka)*, Izdatel'skii Tsentr 'Iunona', Ivanovo, 1999.

de Rougemont, Denis, *Love in the Western World*. Revised and augmented edition, Princeton University Press, Princeton, NJ, 1983 (written 1938).

Rozanov, V.V., *Sobranie sochinenii: O pisatel'stve i pisateliakh*, Izdatel'stvo 'Respublika', Moscow, 1995.

Russkaia staropechatnaia literatura (XVI - pervaia chetvert' XVIIIvv.): Panegiricheskaia literatura petrovskogo perioda, Derzhavinoi, O.A., ed., Nauka, Moscow, 1979.

Rzhiga, V.R., 'Maksim Grek kak publitsist', *Trudy otdela drevnerusskoi literatury* I, 1934, pp. 5-120.

Solov'ev, V.S., *Sochineniia v dvukh tomakh*, Pravda, Moscow, 1989.

Toporov, V.N., 'Tekst goroda-devy i goroda-bludnitsy v mifologicheskom aspekte', in Toporov, V.N., *O mifopoeticheskom prostranstve / Lo spazio mitopoetico*, Izbrannye stat'i. Izd. podg. M. Evzlin i N. Mikhailov. ECIG, Pisa, 1994 (Studi slavi, 2), pp. 245-59.

Uspenskii, B.A., *Tsar i patriarkh. Kharizma vlasti v Rossii (Vizantiiskaia model' i ee russkoe pereosmyslenie)*, Shkola 'Iazyki russkoi kul'tury', Moscow, 1998.

Uspenskii, B.A., 'Postavlenie na velikoe kniazhenie Dmitriia Ivanovicha (1498g.), forthcoming.

Uspenskii, B.A. and Zhivov, V.M., 'Tsar' i Bog. Semioticheskie aspekty sakralizatsii monarkha v Rossii', in Uspenskii, B.A., ed., *Iazyki kul'tury i problemy perevodimosti*, Nauka, Moscow, 1987, pp. 47-153.

Vaiskopf, M., *Siuzhet Gogolia. Morfologiia, Ideologiia, Kontekst*, Radiks, Moscow, 1993.

Vremennik Ivana Timofeeva, Nauka, Moscow-Leningrad, 1951.

Zelensky, E.K., 'Sophia the Wisdom of God - the Function of Religious Imagery During the Regency of Sofiia Alekseevna of Muscovy', in Fradenburg, L.O., ed., *Women and Sovereignty*, Edinburgh University Press, Edinburgh, 1992, pp. 192-211.

NOTES

1. Cf. the literature mentioned by Riabov (1997), p. 111.
2. See ibid., p. 117.
3. The dionysian principle is the 'immeasurable, fixed principle, unstable in its flowing forms, limitless, suffering from incessant separation from itself' (Ivanov, IV, p. 668; from 'The Spiritual Face of Slavdom'), and 'Slavdom' is 'feminine, like the Soul of the World' (ibid., p. 670); whereas the fundamental traits of the apollinian are: 'unity, measure, system, order, balance, the self-sufficient peace of finished forms' (ibid., p. 668). In this article, Russia's femininity is connected with its 'sobornost'' as well.
4. Cf. Hubbs, passim; Billington, p. 20.
5. For example, in his unfinished *Mother*, or in *Knight for an Hour*. Exclamations like the following, from *Sasha*, are not uncommon for Nekrasov: 'Motherland! In my soul I have made my peace, / I have come back to you a loving son.' (Translations from Russian are my own unless otherwise stated).
6. See also his *Autumn Day* (1909): 'Oh, my destitute country, / What do you mean for the heart? / Oh, my poor wife, / For what do you bitterly weep?' and *Russia* (1908): 'Russia, destitute Russia, / For me your grey huts, / Your breezy songs - / Are like the first tears of love!' On the image of Russia as beloved in *On the Field of Kulikovo* see Levinton and Smirnov, pp. 78-9 and 87-93.
7. Belyi, p. 329.
8. Groys, p. 42 (my translation - SB).
9. Quoted in Riabov, op. cit.,1997, p. 106.
10. Berdiaev, op. cit., III, p. 352 (from 'On the Eternally Womanish in the Russian Soul').
11. See Riabov, op. cit., 1997, p. 106.
12. Berdiaev, op. cit., IV, p. 148 (from 'The Spiritual Foundations of the Russian Revolution').
13. Ivanov, op. cit., p. 670.
14. Rozanov, op. cit., p. 261 (from 'L. Andreev and his *Darkness*').
15. Berdiaev, op. cit., III, p. 415 (from 'The Russian Temptation: à propos A. Belyi's *The Silver Dove*').
16. Ibid., p. 421.
17. Quoted in Riabov, op. cit., 1997, p. 117.
18. See, for instance, Berdiaev, op. cit., III, pp. 416-18; and cf. p. 422: 'our cultural intellectual society is perishing from weakness, from a lack of masculinity (from 'The Russian Temptation: à propos A. Belyi's *The Silver Dove*').
19. Berdiaev, op. cit., III, p. 108 (from 'Stavrogin'). See also Ivanov, op. cit., IV, p. 440: '[Dostoevskii] as it were saw before his eyes, how the masculine principle in the mysterious depth of folk life can isolate itself from Christ and how its feminine principle, the Russian Soul-Earth sighs and pines for its promised bridegroom, hero in Christ and god-carrier, finally making up his mind (from 'The Basic Myth in the Novel *The Demons*'). Ivanov saw Lermontov as the first Russian poet who, although unconsciously, turned to the 'eternally-female' and to Sophia as a specifically Russian answer to the problem of the Promethean 'self-designing personality', a problem, introduced into Russian culture, according to him, by Byron (see ibid., pp. 294-5; from 'Byronism as an event in the life of the Russian soul' and ibid., pp. 378-83; from 'Lermontov').
20. Berdiaev, op. cit., III, p. 415 (from 'The Russian Temptation: à propos A. Belyi's *The Silver Dove*').

Social and Amorous Unproductivity from Pushkin to the Silver Age 63

21. For a discussion of the '"implicit" mythologism' of Russian realistic literature, see Meletinskii, pp. 283-4. The present chapter is meant as a contribution to the description of the Russian plot-complex. The modern interest in Russian literary scholarship for this field of investigation, partly developing the ideas of A. N. Veselovskii, partly leaning on the concept of 'semiosphere' as developed by Lotman (1990), or 'conceptosphere' in Likhachev's terms (1993) is witnessed by such publications as Gasparov (1993), *Materialy* (1996), Bocharov (1999). For individual authors, see, for instance, Kleiman (1985), Krivonos (1999). Of related interest is Pliukhanova (1995).

22. See Lotman, 1993.

23. Later examples include Liza from Turgenev's *Home of the Gentry* and Natasha Rostova from Tolstoi's *War and Peace* (the famous dance-scene). In itself, the image is indebted to a wider predilection in Russian Romanticism for 'the artistic (and biographical) stereotype of man as the embodiment of socially typical deficiency and woman as the embodiment of the social ideal' (Lotman 1994, p. 64). The stereotype did not end with Romanticism, however, but proved remarkably productive in the remainder of the nineteenth century. In Gogol's *Dead Souls*, one may reconstruct a hidden plot of salvation through a woman: A. M. Bukharev (arkhimandrite Feodor of the Troitse-Sergieva Lavra) in 1861 published his *Three Letters to N. V. Gogol*, written in 1848 (St Peterburg, 1861), in which he gives an account of what Gogol planned for the third part of his *Dead Souls* trilogy. Most commentators regard this account as a rather truthful reflection of what Gogol had in mind, since it was based on a conversation with him during his visit to the Lavra on October 1, 1851. According to Bukharev, Chichikov would be punished and after that undergo a moral resurrection, particularly stimulated by a female figure:

Perhaps a wonderful Russian maiden, as can be found nowhere else in the world ... would answer to this unprecedented suffering out of generosity and self-effacement ... with an unheard-of, unusual compassion and would start loving him for his feelings and his confession of guilt, which leaves no place for hope and energy; and she would be prepared to carry this unbearable weight together with him (quoted from Mann, op. cit., p. 318).

It is not clear whether this 'helper, of whom he could not even dream in his his former dreams of the children's room' (ibid.) would travel with Chichikov to Siberia, like Ulinka Betrishcheva with Tentetnikov, but Mann (op. cit., pp. 321-2) thinks that there is a strong clue. For Turgenev, see Kagan-Kans, op. cit., pp. 41-55; and cf. Dunham. See also Dostoevskii's panegyric of woman in the last paragraph of his *Something on Lying* (see Dostoevskii, XXI, p. 125). Of course, the Romantic exaltation of woman has its darker sides, as well (Kagan-Kans, ibid.; for Gogol, see note 37).

24. I quote *Evgenii Onegin* from Nabokov's translation (1975).

25. See Grechina, op. cit., pp. 28-30.

26. See Gura 1974, passim. Grechina, op. cit., p. 30, points to the folk concept of love as demonic in nature.

27. For a discussion of these points, see Markovich, op. cit., pp. 7-24.

28. I leave aside the 'personal' variant of this plot-type, in which the hero transforms his own personality: here he either perishes morally or is reborn.

29. See Lotman and Uspenskii.

30. See Lotman, op. cit., 1993, p. 105.

31. See Peterson, op. cit., p. 74. In fact, this recurrent structure had been described as early as 1919 by Gippius.

32. Ibid., p. 76.

33. Loc. cit.

34. Ibid., p. 77.

35. See Paperno, op. cit., p. 80.
36. See Herzen, op. cit., XVI, p. 77 (from 'Emperor Alexander I and V.N. Karazin').
37. See Gogol, op. cit., VI, p. 160 (from 'Petersburg Notes for 1836'). Incidentally, in the phrase 'Moscow is a Russian beard' we find the same oxymoronic combination of sex-characteristics as in Berdiaev's 'he is ever the fiancée' (see note 10). It is interesting to note that Petersburg may reveal female characteristics, as well, but they are invariably treated as negative, demonic (see Krivonos, op. cit., pp. 53-75). We may note here the influence of the Romantic dichotomous conception of woman as demonic/angelic (see ibid., pp. 134-52). In connection with the biblical association of the City with a maiden, a further background may be formed by the antithesis Petersburg-Babylon versus Moscow-Jerusalem (see Vaiskopf, op. cit., chapters two and three).
38. See Riabov, op. cit., 1999, pp. 107-8.
39. Ibid., p. 103.
40. Herzen, op. cit., XX, p. 40. (The italics are Herzen's, and the original is in French.)
41. Ibid., p. 47. (The italics are Herzen's, and the original is in French.)
42. See Riabov, op. cit., 1999, pp. 298-301.
43. In itself, the image undoubtedly goes back to the Old Testament image of Jerusalem as daughter-Sion and bride of Yahweh, contrasted to Babylon as city of debauchery and widow (see Freidenberg, op. cit., 1978 and Toporov, op. cit., 1994). For the reception of this image in sixteenth-century Russia, see Pliukhanova, op. cit., pp. 190-202).
44. Uspenskii (forthcoming) has found some elements of the wedding ceremony in the crowning order of Grand Prince Dmitrii Ivanovich (1498). I should like to thank the author for kindly sharing this information with me.
45. See Rzhiga, op. cit., p. 59; Levinton and Smirnov, op. cit., p. 79.
46. See *Vremennik*, op. cit., p. 333.
47. Quoted in *Panegiricheskaia literatura*, op. cit., p. 179.
48. Hubbs, op. cit., p. 189.
49. From *Pamiatniki Literatury Drevnei Rusi*, op. cit., p. 132.
50. See Pliukhanova, op. cit., pp. 221-32.
51. Zelensky, op. cit., p. 192. Zelensky sustains this thesis with texts by L. Tarasevich and Simeon Polotskii (op. cit., pp. 206-7).
52. See Kantorowicz, op. cit., p. 212.
53. Ibid., pp. 214-7.
54. Ibid., p. 222.
55. Ibid., p. 223.
56. I am grateful to Professor Boris Uspenskii for drawing my attention to this passage from Bacon.
57. See Kantorowicz, op. cit., p. 217.
58. On the image of the bishop's mystical marriage to his diocese in Russia see Uspenskii, op. cit., 1988, pp. 68-73.
59. See Uspenskii and Zhivov.
60. For the image of the city-maiden in Russian culture, see notes 37 and 43.
61. See Andrew, op. cit., pp. 12-13.
62. P. N. Berkov, who credits I. V. Lukin for having introduced 'speaking names' into Russian literature, notes that in his *The Prodigal Improved by Love* (1765), Sofiia is just such a speaking name for a virtuous and wise maiden (see Berkov, op. cit., p. 78). See also his *Idle*

Talker (1765), *Father-in-law and Son-in-law* (1768) and *The Pensive* (1769) and cf. Odesskii, passim. See also Sofiia in Fonvizin's *The Brigadier*, Kapnist's *Chicanery* and D. V. Volkov's *Education*. In the eighteenth century, the Sophia-theme was strongly connected with Russian Freemasonry (see Odesskii, op. cit., pp. 83-4; for some other authors, see Vaiskopf, op. cit., p. 497-8). It would be interesting, though, to investigate the development of the speaking name Sofiia in later Russian literature. Poprishchin's beloved from *Diary of a Madman* and Sonia from *Crime and Punishment* (as was noted by Bem, op. cit., p. 277) immediately spring to mind.

63. See de Rougemont, op. cit., passim.
64. See Dukkon op. cit., (forthcoming).

The Pushkin Text in *Anna Karenina*

by

BARBARA LÖNNQVIST

In the spring of 1873 Tolstoi had already been grappling with a novel about the time of Peter the Great for some years but with meagre results. In a letter to Afanasii Fet on March 17 he says simply: 'My work is not moving' (LXII, p.15).[1] But the very next day something happens. At his morning coffee Tolstoi picks up a book on the windowsill and starts reading. It turns out to be the fifth volume of Pushkin's *Collected Works* in P.V. Annenkov's edition of 1855, including *The Tales of Belkin* and some fragments of unfinished stories. Tolstoi is enthused by his reading and tells Strakhov about it in a letter of March 25:

> I ... picked up this volume of Pushkin and, as always (for the seventh time, I think), I re-read it all; I just couldn't tear myself away, and felt as if I was reading it for the first time. But more than that: he seemed to resolve all my doubts ... And there is a fragment there, 'The guests gathered at the dacha ...'. Without really wishing or meaning to do so, not knowing myself why I did it or what would become of it, I began to plan out all the characters and events, began to take it on; then, of course, I changed, and it suddenly developed so beautifully and sharply, that a whole novel emerged ... a very vivid and fiery novel ... and one which has nothing in common with everything that I'd been toiling over the whole year (Ibid., p. 16).

Tolstoi's wife Sofia Andreevna notes in her *Various Notes for Information* (*Записи разные для справок*) for March 19: 'Yesterday evening Levochka suddenly said to me: "I've written one and a half pages and I think it's good"'.[2] She also writes in a letter to her sister T.A. Kuzminskaia on March 19/20: 'Yesterday Levochka suddenly, unexpectedly began writing a novel from contemporary life. The subject is an unfaithful wife and all the drama that flows from that.'[3] In a letter to P.D. Golokhvastov of March 30 Tolstoi is quite enthusiastic about Pushkin: 'You will not believe that with great delight, the like of which I have not felt for a long time, I have been reading in the recent past, after you had gone, the tales of Belkin, for the seventh time. The writer should never cease studying this treasure' (LXII, p. 18). What could Tolstoi find in Pushkin's 'treasure'? Did his reading leave any traces in the new novel that got off to such a good start when the writer turned to Pushkin's texts?

In his study, *Tolstoi in the Seventies* Boris Eikhenbaum made a textual comparison of *Anna Karenina* and Pushkin's prose fragments, especially the text starting with the words 'Гости съезжались на дачу графини ...' ('The guests gathered at the dacha of the countess ...'). He found some interesting similarities and echoes. For instance, when the guests have gathered at the dacha and accusingly discuss the behaviour of the young Zinaida Volskaia it sounds very similar to the gossiping about Anna Karenina in the salon of Betsy Tverskaia. Eikhenbaum suggests that the last phrase in Pushkin's text could be read 'as an epigraph' for Tolstoy's novel: 'In her there is much good and much less that is bad than people think. But passion will be the ruin of her ...'[4] Even more perceptive is Eikhenbaum's assumption that the scene of the quarrel between Zinaida and her lover Volodskii (in Pushkin's fragment 'На маленькой площади, перед деревянным домиком стояла карета ...' [In the small square, in front of the little wooden house stood a carriage']) lies at the basis of Anna's and Vronskii's last quarrel scene: 'a kind of summary for the final quarrel between Anna and Vronskii'. Eikhenbaum notes the similarity in situation: Volodskii-Vronskii leaves the house in a carriage while Zinaida-Anna follows his movements through the window.

I would like to deepen the analysis by pointing to a very telling detail - the *gloves* of the lover. In Pushkin's text we read: 'Valerian was no longer listening. He *was pulling tight a glove he had put on some time before* and kept glancing outside impatiently' (my emphasis).[5] And in Tolstoi: 'She went over to the window and saw him *take the gloves without looking up* ... Then, without looking out of the window, he settled himself in his usual position in the carriage, with one leg crossed over the other *and, putting on a glove*, disappeared round the corner' (my emphasis: XIX, p.333).

The gesture of pulling on the gloves works in both texts as a sign of parting, a forewarning of the final farewell. Vronskii's departure is even delayed because of the gloves, as if to give Anna a chance to regret and not to let Vronskii depart in anger.

> She heard his steps in the study, and then the dining-room. He stopped at the dining-room. But he didn't turn to her, but only gave instructions that they should let Voitov have the stallion in his absence. Then she heard the carriage being brought round, its door being opened, and he went out again. But then he came back into the hall, and someone ran upstairs. It was his valet who had run back in for the gloves he had forgotten (XIX, p. 333).

At the same time the attention given to the gloves highlights this object in the text and lends it a deeper meaning, which we may compare with the importance of Anna's red bag in her death scene. Using the language of cinema Shklovskii comments on this feature: 'The realism of both Pushkin and Tolstoi is based on their using a great number of *close-ups* instead of general shots'.[6] In Pushkin as well as in Tolstoi, that is, the Tolstoi of *Anna Karenina*, objects held in such close focus are thus drawn into a network of meaning, and pure description is replaced by symbolic telling. Perhaps this is what Tolstoi had in mind when he said: 'In the great poets, in Pushkin, this harmonious correctness of the distribution of objects is taken to perfection' (LXII, p. 22). Later Tolstoi emphasized that everything superfluous should be removed from the text in order to attain the clarity and concentration of the ancient Greeks ('there should be nothing superfluous, as in all of ancient Greek literature'.)[7]

When he started to write *Anna Karenina* he was also revising *War and Peace* and in several letters he criticizes his previous work as 'too wordy' ('многословная дребедень'). A tight structure with high inner coherence ('гармония') seems to be the textual feature that made it possible for Tolstoi to compare Pushkin with Homer and consider their works 'the right kind of art':

> Reading gifted, but unharmonious writers (and the same for music, painting) irritates and, seemingly, encourages us to work and broadens the field; but this is a mistaken perception; but reading Homer, Pushkin *compresses the field* and, if it does rouse one to work, then there is every reason for it (my emphasis: LXII, p. 22).

Although *The Tales of Belkin* are mentioned in Tolstoii's biography as an activating influence on his work with the new novel, no textual comparison has been made like the one Eikhenbaum made for the Pushkin fragments. I would therefore like to compare some details in *Anna Karenina* with the Belkin tale *Peasant-Lady*. A possible link between Pushkin's text and Tolstoi's is Princess Betsy Tverskaia, the cousin of Count Vronskii. As has already been established the gathering of the guests at Betsy Tverskaia finds its source in Pushkin's text 'The guests gathered at the dacha of the countess ...'. But the name of the princess, Betsy, brings us to the daughter of the anglomaniac Muromskii in Pushkin's tale: '... the daughter of my anglomaniac, Liza (or Betsy as Grigorii Ivanovich usually called her') (p. 148). Furthermore, an unexpected affinity arises from their surnames, Betsy *Muromskaia* and Betsy *Tverskaia*, both names being based on the names of ancient Russian cities. Besides, both women play on a certain 'English' appearance.[8] Thus, when Liza-Betsy wants to disguise her 'Russian face' from her neighbour's son, she borrows a jar of English ceruse from her governess, Miss Jackson, and whitens her face to make herself appear 'foreign' to her suitor, who knows her only as a red-faced peasant girl. A whitened face is a marked trait of an Englishwoman in Pushkin's tale:

> The table was set, and breakfast ready, and *Miss Jackson, her face already whitened*, and corseted into an hour-glass shape, was cutting the thinnest of

tartines. ... instead of Liza there entered *Miss Jackson, whitened*, corseted, with downcast eyes and giving a small curtsy ... (my emphasis: pp. 155, 162).

Tolstoi's Betsy also appears pale and powder-covered:

> Princess Betsy left the theatre before the end of the last act. She had only just had time to go into her dressing-room, *sprinkle her long pale face with powder*, wipe it off, adjust her hair and order tea in the large drawing-room, when her friends started arriving one after another at her enormous house on the Bolshaia Morskaia (my emphasis: XVIII, p. 140).

But Betsy Tverskaia's 'Englishness' is further developed in Tolstoi. The language of her salon is peppered with English expressions (while in Muromskii's house only 'my dear' is heard):

> '"Tell us something amusing. But not spiteful," said the envoy's wife, who was a great expert in elegant conversation, which the English call *small-talk* ...'; '"It's never too late to repent," the diplomat said, quoting the English saying ...'; '"Your Rambouillet is at full strength," Karenin said, looking round all the company ... But Princess Betsy could not stand this tone of his, *sneering*, as she called it ...'; '"How pleased I am that you've arrived," Betsy said ... "We'll manage to have a real heart to heart over tea, *we'll have a cosy chat*, won't we?" she turned to Anna ... And indeed, over tea ... they had *a cosy chat*, as Princess Tverskaia had promised before the guests arrived. They had a really good gossip about the people who were expected ...' (XVIII, pp. 141, 146, 148, 312, 313-14: italics indicate English in the original).

The conversation finds its counterpart in the game of croquet, the main pastime of the guests: '"But you should have gone," Betsy turned to Tushkevich, "You and Masha could have tried the croquet lawn where they've cut it" ... Tushkevich came in, announcing that the entire company was waiting for croquet players' (XVIII, pp. 312, 318).

Betsy's 'English' life is characterized by luxury and idleness, traits repeated in the life of her cousin Vronskii.[9] If the 'English way of life' at Muromskii's estate is depicted with Pushkinian irony, as a kind of whim on the part of the landowner, the 'Englishness' at Vronskii's estate takes on a different colouring. At Vozdvizhenskoe life is construed in accordance with *modernity*, the essence of which is to bring new appliances into the Russian household. The main English trait is the introduction of *machinery* into processes that earlier were done by hand or by manpower. Such a mechanization of life even reaches the grotesque when Tolstoi describes the nursery, where Anna's and Vronskii's baby roams about. An aura of 'foreignness' ('not ours') surrounds the little girl since her birth when Miss Edward was hired to take care of the 'baby'. The foreign form of her name (Annie) is used in the Vronskii household as well:

> In the nursery the luxury which had struck Daria Aleksandrovna throughout the house, struck her even more. Here there were *little carts ordered from England*, and *appliances for teaching babies how to walk*, and a specially designed divan like a billiard table, for children to crawl on, and swings and special, new baths. *All this was English*, solid and sturdy and obviously very expensive (my emphasis: XIX, p. 193).

Not only has machinery taken hold of Vronskii's house, but the day is equally *divided into hours*, as the princess Varvara explains to the visiting Dolly Oblonskaia: 'And then, c'est un intérieur si joli, si comme il faut. Tout-à-fait à l'anglaise. On se réunit le matin au breakfast et puis on se sépare. Everyone does what they like before dinner. Dinner is at seven'. (XIX, p. 196: French in original)

The guests at Vozdvizhenskoe are not united organically by some common work as at Levin's Pokrovskoe, where every activity has some practical meaning: the women cook jam on the veranda, the men hunt, children and grown-ups pick mushrooms together. To Anna's sister-in-law, Dolly Oblonskaia (whom the author calls Daria Aleksandrovna throughout her visit to Vozdvizhenskoe, thus signalling her 'un-Englishness') life on Vronskii's estate seems both luxurious and unnatural. It makes her think of playing at theatre:

> But during the game [of tennis] Daria Aleksandrovna felt unhappy. She did not like the playful tone kept up between Vasenka Veslovskii and Anna, nor the common unnaturalness of grown-ups when they play a children's game and there are no children there. ... All this day it had seemed to her that she was on stage with better actors than herself and that this poor acting of hers was spoiling the entire show (XIX, p. 211).

In Pushkin's tale Muromskii's English way of life is a matter of laughter and comedy, well expressed in the words of the landowner's neighbour Berestov: 'Why should we be ruining ourselves living English style! Having our Russian fill is good enough for us!' (p. 146). In reverse, Tolstoi's description of Vronskii's 'English' estate takes on a menacing note. The modern way of living at Vozdvizhenskoe is coloured by falsity and mechanization, and Anna's constant changing of clothes has none of the merriment connected with Betsy's mummery, but arises from her unconscious need to cleanse herself from 'stains'. Tolstoi underscores that Anna changes clothes *four* times during Dolly's one day at the estate: '"Now I'm going to change, and I'll send a girl to you ... Now we must go and change. You as well, I think. *We've got all dirty at the building-site*

... Yes, we're very correct here," she said, as if apologizing for her own elegance' (my emphasis: XIX, p. 204).

Even if changing clothes for lunch and dinner was part of the aristocratic etiquette, Tolstoi contrasts Anna's new and luxurious outfits with Dolly's 'one single dress': 'She had nothing to change into, as she was had already put on her best dress; but, in order to signal in some way that she had prepared for dinner, she asked the maid to brush her dress, changed the cuffs and ribbon, and put some lace on her head' (XIX, p. 204).

The changing of clothes, like the rebuilding of the estate and the introduction of new harvesting methods are all signs of a will to renewal. Vronskii desperately tries to change the situation. All the activity is, however, a substitute for the great change that does not take place – Anna's divorce from Karenin and her marriage to Vronskii (which, by the way, would make little Annie *his* daughter - one of his main concerns).

If the English governess of Betsy Muromskaia, Miss Jackson, is only laughable with her ceruse and tight corset, the Englishwoman taking care of Anna's and Vronskii's daughter is presented as having moral flaws:

> Hearing Anna's voice, a smart, tall English woman, with an unpleasant face and lewd expression, hurriedly shaking her blond curls, came into the room and immediately began justifying herself, even though Anna had not accused her of anything. To every word of Anna's the English woman kept mutterring hurriedly: '*Yes, my lady*' (XIX, p. 193: italics indicate English in original).

Her manner of speaking suggests a mechanical doll (the repeated 'yes, my lady') and makes her part of the furnishings that creates the unnatural atmosphere of Vozdvizhenskoe. Dolly connects her unpleasant looks ('with an unpleasant face and lewd expression') with the abnormal family situation at the estate:

> The only explanation Daria Aleksandrovna could find for the fact that Anna, with her knowledge of people, could have taken on for her little girl such an *unsympathetic, unrespectable* English woman, was that a good nurse would not have entered such an *irregular* family as Anna's was (my emphasis: XIX, p. 194).

In *Anna Karenina* Vronskii's anglicized estate is set off against Levin's Pokrovskoe. If everything at Vozdvizhenskoe is 'brand new' and of foreign origin, Levin cherishes the old and proven Russian way of life. The opposition between the two estates is revealed in a number of details. Very telling are all the worn and mended objects that Daria Oblonskaia brings with her from Pokrovskoe on her visit to Vozdvizhenskoe. Her carriage, borrowed from Levin, has 'mended mudguards', the coachman is dressed in an old kaftan and the horses are of different colour. Daria herself has by mistake taken an old 'patched dressing-jacket' with her, and Tolstoi points out that while 'at home' she had been proud of the patches and mendings - a sign of care and thriftiness, they seem awkwardly out of place at Vozdvizhenskoe: 'Daria Aleksandrovna ... was ashamed in front of the maid because of her mended dressing-gown which had been packed by mistake, as luck would have it. She was ashamed on account of the very same patches and darns of which she was so proud at home' (XIX, p. 191).

Tolstoi's valorizing of objects which have been 'patched-up', 'mended', 'covered', as it were, could be read as a symbolic development of the name *Pokrovskoe* ('pokrov/pokryvalo: veil, cover').[10] Life on Levin's estate is strongly connected with marriage, motherhood and protection. Pokrovskoe connotes celebration of family life: Kitty (by now the Russianized Katia) is expecting her baby and her sister Dolly/Daria with her many children is a constant guest at Levin's.

It could well be that Tolstoi's opposition of the two estates was also inspired by Pushkin's tale *Peasant-Lady*. The anglomaniac Muromskii has as his neighbour the landowner Berestov, whom he considers 'a provincial bear'. At Vronskii's estate Levin is criticized in similar tones. He is 'behind his time' and his views are on the whole 'Turkish', as the guest Veslovskii puts it.

> Sviiazhkii had begun talking of Levin, telling them about his strange views that machines were only harmful for Russian agriculture.
> 'I don't have the pleasure of knowing this Mr Levin,' said Vronskii, smiling, but he probably hasn't seen the machines he condemns. But if he has seen them and tried them, then somehow or other they must have been Russian, and not actually imported. And what might be his views?'
> 'Turkish ones, in general,' said Veslovskii, turning to Anna with a smile.
> 'I like him very much, he and I are great friends,' said Sviiazhskii, smiling good-naturedly, 'Mais pardon, il est un petit peu toqué; for example, he asserts that the zemstvo and arbitration boards - that all this is unnecessary, and he doesn't want to take part in any of it' (XIX, pp. 208-9).

In Pushkin's story the word 'медведь' ('bear') characterizes the landowner Berestov as something unpolished and wild (and of course 'truly Russian', like the 'береста' [birch bark] that the reader associates with his name). In Tolstoi we also find a bear image connected with Levin. It runs through the whole novel beginning with Levin's and Kitty's encounter at the skating rink and the mentioning of Levin's old nickname for his would-be wife 'tiny bear'.[11]

In Pushkin's tale Muromskii's anglomania is presented as light-hearted comedy, masquerade and fun. The Englishness that imbues Vronskii's estate just like his cousin Betsy Tverskaia's life is of a more menacing kind. It connotes falsity and estrangement from real life. At Vozdvizhenskoe Anna and Vronskii live in a *fictive* world, playing at marriage, thus acting out the *English novel*[12] that Anna was reading on the train just before Vronskii declared his love to her. And Anna literally closes her eyes (embodied in her increasing habit of прищуриться [screwing up her eyes]) at the clashes with reality that result from this make-believe attitude. Tolstoi's moral verdict is unambiguous: Man should not live by fiction. Life is not to be constructed by someone's personal will, it can only be carefully 'mended', just like Daria Oblonskaia mends her old jackets and patches up her marriage with Stepan Arkadievich. From a moral point of view she seems to be the real heroine of Tolstoy's novel. Maybe this is where the two great 'realist' writers meet. Time has transformed Pushkin's faithful wife Tatiana into Daria Oblonskaia, while Anna has sprung from a different aesthetics, that of the romantic heroines who live out their love story and perish tragically.

NOTES

1. Tolstoi is quoted from the Jubilee edition: *Polnoe sobranie sochinenii*, I-XCI, Gosudartsvennoe izdatel'stvo khudozhestvennoi literatury, Moscow, 1928-64. Only the volume and the page number will be given after each quotation.
2. S.A.Tolstaia, *Dnevniki v dvukh tomakh*, I, 1862-1900, Khudozhestvennaia literatura, Moscow, 1978, p. 500.
3. Quoted from L.N. Tolstoi, op.cit., LXII, p. 577.
4. B. Eikhenbaum, *Lev Tolstoi. Semidesiatye gody*, Khudozhestvennaia literatura, Leningrad, 1974, p. 149.
5. A.S. Pushkin, *Polnoe sobranie sochinenii v desiati tomakh*, VI, Izdatel'stvo Akademiia Nauk SSSR, Moscow, 1957, p. 573. All Pushkin quotations are from this volume. Only the page number will be given after the quotation.
6. Viktor Shklovskii, *Energiia zabluzhdeniia. Kniga o siuzhete*, Sovetskii pisatel', Moscow, 1981, p. 147.
7. Quoted in Eikhenbaum, op.cit., p. 69.
8. The 'Englishness' contrasts ironically with the surnames of the ladies – Murom and Tver' being geographical names semantically connected with the idea of being 'very Russian'.
9. For a more detailed analysis of 'Englishness' in *Anna Karenina*, see Barbara Lönnqvist, 'The English Theme in *Anna Karenina*', *Essays in Poetics*, XXIV, 1999, pp. 58-90.
10. On a realistic level the name Pokrovskoe derives of course from the village church devoted to Pokrov Bozh'ei Materi (The Feast of the Protection/ Protective Veil of the Virgin). But in Russian folk belief the holiday of Pokrov is connected with marriage and pregnancy: see Dal', V., *Tolkovyi slovar' zhivogo velikorusskogo iazyka*, Gosudarstvennoe izdatel'stvo inostrannykh i natsional'nykh slovarei, Moscow, 1955, III, p. 247 for sayings illustrative of these beliefs.
11. The bear image undergoes a complex metamorphosis in the novel: see Barbara Lönnqvist, '"Medvezhii" motiv i simvolika neba v romane *Anna Karenina*', *Scando-Slavica*, XLI, 1995, pp. 115-30.
12. There are textual similarities between the story of the English novel Anna is reading in the train ('as Lady Mary rode along ... And teased her sister-in-law and amazed everyone by her boldness' XVIII, p. 107) and what unfolds during her sister-in-law Dolly's visit to Vronskii's estate.

On the Subjectivism in Pushkin's Universality: The Case of Rozanov

by

HENRIETTA MONDRY

In work published in connection with the bicentenary of Pushkin's birth, the problem of the way he is perceived has aroused some interest. For example, in an article by V. Nepomniashchii 'The Pushkin phenomenon in the light of the obvious',[1] the question of the special features of the perception of Pushkin is seen as one of the methodologies of a scientific approach. Using the concept of science as a subject for objectivist philosophy, Nepomniashchii writes that the whole of the existing literature on Pushkin, in spite of its vastness, does not comprise anything 'integral' (p. 195). By 'integral', as implied by the title of his article, he means a phenomenological or existential approach. Interestingly, Nepomniashchii takes a phenomenological approach to be synonymous with one that is objectivist or philosophical. However, the most important phenomenologist philosopher of the twentieth century, Merleau-Ponty in *The Phenomenology of Perception,* contrasts a phenomenological methodology that is sensory and experienced existentially with the philosophical pseudo-objectivism both of empiricism and theorizing intellectualism.[2]

Although Nepomniashchii writes of the advantages of a phenomenological approach, he is critical of a subjectivist approach to Pushkin, which he designates the 'my Pushkin' type of approach (p. 198). At the same time he stipulates that such a method of perception, since it is a 'self-portrait' method (p. 200) with Pushkin as a 'mirror' (p. 198) in which the reader is reflected, cannot be scientific. Referring to the subjective approach as one of 'multiplicity' and 'fragmentation' (p. 200), the critic rejects it, since it is characterized by the 'indifference' and 'emptiness of an alienated and laboratory relationship to its subject'. Still, Nepomniashchii's criticism of subjective approaches to Pushkin appears inconsistent, in that it is precisely in the 'my Pushkin' type of approach that a phenomenologically interested relationship is expressed, one based on a dynamic relationship between reader and poet, in which the object being perceived is inseparable from the subject perceiving. To employ the terminology of the phenomenologist Gilles Deleuze, relationships of 'becoming' are established[3] between reader and writer and his/her text, as a result of which the object of investigation loses its absolute autonomy and forms a *subject/object assemblage,*[4] which cannot be a model for what the critic calls 'an alienated and laboratory relationship to its subject'

(p. 200).[5] If such a properly understood phenomenological methodology is employed, the object of perception is raised to the level of the actual perceiving subject.[6]

It is remarkable that in an article by Elena Zinger written for Pushkin's bicentenary, 'The memory of a dear one is immortal in me ...' (which appeared at the same time as Nepomniashchii's in *Novyi Mir* in 1998) the author's position on her approach to the Pushkin theme is expressed through the methodology of an intuitive search.[7] Elena Zinger compares her own method with the associative 'slow-reading' (p. 121) of Pushkin proposed by Gershenzon in 1923. She reminds her readers that the Gershenzon approach was criticized by Tomashevskii, who saw its major shortcoming as 'the appearance of meanings where there were none' (p. 121). Polemicizing with the objectivist rhetoric of Tomashevskii, she tells us that the first creative impulse to a scientific search in her own work on Pushkin was the kind of association Tomashevskii would have called 'spontaneous and parasitic' (p. 121). What is significant is the fact that the theme of Zinger's work on Pushkin is a theme from an event in his personal life: the theme of the connection between the fate of the poet and his poetry (the theme of the reflection of meeting Amaliia Riznich in the writings of Pushkin). An essential point for the present chapter is the fact that Zinger's methodological position, which has regard for the author's own concerns, reveals itself in the way she develops her theme, eliminating the distinction between life and literature.

Amongst recent work on perceptions of Pushkin, we should especially note Paul Debreczeny's *Social Functions of Literature: Alexander Pushkin and Russian Culture,* which concerns itself with features of perceptions of Pushkin in the nineteenth century.[8] Debreczeny has applied to this question a number of models drawn from disciplines related to the study of literature. He attempts to define the specific features of individual and group perceptions of Pushkin's writings and personality, on the basis of models taken from sociological, psychological and psychoanalytical works by theoreticians from a wide range of schools. The models he uses include the well-known concepts of Aristotelean catharsis, which through the aesthetic act of the perception of art acts as a purifier; Freudian sublimation, by which the *id* gains a victory over the *ego*; the concept of compensating for the shortcomings of life's realities by escaping into the wide macrocosmos of *literary* reality. He devotes one chapter to an analysis of the place of Pushkin's personality, and works in the psycho-analytical search and self-reflection of Marina Tsvetaeva. Although Debreczeny deals with the question of the reception of the author and his writings, he makes no direct references to post-structural approaches to the mutual relationships established between reader and text. In spite of his attempts to use inter-disciplinary models for a reader's perception of a text, Debreczeny keeps within the framework of philosophical objectivism. Notwithstanding his references to the work of Vygotsky on child psychology and his observations of Tsvetaeva's self-reflection of bisexuality, the readers in Debreczeny's book are not differentiated by gender or by sexual orientation. The difference in readers' perceptions is basically defined by categories of class, not by categories of age. Thus the reader's subjectivism which creates a text is excluded from a book devoted to the perception of literature.

Different from Debreczeny, whose book lacks a clearly expressed standpoint on the polemical non-acceptance of post-structuralist theories, is V.S. Baevskii's work on Pushkin's religiosity ('Biblical themes, motifs and images in Pushkin's *The Gypsies*' of 1996), in which Baevskii expresses his non-acceptance of subjectivism in interpreting Pushkin's work.[9] Criticizing the ideas of 'the opposite interpretation', Baevskii refers to the perception of Pushkin in the writings of those active in Russian culture at the beginning of the twentieth century, 'the bearers of a new religious consciousness', as an example of scientific objectivism.

In the present chapter, an attempt will be made to focus on a model for perceptions of Pushkin ignored by Debreczeny and rejected by Baevskii and Nepomniashchii. It may be called 'consciously subjectivist', but its purpose is to express the philosophical position of the actual reader. I propose as my reader-creator, someone who generates a personal perception of Pushkin's writings and life, a representative of Russian culture from the beginning of the twentieth century - Vasilii Vasilevich Rozanov (1856-1919). My aim is a simple one - to demonstrate that in Rozanov's work on Pushkin, subjectivism as a philosophical methodology is programmatic. Rozanov's phenomenological position as a philosopher of life is revealed in the selective interest he took both in everyday events in Pushkin's life, and in his writings - an interest based on the principle of recognizability. For Rozanov what is interesting in Pushkin is only what he finds of interest in himself. This principle of 'interestedness' applies without exception to Rozanov's perception of the world in the widest possible variety of its representations - objects of decorative and applied art (sculpture, ancient coins),[10] the hero of a work of literature, or one of his many acquaintances.[11] Using this kind of 'contemplation' perception,[12] Pushkin's uniqueness loses any meaning.[13] From Grigorev's 'Pushkin is our everything' Pushkin becomes *Pushkin as everything*. The perception of Pushkin's personality by his contemporaries and successors, and Pushkin's own orientation towards this myth-making character, simply collapses. If one uses Rozanov's perception methodology Pushkin becomes as 'small'[14] or as 'great' as Rozanov 'contemplating' him.

For Pushkin's centenary celebrations in 1899, Rozanov wrote a fairly routine article on Pushkin with the routine title of 'A.S. Pushkin'.[15] In it he used such commonplace formulae as 'today marks the first centenary celebration of the principal luminary of our literature' (p. 37), and employed banal phrases like 'Pushkin is a national poet'. By 1899 Rozanov had developed his own special style and was the author of the sensational *In the World of the Unclear and*

Undecided. Yet he wrote an article on Pushkin which he himself described as 'a few pitiful copper coins' added to what had already been said, an article 'without any claims to originality or novelty'.

A year later Rozanov suddenly published an article which he enthusiastically entitled 'Something new on Pushkin' ('Кое-что новое о Пушкине'). What enabled him to discover a new theme in Pushkin, a theme which turned what he had called the 'copper coins' of banality into gold? Rozanov is so excited about the theme he has discovered that, forgetting about the epithets he used to describe the poet a mere year ago, he contemptuously enumerates the routine and worn-out themes on which literary historians have concentrated. Themes like 'Pushkin as a human being', 'Pushkin as a national poet' (p. 57). What new problems has Rozanov found in Pushkin?

Rozanov is in such a hurry to state his new theme that as early as the second paragraph he identifies it as 'The Jew and Pushkin ...' (p. 57). He at once sets out the problems connected with this theme on the basis of a parallel drawn between Pushkin and the Jew in *The Covetous Knight* and defines it as follows: 'What is there in common between the petty merchant and the most generous of mortals? What mutual comprehension is there?' (p. 57). Rozanov quotes some lines of dialogue between Albert and the Jew in *The Covetous Knight,* drawing particular attention to the words of the old Jew:

> How can one know?
> Our days are numbered not by us:
> Yesterday the young man flourished, today he is dead,
> And now four old men
> Carry him to the grave on their bent shoulders. (p. 58)

Rozanov is not interested in what Albert says, his attention is focused on the old Jew, whose thoughts he identifies with those of Pushkin. According to Rozanov Pushkin divined and defined 'the universal' in Jewishness, its oldness: 'What oldness there is in the reply, what wise oldness!' (p. 58).

Rozanov further develops the idea of Pushkin's perspicacity regarding the role of the Jew in European civilization by using the example of an unfinished fragment from *Beginning of a Story* by Pushkin: 'In the Jewish hut there is an icon-lamp'. Here Pushkin describes a scene in a Jewish house, where an old man is reading an ancient book by candlelight, an old woman is preparing a meagre evening meal, and a young Jewess is weeping. The scene is interrupted at midnight by a heavy knock at the door. Rozanov admits that he does not know what Pushkin was trying to say in this unfinished fragment. He suggests it might be a version of the mediaeval theme from the history of the persecution of the Jews in which 'the unknown traveller' is either 'a patrol, the inquisition, or a member of some other legal body' (p. 60). However, Rozanov as a philosopher is not interested in the development of the subject of the story, but in the theme of the family and Jewry. He believes that Pushkin guessed that the very essence of Jewry, what he calls its treasures, lies in its feeling for family and religion. He notes that Pushkin realized that the Bible is understood by Jews differently from the way it is understood by European peoples. He formulates the idea as follows: 'Biblical theism is in fact family theism' (p. 60). Then, as though he has suddenly remembered that he is supposed to be writing about Pushkin, he adds, '[a]nd Pushkin understood this and tacitly showed it' (p. 60).

In order to understand the mechanics of Rozanov's selection of so-called new themes in Pushkin, we should note that by the time he wrote his second Pushkin article, he had already worked out for himself the theme of the contrast between ancient religions and Christianity. Similarly, by 1900 he had already linked the theme of sex with the theme of religion and the family, expressed in 'The Family as Religion' (1898), and 'Marriage and Christianity' (1898). By the time he wrote his second Pushkin article, the polemics around his published views on the metaphysical essence of sex were in full swing. In *From the Riddles of Human Nature* (1898), Rozanov had proclaimed himself the rehabilitator of the idea of family, the apologist for the pantheism of paganism, and the reformer of the asceticism of Christianity. The theme of sex and the body in ancient pre-Christian religions was heard in this work as a polemic against the bodilessness of the New Testament[16] But the theme of Judaism and Jewry, with all its complicated acceptance-rejection dynamic, as Efim Kurganov has recently shown,[17] was to be developed by Rozanov in works written after 1900. By the time he came to work on the 1900 article on Pushkin, the theme of Judaism had become fixed in his mind as that of demonstrating that there was in the Old Testament a deferential attitude towards sexual and family feelings. On the other hand, the motif of competition with Jewish fecundity,[18] which was to become the dominant theme in *Solitaria* (1911) and *Fallen Leaves* (1912),[19] had not yet been articulated in the works of 1898 as one of semitism, but had been introduced as the theme of the difference in attitude towards sex and family in the Old and New Testaments. The incompleteness of Rozanov's thoughts on the destinies of semitism are revealed in the vagueness with which the philosopher interprets the theme of Jewry in Pushkin. This is precisely the reason why, addressing it in the Pushkin article, he breaks off with the stipulation that the question of 'Pushkin's attitude to semitism' so far remains unresolved. Having noted the theme, Rozanov cannot bring himself to develop it more fully as a Pushkin theme, just as he had hitherto failed to articulate its problems.

The article 'Something New on Pushkin' (1900) is also significant for an understanding of the way Rozanov perceives biographical and literary material. It contains the methodological key to what his creative impulse clearly was. It is noteworthy that the stimulus that turned him to Pushkin, prompting him to write the article, was a recently published article by P. Shchegolev, 'Immodest Guesses' ('Нескромные догадки') of 1899. This article contained information on people of Pushkin's time, who were known to him personally, and these were interpreted by Shchegolev as literary prototypes. Rozanov read the article with the new biographical information linking concrete historical figures with characters in Pushkin's works and became animated. He became animated precisely as a 'philosopher of life' learning something new about Pushkin's life. He is interested in the fact that Ineza in Don Juan is derived from Amaliia Riznich, and that behind Laura lies the frivolous Anna Kern. Rozanov interprets this as Pushkin saying farewell to the amorous adventures of his youth before his marriage to Natalia Goncharova. As a 'contemplator' of life, Rozanov adopted his own approach, moving from biographical data, information about the poet's life to an interpretation of the texts. This demonstrates the essential features of his methodological standpoint, and it also contains a polemical element. Thus in an article on Solovev, 'To the Memory of Vl. Solovev' ('Памяти Вл. Соловьева') of 1900, written in the same year as the article on what was new in Pushkin, Rozanov accuses him in his book *Pushkin's Fate* (*Судьба Пушкина*) of 'theoretical speculation', 'unsupported by knowledge of life' (p. 67). He further criticizes Solovev for 'having little feeling for actuality, for the earth ...' and writes that 'in his sad family history Pushkin has been caught in the snare' of Solovev's abstract ideas ('To the Memory of Vl. Solovev', p. 67).

This pattern of an awakening of interest in Pushkin as a result of information about his life and times was repeated in 1916. Once again Shchegolev published new documents. In the same year Rozanov responded to this with a new free interpretation. This time the two themes - that of sex and that of the family - which with some artificiality had been joined together in the 1900 article, were combined into a single theme and used to explain the reasons for Pushkin's death. It is significant that between writing the two articles reacting to biographical material Rozanov showed no great interest in Pushkin. In the period from 1900 to 1916 he published another anniversary article on Pushkin ('Returning to Pushkin [for the seventy-fifth anniversary of the day of his death']' in 1912), and also an article dedicated to Pushkin and Lermontov. The anniversary article again includes such commonplace rhetoric as 'Pushkin is calmness, clarity, balance' (p. 366). And although the second article is called 'Pushkin and Lermontov' (1914), it is devoted to the demonism of Lermontov, not to the dullness with which Pushkin is represented. Lermontov interests Rozanov as a demonic phenomenon, whose life linked the metaphysical with the physical. For his part, Pushkin is again the recipient of the sort of banal epithets he earned in the first anniversary article about him: 'Pushkin is a poet of world harmony - order, concord, happiness' ('Pushkin and Lermontov', p. 602). In this article Pushkin is important to Rozanov only as part of his model for a schematic antinomy, the antithesis of Lermontov: in Pushkin there is the stasis of life, whereas in Lermontov there is a farewell to life and a movement towards death.

In 1916 Rozanov published a striking article on Pushkin: 'The End of Pushkin (Concerning P.E. Shchegolev's new book *The Death of Pushkin*)'. Again he reacts against Shchegolev, using a document as his starting point, but it is as if, in so reacting, he is destroying the document's importance. He writes that, although Shchegolev spent 15 years searching the archives for an explanation of the reasons for Pushkin's death, he, Rozanov, finds the story of that death 'blindingly clear' in its own right (p. 643). He draws the reader's attention to the cynical explanations given by Pushkin in the first published letter to his wife on the 'true nature of his urges', 'the true nature of the attentions' being paid to her, in which Pushkin, according to the philosopher, uses uncensored, obscene language. Furthermore Rozanov describes Pushkin's own philandering as the behaviour of a pantheist. Being an expert observer of life, the philosopher seeks an explanation for the poet's behaviour in the modes of behaviour prevalent in Pushkin's day. Rozanov describes relationships between the sexes in high society at the time of Alexander I as a 'universal lover' time, when infidelity was regarded as normal conduct and fidelity was regarded as miraculous. His conclusion on the reasons for Pushkin's death is simple - it was not infidelity that Pushkin found intolerable, but *talk* of infidelity. Infidelity may have been normal conduct, but talk about it was not. Infidelity may have been one of the components of 'society chic', but talk of 'horns' was in a different category (p. 643). As a writer of immortal epigrams, Pushkin was well aware of the value of verse on cuckoldry, and found intolerable what the philosopher calls the moment when he was given 'a dose of his own poison'(p. 643).

The two themes of Rozanov's philosophy of sex are derived from the two themes developed by Rozanov in his writings on Pushkin: on the one hand, wisdom and the importance of the role of the family in Judaism and, on the other, the theme of Pushkin as someone failing to play the part of an Old-Testament husband in his marriage. Both themes are linked with questions of everyday life and behaviour, and relate to the question of the family and sex. According to Rozanov, in the first theme Pushkin 'understood and silently indicated'(p. 60) the role of the family as a pillar of the religious spirit of Jewry; in the second the philosopher demonstrates how Pushkin the pantheist failed in his life to carry out the role of a patriarch, a husband to his wife.[20] He notes that by addressing his wife in letters in the tone used to address a coquette or housemaid [21] Pushkin in his cynicism had left his wife without a husband even while he was still alive. Pushkin chose not 'one wife', 'one wife for life' (p. 645), as wives are chosen in the Old Testament, but made his choice as a 'pantheist', choosing beauty that was 'purely corporeal' (p. 645). The meaning of Rozanov's interest in Pushkin lies in his choice of these two themes. Both of them are component parts of his philosophy of sex, in which questions of family and sexuality are simultaneously the object and method of his investigation of life.

The essential subjectivism of Rozanov's position is a basic programmatic principle. He devised a synthesis of the subjectivism of perception and the objectivism of philosophy. Thus, in Merleau-Ponty's definition, 'the external world' represents a 'text', which 'is not copied, but composed' (p. 9).[22] Pushkin's writings and the events in his life were the external world *composed* by Rozanov in his interpretation of the poet. In a letter to Hollerbach (Letter 24, August, 1918) Rozanov himself formulated this philosophical position as follows:

> When you 'write about Rozanov', you do not write entirely about him, you also include your own fallen leaves 'what I think', 'feel', 'what occupies me', 'how I live'. This is a form both full of egoism and without egoism. In fact human beings *have something to do with everything and nothing to do with anything*. Essentially they are concerned only for themselves, but in such a way that their concern for themselves includes a concern for the whole world (p. 536).[23]

The problems of comprehension had occupied Rozanov since the time of his first philosophical treatise, *On Comprehension* (*О понимании*) of 1886. But it was only when he discovered a new form which eliminated the bipolarity of the subjective and the objective that he was able to find adequate expression for the process of perception. By 1918 the philosopher had finally established an element of subjectivity in the process of comprehension and perception. This subjectivity, however, did not interfere with the discovery of an ultimate truth. Rozanov recognized the originality of his position in creating new 'forms' (p. 536), defining them as 'a special combination of egoism and non-egoism' (p. 536). He sees the element of 'fabrication' in the process of comprehension as an integral part of the act of perception, but one which does not act as an obstacle to the search for complete cognition:

> But human beings eternally fabricate and here we have the peculiar feature that even fabrications do not destroy truth, do not destroy the fact: every reverie, every desire, every web of thought will play its part ... And when I think that this is what I have done with my 'self', have done since 1911, of course no single human being will be *expressed* on such a scale and at the same time be again subjective ... (p. 536).

This kind of perception in which there is no distinction between objectivity and subjectivity became fundamental in the existential world-view of twentieth-century phenomenologists. For example, Georges Bataille, who exerted considerable influence on the development of post-structuralist critical theories, defined the philosophy of perception as a process of the self-expression of an 'individual', not of 'inseparable humanity'.[24] Rozanov as an individual in his interpretation of Pushkin expressed two *idées fixes* of his world-view - the theme of Jewry and Judaism and the theory of sex. In a letter to A.A. Izmailov (August, 1918) Rozanov referred to himself as 'a genuine and truly the last Jewish prophet'(p. 126).[25] He discovered in Pushkin the theme he called 'the Jew and Pushkin' as a projection of 'his own concerns', of himself, onto the world-view and personality of Pushkin.[26] Having devoted his whole life and work to what he himself defined as 'the sermon of sex' (*Fallen Leaves*, p. 132), Rozanov found in Pushkin's personal life a confirmation of his theory of sex, constructed on a synthesis of religiosity and sexuality. In Rozanov's interpretation Pushkin understood the unique role of Jewry in the history of religion and the family and emerges as the equal of Rozanov himself, treated by him as a *subject*. On the other hand Pushkin, who proved to be a poor husband, a philanderer and a pantheist, was still an *object* for study. In the former regard the boundary between Rozanov and Pushkin is eliminated; in the latter a barrier of alienation is erected. In the alienation process Rozanov remains a 'Jewish prophet', while Pushkin lapses into paganism. Nevertheless such patent objectivity is in its turn subjectified in the context of a knowledge of Rozanov's own personal life. Taking into account modes of conduct in Rozanov's time, when he himself took part in orgiastic sessions and ritual dances which involved stroking one's partner's genitals,[27] his claim that his time in history was part of his objectivity fails to be convincing. By finding his explanation for Pushkin's behaviour in the norms of fashionable behaviour at a particular time in history, Rozanov proves to have brought only an apparent objectivity to his evaluation of the poet's conduct. By taking part in rituals which apparently were intended to revive paganism, Rozanov was behaving like Pushkin, the so-called 'pantheist'. Thus both the first and second themes developed by Rozanov in his perception of the poet Pushkin, leave Pushkin filtered through the perception prism of the philosopher's subjectivism. Here there is an ironic paradox, the essence of which lies in the fact that Pushkin can be simultaneously a biblical prophet and a pantheist in the same way that Rozanov can be a Jewish prophet and a pagan. Given such a subjective interpretation of Pushkin on the part of Rozanov, the only element of objectivity to be found is in the modes of conduct at the beginning of the twentieth century, when it was fashionable to try to create a new organically integrated theogony on the basis of a synthesis of Judaism, Christianity, forms of paganism and Buddhism. Historical contextuality, which Merleau-Ponty calls a phenomenological 'field' of perception, or 'field' of vision[28] expresses an ambivalency between objective and subjective perceptions which is programmatically important for phenomenology. This *subjective objectivity* is of prime importance for the essential life philosophy of Rozanov himself.

In post-structuralist critical debates, the development of which was strongly influenced by phenomenological methodology, relationships of bipolarity are removed from the connection between subject and object. Self-knowledge is acquired at the expense of knowledge of the world and the world comes to be known through the prism of knowing oneself in the world. Rozanov looked at the world through the prism of the 'gaze' described by Lacan,[29] in which the gaze carries a charge of self-expression and recognition of oneself in others. Between object and subject a single continuum is created.[30] Rozanov's recognition of Pushkin came from his recognition of Pushkin in himself, and of himself in Pushkin. It is in this new, phenomenological sense that finally Pushkin actually does become 'our everything'.

NOTES

1. V. Nepomniashchii, 'Fenomen Pushkina v svete ochevidnostei' ('The Pushkin phenomenon in the light of the obvious'), *Novyi Mir*, VI, 1998, pp. 190-215.
2. See, for example, the work of Monika Langer on the essential features of Merleau-Ponty's perception of the world and the following important definition of the radical difference between a phenomenological methodology of perception and objectivist approaches: '... in deliberately employing the word *field*, phenomenology emphasises the irreducibility of the world and the perspectivity of reflection. Reflection thus understood is not the surveying of a world spread out as a spectacle for a disembodied, all encompassing Thinker. It is, rather, an activity of an individual philosopher and is always conditioned by the latter's concrete situation in the world. If it is to be truly radical, phenomenological reflection will need to reflect on itself, maintain a constant awareness of its own source in an unreflective experience and recognize that it invariably transforms that unreflective experience in submitting it to reflection.' See Monika Langer, *Merleau-Ponty's Phenomenology of Perception. A Guide and Commentary*, Macmillan, London, 1989, p. 19.
3. Gilles Deleuze, 'Literature and Life', translated by Daniel M. Smith and Michael A. Greco, *Critical Enquiry* XXIII, 2 (winter) 1997, pp. 225-30.
4. Gilles Deleuze and Felix Guattarri, *Anti-Oedipus: Capitalism and Schizophrenia*, translated by Robert Hurley, Mark Seem and Helen R. Lane, Athlone, London, 1984.
5. Réné Scherer, 'On Four Formulas That Might Sum Up The Deleuzian Philosophy', *Angelaki* II:3, 1997, pp. 173-7.
6. Ibid., p. 173.
7. E. Zinger, 'Vo mne sviashchenna pamiat' miloi' ('The memory of a dear one is immortal in me ...'), *Voprosy literatury,* March-April, 1998, pp. 121-52.
8. Paul Debreczeny, *Social Functions of Literature: Alexander Pushkin and Russian Culture*, Stanford University Press, Stanford, 1997.
9. V.S. Baevskii, 'Bibleiskie temy, motivy I obrazy v *Tsyganakh* Pushkina' ('Biblical themes, motifs and images in Pushkin's *Gypsies*'), *Russkaia filologiia*, Smolensk Pedagogical Institute, Smolensk, 1996, p. 7.
10. See Henrietta Mondry, 'O "nekrasivoi" androginnosti: statuia kak politika tela u V.Rozanova' ('On "ugly" androgynousness. The statue as the body politic in V.Rozanov'), *Russian Literature*, XLVIII-I, July 2000, pp. 71-86.
11. See A. Danilevskii's correct conclusion, 'Rozanov in the world of literature primarily perceived himself, constantly projecting himself onto various literary characters ...', in Aleksandr Danilevskii, 'V.V. Rozanov kak literaturnyi tip', in *Klassitsizm I modernizm*. ('V.V. Rozanov as a literary character', *Classicism and Modernism*). Universities of Tartu and Stockholm, Tartu, 1997, pp. 112-28.
12. See Viktor Erofeev, 'Raznotsvetnaia mozaika rozanovskoi mysli', in *V.V. Rozanov. Nesovmestimye kontrasty zhitiia* ('The multicoloured mosaic of Rozanov's thought', in *V.V. Rozanov. The Incompatible Contrasts of Life*), Iskusstvo, Moscow, 1990, pp. 6-36 (p. 9).
13. The theme of Pushkin's uniqueness provides the basic thrust of Nepomniashchii's article. In it, despite his claim to be concerned with phenomenology, the concept of 'phenomena' is used synonymously with that of uniqueness.
14. Compare Pushkin's utterance on the uniqueness of the personality of a poet in connection with Byron's death and popular rumours about him: '... *He is small, like us, he is vile, like us!* You lie, you scoundrels: he is both small and vile, but not like you, - in a different way'. Quoted by Iurii Lotman in *Roman A.S. Pushkina 'Evgenii Onegin'*.

Kommentarii (A.S. Pushkin's Novel 'Yevgeny Onegin', A Commentary), Prosveshchenie, Leningrad, 1980, p. 26.

15. All quotations from Rozanov's writing on Pushkin are from the following edition: V.V. Rozanov, *O pisateliakh I pisatel'stve* (V.V. Rozanov, *On Writing and Writers*), Respublika, Moscow, 1995.
16. George F. Putnam, 'Vasilii V. Rozanov: Sex, Marriage and Christianity', *Canadian Slavic Studies*, III, 1971, pp. 301-26.
17. Efim Kurganov, 'Vasilii Rozanov I bibleiskii mir' (Vasilii Rozanov and the Biblical World), *Russkii evrei*, IV, 1997, pp. 28-31.
18. Henrietta Mondry, 'Race and Stereotype: Soloviev, Rozanov and Jewish Sexuality', *Jewish Affairs*, LII, 3, 1997, pp. 141-6.
19. Compare, for example, the following utterance by Rozanov: 'A continuation into the future of the Christian rejection of sex will have as its consequence an increase in the triumphs of Jewry. That is why my preaching of sex is so timely'. V.V. Rozanov, *Opavshie list'ia*, in *Izbrannoe (Fallen Leaves*, in *Selected Works)*, A. Nemanis, München, 1970, pp. 81-426, p. 132.
20. It is significant that it is precisely in Pushkin's concern to create a home and family that Iurii Lotman sees the embodiment of the poet's patriarchal ideal: thus, for example, 'The poetry of the patriarchy of family, an idyllic picture of the family nest ...' See Iu. M. Lotman, *Aleksandr Sergeevich Pushkin. Biografiia pisatelia. (Aleksandr Sergeevich Pushkin. A Biography of the Writer)*, Prosveshchenie, Leningrad, 1980, p. 204.
21. Significantly, Lotman sees in the use Pushkin makes of the lexis of the common people in his letters to his wife an indication of intimacy, a mark of the establishment of 'the norms of family style': ibid., p. 202.
22. See, for example, 'the text of the external world is not so much copied as composed' in Maurice Merleau-Ponty, *Phenomenology of Perception*, Routledge, London, 1962, p. 9.
23. V.V. Rozanov, *Pis'ma k E.F. Gollerbakhu*, in *Izbrannoe (Letters to E.F. Hollerbach*, in *Selected Works)*, A. Nemanis, München, 1970, pp. 515-64, p. 536.
24. See 'A philosophy is a coherent sum or is nothing, but it expresses the individual, not indissoluble mankind' in Georges Bataille, *Theory of Religion*, trans. Robert Hurley, Zone Books, New York, 1989, p. 11.
25. V. Rozanov's letters to A. Izmailov. *Novyi Zhurnal*, CXXXVI, 1979, pp. 121-6, p. 125.
26. It is significant that in his *Pushkin's Wisdom* Gershenzon will repeat Rozanov's description of Pushkin as a man endowed with Old-Testament wisdom and burdened by the knowledge of an Ahasuerus: 'on his face the dusty wrinkles of Ahasuerus show through, from his eyes looks the heavy wisdom of the millennia', '... through his thought flows a stream of Old-Testament experience'. Gershenzon was in correspondence with Rozanov. See M. Gershenzon, *Mudrost' Pushkina (Pushkin's Wisdom)* (1919), Ann Arbor Reprint, Ardis, 1983, p. 13, p. 14. For Rozanov's correspondence with Gershenzon see V. Proskurina, 'Perepiska mezhdu V.V. Rozanovym i M.O. Gershenzonom, 1909-1918' ('The Correspondence between V.V. Rozanov and M.O. Gershenzon, 1909-1918'), *Novyi Mir*, 3, 1991, pp. 215-42.
27. For this see Rozanov's letter 30 to Hollerbach of 6.10.1918, in *Selected Works*, A. Nemanis, München, 1970, pp. 549-52.
28. See Langer, op. cit., p. 19.
29. Lacan himself notes that the work of Merleau-Ponty was a significant influence on the formation of his theory of the symbolic gaze: see Jacques Lacan, 'What is a picture?' in *The Four Fundamental Concepts of Psycho-Analysis*, Norton, New York, 1978, pp. 105-19
30. This type of philosophical subjectivism has nothing in common with the ideological falsificatory interpretation with which V.S. Baevskii confuses it. As far as the model of Marina Tsvetaeva's reading of Pushkin is concerned, Debreczeny's interpretation lacks one post-

structuralist schema which seems to me productive. He notes that a perception of Pushkin was influenced by two representational images of Pushkin - one in portraits, one in sculpture. Thus, when she was a child, the *corporeal* Pushkin was perceived by the future poetess sensorially, through his 'dark' (*My Pushkin*) corporeality. By perceiving her own *déclassé* situation through a corporeal connection with the dark poet Tsvetaeva created in her writings and life the myth of her 'Jewishness', in which Jewishness is synonymous with the image of the 'colonial' Other. Her bisexuality was for Tsvetaeva a sign that she belonged to the polyvalent conglomerate of the Other. Seeking for an explanation for her bisexuality, she found a way out for her own desires by creating relationships with Pushkin and his characters. Using the terminology of Gilles Deleuze one may call the latter 'assemblages', or the machines of these desires. Gilles Deleuze and Felix Guattari, *Anti-Oedipus: Capitalism and Schizophrenia*, translated by Robert Hurley, Mark Seem and Helen R. Lane, Athlone, London, 1984.

Tsvetaeva's Three Pushkins

by

DIANA L. BURGIN

Although there is hardly a Russian poet who has not claimed a posthumous creative and personal intimacy with Pushkin, Marina Tsvetaeva's takes second place to none in terms of its fervour, durability and range. If we are to credit one of F.A. Stepun's reminiscences of Tsvetaeva, during a difficult time in her, and Russia's, life, Pushkin offered her the support and protection of a guardian angel. Stepun recalls:

> In autumn 1921 Tsvetaeva and I were walking down Tverskoi Boulevard ... I felt scared listening to her, but she was not scared to talk: she believed that in Moscow, not only Lenin was in power in the Kremlin, but Pushkin reigned as well, at the Monastery of the Passion. 'Oh,' she exclaimed, 'nothing is frightening with Pushkin as company'. As she walked with me toward Nikitskii Gates, she thankfully sensed his sadly downcast gaze following her and giving her his blessing (6/79).[1]

Tsvetaeva's work is peppered with references to Pushkin and contains a number of writings devoted solely to him, such as the 1913 poem, *Meeting with Pushkin*, the 1931 lyric cycle *Poems to Pushkin*, and the 1937 autobiographical prose work *My Pushkin*, which she described as 'my early childhood: Pushkin in the nursery - amended to read: *in mine*' (6/450). Her caveat notwithstanding, the Pushkin of Tsvetaeva's 'early childhood' has almost all the earmarks of her mature Pushkin, illustrating her own belief that 'what one knows in childhood, one knows all one's life, but what one doesn't know in childhood - one doesn't know all one's life' (5/81).

In 1931 Tsvetaeva wrote to Boris Pasternak: 'I've been with Pushkin, mentally, from the age of 16 - always walking, never kissing, not once, - not the slightest temptation to' (8/443). This comment makes clear that Tsvetaeva considered her mature relationship with Pushkin to be a dynamic, female-male, but emphatically non-sexual marriage-of-the-minds, which offered a model for creative intimacy between the Original Russian Poet and herself, specifically as a Russian *female* poet (not a poetess!). Creatively and personally, Tsvetaeva wished to be loved by Pushkin without earning the 'contempt' she believed he had, 'like all his ilk', for 'the women he loved' (8/452), except his wife, who she considered the most contemptible of all his women. Tsvetaeva wanted to be not Pushkin's real, but his ideal wife.

In numerous comments, Tsvetaeva reveals an extraordinary preoccupation with Pushkin's national poetic bloodline, so to speak. She considers Pushkin's poetic blood to be as pure as his actual blood was mixed. For her, the sign of poetic blue blood is Pushkin's immortal life and his nation's undying love. As she explains to Rilke: 'A Pushkin, a Blok and - to name them all at once - an ORPHEUS - can never die since he is dying in fact in the present (eternally!)' (7/59). Tsvetaeva argues that the Pushkin line in Russian poetry passes from Pushkin directly to Blok not because of 'an inner kinship' between them, but because of the 'sameness' of the Russians' love for them 'that makes them kin' (4/56). Among Tsvetaeva's living contemporaries, the Pushkin-Blok poetic bloodline produced 'her great friend in both life and work', Boris Pasternak, of whom she writes: 'one never knows, who is bigger in him, the poet or the man? *Both are bigger!* A very rare case among creative people, although, in my opinion, *the way it should be*. That's how Goethe was - and Pushkin - and, from our time, Blok' (7/313). Tsvetaeva fits herself into Pushkin's poetic bloodline and proves the trueness of her poet's identity in observing that '*all* real [poets] have known their own worth - beginning with Pushkin', and that she is exceptional even among real poets because she is 'the first after Pushkin who has delighted *so* in his own strength, so - openly, so - dispassionately, so - single-mindedly!' (7/396).

Tsvetaeva felt a great need to base her kinship with Pushkin on a factual as well as 'mental' foundation. She set store by any personal contact she, or members of her family, chanced to have, however indirectly, with Pushkin's blood relatives. In *My Pushkin* she highlights her 'seeing' at the age of three Pushkin's son, Alexander, in her childhood home in Three Ponds Lane when the latter visited her parents. That visit of what Tsvetaeva considers 'the dual monument' of Pushkin's 'glory and his blood' (at the time she saw Pushkin's son, she knew Pushkin only as his monument in Moscow, that is, as Pushkin-Monument), represents to her, 'a whole lifetime later', her having 'had, before Pushkin, before Don Juan, a visit from [her] own Commendatore' (5/65). Having her own Commendatore identifies Tsvetaeva as a proto-Don Juan herself, and therefore, might pose to some readers a question she never asks: Did she have her own Doña Anna, and if so, who was she?

As an adult, Tsvetaeva met two women who were related to Pushkin, by blood and by marriage, respectively: his granddaughter, Elena Aleksandrovna Pushkina (1889-1943); and the painter Natalia Goncharova, 'the great granddaughter of N. N. Goncharova, Pushkin's fateful wife' (6/376). Tsvetaeva's friendship with Natalia Goncharova seemed to her, with nostalgic hindsight, to have begun in the childhood world of *My Pushkin* because Pushkin's son, who visited her Three-Ponds-Lane house, 'would drive past the Goncharovs' house - adjacent to [the Tsvetaevs']' (8/447). Thus, in *My Pushkin*

Tsvetaeva writes the origin of her bondings with Pushkin, bondings that express her own most urgent issues of existential, poetic, racial and sexual identity.

The writing of Tsvetaeva in general provides a refuge for the unregenerate essentialists among us who can take vindictive pleasure in Tsvetaeva's penchant for knowing and naming what reality, people and things *are*. Nowhere is her essentialism more obvious than in *My Pushkin* where she repeats the name Pushkin 146 times, mainly in the nominative case. More essentially revealing, 26 of Pushkin's nominative case appearances occur in predicate sentences of the type: 'Pushkin is X', sentences that affirm Pushkin's immutable essence for Tsvetaeva in particular - he is, after all, *her* Pushkin - but by implication, for any right-thinking Russian.

And who *is* Pushkin? In *My Pushkin* he has an abundance of names: 'Pushkin is the man taken away (уводимый)' after a fatal duel; 'Pushkin is a poet', Tsvetaeva's and Russia's 'first poet'; 'Pushkin is a Negro' (like all poets); 'Pushkin is Pushkin-Monument', 'Pushkin is Pushkin', 'Pushkin is a symbol', 'Pushkin is a *fact* ...', and so on. That some of these Pushkin identities contradict each other merely enhances Pushkin's greatness, indicating his all-encompassing, divine nature. Who but a god can *be* human and divine, dying and living, fact and symbol, wholly self and his others?

In view of Tsvetaeva's insistence on calling Pushkin by his right names, it is ironic that from the very beginning of *My Pushkin* she uses him as a cover-story for a personal mystery narrative: 'It begins like a chapter in the bedside reading of all our grandmothers and mothers - *Jane Eyre* - the secret of the red room. In the red room stood a secret bookcase' (5/57). Here we have a classic tease, for Tsvetaeva delays telling 'the secret of the red room' for some eight pages. First, she backtracks into the secret's prehistory. Then, a few pages later, she delves into its pre-prehistory, which involves little Musia's relationship with Pushkin-Monument, 'a black man taller than everyone and blacker than everyone - with head inclined and hat in hand' (5/59). Pushkin-Monument teaches her many 'first lessons' - in numbers, in scale, in materiality, in hierarchy, in thought, and, most essential, he confirms for her that 'out of a thousand clay figurines, even placed one on top of the other, you cannot make a Pushkin' (5/61).

When Tsvetaeva finally reveals the secret of the red room she broadens it to include the whole Eden of her childhood: 'But what about the secret of the red room? Ah, the whole house was secret, the whole house was - a secret! Forbidden bookcases. Forbidden fruit. That fruit - a volume, a huge blue-violet volume with a horizontal gold inscription - Collected Works of A. S. Pushkin' (5/65).

Tsvetaeva's Pushkin was secret because he 'infected [her] with love. *With the word* - love' (5/68), specifically, the transgressive tragic love of Tatiana and Onegin. Their love aroused her desire for a slightly-more-homosexual-than-heterosexual, but more a suprasexual desire for love, a secret desire she kept from her mother, who did not suspect that she 'was not in love with Onegin, but with Onegin and Tatiana (and, perhaps, a little more with Tatiana), with both of them together, with love. And ever afterwards', Tsvetaeva continues, 'I have not written a single thing without first falling in love with the two of them (with her - a little more), not with the two of them, but with their love. With love' (5/71). The most deep-lying 'secret of the red room', of the madwoman in the Tsvetaevan house who burns with somewhat-lesbian, graphomaniacal desire is that Pushkin infected her with want of her own.

The mystery of Pushkin's homoerotic agency for Tsvetaeva may lie embedded in her version of how he came to be, her genesis of the Original Russian Poet:

> Pushkin is *fact* overturning theory. Before birth racism was overturned by Pushkin at the very minute of his birth. But no - earlier: on the day of the marriage of Peter the Great's Negro, Osip Abramovich Gannibal with Maria Alekseevna Pushkina. But no, still earlier: on the day unknown to us and at the moment when Peter first fixed upon the Abyssinian boy Ibrahim his black, bright, gay and terrible gaze. That gaze was the command for Pushkin *to be* (5/62).

Tsvetaeva's narrative movement backward to Pushkin's original - immaculate - conception takes the reader first to the heterosexual cover-story of his grandparents' marriage, and then, further back, to the proto-engendering imperial Word of command issued through the great (and bisexual) tsar's gaze on an Abyssinian boy. Pushkin, the Original Russian Poet, is the forbidden fruit of mixed-race, mixed-class, but same-sex desire in its purest variant: Platonic man-boy love. Pushkin is the original pure-bred hybrid and as such, the agent of the female Russian poet's writing.

Through the Onegin-Tatiana model, Pushkin also taught the precocious child-Tsvetaeva what heterosexual love was: '*This* is love: when there's a bench, on the bench a she, then he comes and talks the whole time while she does not say a word' (5/70). For a woman, love for a man means losing one's tongue, losing language. No wonder that the Onegin-Tatiana love aroused in Tsvetaeva a lifelong 'passion for unhappy, unreciprocated, impossible love' that made her lose any desire 'to be happy' and 'condemned' her 'to - *nonlove*' (5/71). In Russian fin de siècle letters, both 'impossible love' (cf. the lyrics of Poliksena Soloveva) and 'nonlove' (cf. the lyrics of Zinaida Gippius) can be argued to be euphemisms for 'lesbian love'.

Pushkin, however, was also the origin of Tsvetaeva's idea of non-sexual 'tender love', which he conveyed to her, homoerotically enough, in the word подруга (female friend): 'The word *podruga* - most loving of all words - sounded to me for the first time, addressed to an old woman. 'Подруга дней моих суровых - голубка дряхлая моя! (Friend of my severe days - my frail little dove!') ... I would say the word "подруга", I would say: "голубка (little dove)" - and I would feel a sharp pang' (5/80).

Tsvetaeva carried from her nursery into maturity a Pushkin who answered most of her own creative and personal needs for a true, undying, transgressive Russian poet. The only two important aspects of Pushkin that were not part of her childhood Pushkin were his relationships with Nicholas I, his tsar, and Natalia Goncharova, his wife.

According to Tsvetaeva, 'Pushkin feared Nicholas, deified Peter, and loved - Pugachev' (5/367). In an unpublished fragment of her essay, 'Pushkin and Pugachev', she noted, perhaps trying to justify her divine poet's fear of a merely mortal emperor: 'One has to admit that Pushkin was exceptionally unlucky with Nicholas since Nicholas was not only not artistic, he was anti-artistic, and it is even somehow shameful for us to see them - together' (7/714). The published essay 'Pushkin and Pugachev', in the first part of which Tsvetaeva reads *The Captain's Daughter* homo-erotically, emphasizing Grinev's (alias Pushkin's) platonic love for Pugachev, explains Nicholas I's feeling for Pushkin by contrasting it to Peter I's feeling for Pushkin's grandfather: 'Pugachev does not need Grinev for anything: he needs him for his soul ... The way a Russian tsar loved the Negro Ibrahim. The way Nicholas I did *not* fall in love with Pushkin' (5/503).

As for the colourless beauty, Natalia Goncharova, Tsvetaeva deals with Pushkin's feelings for her in her 1929 prose work, *Natalia Goncharova*. She begins her investigation into what I would call 'the secret of the white wife' by affirming the existence of three Pushkins and asking which of the three Goncharova married:

> There are three Pushkins: Pushkin - through the eyes of those who love him (friends, women, poetry lovers, students), Pushkin - through the eyes of the curious (all those who caught the latest gossip about him more avidly than they caught his last line of verse), Pushkin through the eyes of those who judge him (the tsar, police, Bulgarin, x's, y's, posthumous assessments), and, finally, Pushkin - through the eyes of the future - *us* (4/80-1).

Tsvetaeva contends that Goncharova married 'neither the first [Pushkin], nor the last for they are the same. Perhaps, [she married] the second - the Pushkin of gossip - and - however cruel it may be to say - most truly, Pushkin as seen by the judges, the Court' (4/81).

Tsvetaeva sees Goncharova-Pushkin as the starkest of contrasts - white-out (пробел) and Pushkin. The fact that Goncharova was 'simply a beauty', and Pushkin was 'simply a genius' explains Pushkin's otherwise unfathomable attraction to his wife: 'The pull of the genius - of overfullness - to empty space ... He wanted nullity for he was all things' (4/85). 'There are pairs - similar [to

Pushkin-Goncharova]', Tsvetaeva concludes, 'but they are pairs who are separated, almost torn apart. Siegfried, not having known Brunhilde, Penthesilea, not having known Achilles. And there are fateful pairs who exude a feeling of being condemned from within, without hope in this world or that. Pushkin-Goncharova' (4/85).

Because of his fateful match with Goncharova, Pushkin acquires mythic-hero status, being for Russian culture what Siegfried is for German culture and Achilles for ancient Greek. Interestingly, Goncharova is not, as might be inferred by these analogies, catapulted into the queer company of semi-divine warrior-maidens like Brunhilde and Penthesilea - if any woman is to be Pushkin's Amazon it would have to be Tsvetaeva herself. Rather, Goncharova receives one of Tsvetaeva's most disdainful mythical identities; she is merely 'a guiltless, wordless woman - Helen - a doll, an instrument of fate' (4/85).

Although Tsvetaeva clearly conveys that *her* Pushkin, unlike Goncharova's, is Pushkin 'through the eyes of those who love', all three Pushkins are perceptions which she embraces and makes manifest in her works. For she is writer, gossiper and reader of Pushkin: those who see Pushkin through loving eyes see Pushkin writing, those who see Pushkin through curious eyes see Pushkin being different, and those who see Pushkin through judging eyes are trying to read him, the immortal, mortally. It is namely Pushkin's three-in-one nature that makes creative intimacy with him possible for a Russian female genius-poet, and Tsvetaeva ultimately finds a fluid identification with Pushkin in his eternal processes of writing, being Other, and being (mis)read.

Tsvetaeva was a lonely person who both cultivated and complained about her aloneness. 'My favourite form of intercourse', she wrote in a 1922 letter, 'is otherworldly: dream: having a dream. And my second favourite is letters' (6/225). Given her love for Pushkin, it is not surprising that she used all her favourite forms of intercourse - poems, letters, dreams - to communicate about and with him, and that the 'otherworldly' relations she enjoyed with Pushkin proved far more satisfying than her real-life meeting with his blood relative, his granddaughter. This meeting occurred (on 10 July 1931) in the midst of her writing *Poems to Pushkin*, the first of which, 'Scourge of gendarmes, god of students' ('Бич жандармов, бог студентов'), was completed on 25 June 1931. Around that time Tsvetaeva wrote in her notebook the draft of a letter to Pasternak in which she meditates on Pushkin's blood, immortality and creative legacy to Russian poets. On July 19, nine days after meeting Pushkin's granddaughter-by-blood, Tsvetaeva completed *Poems to Pushkin*. Then, she had a dream about Pushkin, the contents of which would lead her in rereading it seven years later, to a secret aspect of her identification with him. Thus, over a period of about two months in the summer of 1931, Tsvetaeva communicated with Pushkin intensely via lyric, letter, life and dream. In the remainder of this chapter I shall examine each of these closely interrelated, but distinct Tsvetaevan encounters with Pushkin.

Tsvetaeva characterized her *Poems to Pushkin* as 'dangerous', 'revolutionary', 'having nothing in common with the canonical Pushkin, but having everything to do with the opposite of the canonical' (6/449). The classically Tsvetaevan opposition - canonical 'they' vs. noncanonical 'I' - is felt particularly keenly in the first poem of the cycle, 'Scourge of gendarmes ...', in which the 'happy, confident' voice of Tsvetaeva writing poetry takes the offensive against 'them' - White émigré Pushkinists. They, in the opinion of the poet-I, are trying evilly to construct a Pushkin who essentially was *not*. The poet expresses caustic incredulity at the critical establishment's false notions of Pushkin in a series of mocking rhetorical questions, on the singsong rhythm of which she structures the poem.

Each stanza of 'Scourge of gendarmes ...' - composed of two parts, a quatrain and a couplet - follows a set pattern: first, the poet affirms one of her (the real) Pushkin essences; then, she uses her affirmation of her real Pushkin to question the canonical (their) construction of Pushkin. Undermined by essentials, the canonical Pushkin totters in shaky role-plays, its performance scripted contrary to Pushkin *fact*. The first stanza establishes the metrical, syntactic and rhetorical polemic the poet engages in throughout the poem:

Бич жандармов, бог студентов,
Желчь мужей, услада жен,
Пушкин - в роли монумента?
Гостя каменного? - он,

Скалозубый, нагловзорый
Пушкин - в роли Командора?

Scourge of gendarmes, god of students,
Gall of husbands, joy of wives,
Pushkin - in the role of statue?
Guest of stone? - he, then, arrives,

Teeth shown naked, brazen-facèd,
Pushkin - playing Outraged Pater?

The poet goes on to offer a number of antinomies made up of her real Pushkin, on the one hand, and the critical establishment's role-playing Pushkin, on the other. For example, the poet's 'salty Pushkin' versus their 'Pushkin in the role of lexicon'; the poet's 'African intransigent' versus their 'Pushkin in the role of schoolmaster'; the poet's 'Russian classic who called the sky of Africa his own, and the Neva's - vile' versus their 'Pushkin in the role of rabid Russophile', and so forth.

The Pushkin whom Tsvetaeva cherishes and defends is the passionate African outsider who embodies 'Pushkinian rebellion'. Her Black Rebel Pushkin, however, could as easily represent Tsvetaeva's own rebellious genius, as constitute the essential Pushkin who may well be beyond recovery beneath the superstructure of cults built over him. Yet, Tsvetaeva does not treat Pushkin as a biographical subject of a putative real life: rather, she uses him as her Pushkinian weapon in her larger, lifelong struggle against middle-class morality, materialism and moderation: 'The ignominy ... of being gold and the mean'. In the end, however, Tsvetaeva's Pushkin, like the Pushkin of so many of his latter-day Russian idolaters, is liberated from one set of stereotypes only to be projected into another. Her Pushkin seems, also, to be playing a role - of the grinning, lusty Negro, frightening in his fury; the Negro of Marina the Great is not so much a Black Pushkin as a Pushkin in blackface, rampaging in 'white infuriate rage', grimacing so widely that his throat is revealed.

Nevertheless, Pushkin's ethnic otherness attracted Tsvetaeva more than any other *fact* about him. She insists everywhere on his African blood, and, on the basis of his ethnicity alone, she develops her sincerely anti-racist idea of the proudly different 'race' of Russian poets that Pushkin originated. She approaches Russian poethood as if it were a genetic trait, but a genetic trait that a poet, if he has genius, can and should nurture in himself. Thus she writes to Pasternak:

> ... Your mug ... looks like something from a colonial exhibit. You were thinking of yourself - an Ethiopian? A Negro? About your connection - via blood - with Pushkin-Gannibal-Peter ... If you, and I really advise you to, Boris, only sensed the negro blood in yourself (NB! in 1916 some professor wrote a two-volume study, arguing that Pushkin was a Jew, i.e. a Semite) ... (8/442).

This letter, which Tsvetaeva was not sure whether she sent or not, compels attention on several counts. First, Tsvetaeva's parenthetical note about a professor who argued that Pushkin was a Jew represents, most probably, her confused recollection of a well-known essay - hardly two volumes long! - published in 1899 (perhaps Tsvetaeva read it in 1916) by the anthropologist, D. N. Anuchin.

In 'A. S. Pushkin (An Anthropological Sketch)', Anuchin concludes that:

> a certain semitic strain was characteristic of Pushkin's physical type, as indicated by his death mask and many portraits, which is to be expected since the African blood that flowed in his veins was Abyssinian, and Abyssinians are part semitic ... Both during Pushkin's

life and more recently, persons who have been considered the most similar in appearance to Pushkin in terms of hair and facial type, have usually turned out to be Jews.[2]

However repulsively ludicrous Anuchin's 'scientific' conclusions may be - based as they are on death masks, portraits, and received opinion - and however supportive they are of the 'racial theory' which Tsvetaeva claims to disavow and argues that the *fact* of Pushkin repudiates, she appears to have been not only intrigued, but creatively inspired by Anuchin's conclusion that Pushkin's African blood contained a semitic admixture. 'TRANSPOSE IT', Tsvetaeva commands in her *nota bene*, 'that is, write a two-volume study, or a single couplet of your own, arguing that Pasternak is a Negro' (8/442).

Tsvetaeva's works show her tendency to conflate Negroes and Jews, who, in her eyes, share with poets the status of outsiders and objects of persecution. In *My Pushkin* she argues that all poets are Negroes. In section twelve of *Poem of the End* (1924) the poet exclaims: 'In this most Christian of worlds Poets are yids! (жиды)'. In her epistolary appeal to Pasternak to 'sense the Negro blood in himself', Tsvetaeva may have been moved by the fantasy hope that the one Russian poet she considered her poetic brother, could realize his Pushkin essence more easily than she could hers not only because of his gender, but because of his 'secret' Jewish blood. Conversely, one has to suppose that she fantasized a sibling relationship with Pasternak in part because of his Jewish roots, which brought him, and her as his sister, closer by blood to Pushkin. If there is anything for a poet in Tsvetaeva's eyes to take more pride in than an African ancestry, it would have to be an African-Semitic one. For 'those who love him' as Tsvetaeva does, Pushkin is not only a 'god of students', but a god of outcasts, Negro of Negroes and very Jew of very Jew.

Since Pushkin's blackness plays such a crucial part in Tsvetaeva's essentializing him, one can understand her disillusionment at the reality of Pushkin's blood, which she encountered in his granddaughter: '(A tow-haired, white-browed, white-eyed German woman, a nobody, fish-like, with a mouth full of cold suet stuck to her palate, speaks with a greasy burr,) ... I recite *Poems to Pushkin*, bursting with excitement - that I'm reciting for his *granddaughter*. Bursting - all alone, since she doesn't understand *anything* and shows no response - at all)' (8/447). Elena Pushkina contradicted Tsvetaeva's real Pushkin on every count, prompting her to ask '*who* was "Sashka" married to, so that his offspring should have absolutely no feature of Pushkin's?' (8/448). Pushkin's granddaughter also poses a mystery, 'the secret of heredity: *What, then*, and *where, then*, is BLOOD'. (8/448)

Tsvetaeva resolves this mystery in a way that subverts her entire 'otherworldly' reality. Since Pushkin is Tsvetaeva's 'dream' and her poetic peer while his granddaughter, her chronological peer, 'is his living blood and life, his material proof', she is forced to admit 'a truth contrary to [her]self and *alien to*

[her] whole life, namely, life (the living) may be incomparably stronger than the most exceptionally strong, exceptionally alive dream' (8/449). This may well have been the 'last lesson' that Pushkin taught Tsvetaeva, a last lesson of greater magnitude than all the first ones she absorbed as a child and an essential reality corrective for so fantasy-driven a poet as she. Nine days after enduring the moral death of reading to Elena Pushkina's non-comprehending, unresponsive, anti-Pushkin ears 'Scourge of gendarmes ...', 'the most comprehensible' of her *Poems to Pushkin*, 'the poem from which the others take off,' Tsvetaeva completed her Pushkin cycle. Only then did she indulge in her favourite form of intercourse with Pushkin, having a dream about him:

> A hospital. Some kind of a nurse alerts me in French that there's nobody with him now, that I can go in. A corridor. Wards. Which one? The nurse points to the third open door on the left. I - to her: 'But how will I know him?' I can't see a thing. I go in. There's no window, light comes in from the door. It's grey. Visitors along the walls. I see Volodia Sosinskii (already!) doing a sketch. Directly opposite the entryway, in the middle of the room - a bedstead. On it Pushkin. To the left another bed, empty. Someone, seeing me: 'And this is Marina Tsvetaeva, our best poet'. I stand on my knees in the space between the beds, he offers - I take - his hand. 'Well, then, *Masetochka*, have you come to watch how people die? Farewell, Masetochka?' 'Farewell, fellow-countryman!' (Of poetry's country, of course, but here I recall that he is more a Petersburger than a Muscovite.) *Very* like, *he* is as he actually was. Small face and body. Enormous, rolling whites of the eye, the colour of his eyes is blue-*green*, from fever. *His* brow, hair, side-whiskers. *His* mouth. From which portrait - I don't know, *not* a photo of a portrait, a composite - of them all. The voice - I can't say otherwise than - elegant, playing, light, with an *almost*-ironic intonation - even on his death bed - of play. (8/451)

Tsvetaeva contextualizes the dream about Pushkin with a pre-dream dream of a conversation with Pushkin's 'murderer', Nicholas I. According to her notion of three Pushkins, this conversation represents an exchange between a lover of Pushkin (Tsvetaeva) and *the* judge of Pushkin (the tsar). In Tsvetaeva's subconscious, Nicholas's motivation for killing Pushkin is implied in the one thing Tsvetaeva later recalled the tsar saying to her in the dream: '"One cannot be simultaneously the first poet of Russia and the husband of the country's most beautiful woman"', as if such double good fortune would strain any reader's credulity (as well as incur the envy of the gods). As the dreamer, Tsvetaeva can be all the people in her dream, including Nicholas, her own and Pushkin's adversarial judge. Therefore, the tsar-judge and critical reader within Tsvetaeva expresses the logical impossibility - in realism and humdrum reality - of possessing too much good fortune, genius and beauty. The same principle operates in this dream as controls the poetic world of Tsvetaeva's *Mountain Poem*, to take one example: 'The gods take vengeance on their likenesses' (3/28). By having both genius and beauty, Pushkin evoked the envy of the gods who wrought their revenge through Nicholas I, the anti-artistic tsar-father. In her above-cited draft letter to Pasternak, Tsvetaeva explains the higher justice and purpose of Pushkin's death: 'After all, Pushkin was killed because, by reason of his death, he would never die, he would live eternally, he would go walking with me around Meudon in 1931 (Pushkin was killed because he was invented to be immortal)' (8/442-3).

Tsvetaeva's dream about Pushkin is a dream of parting that is appropriate to the poet's just having completed her *Poems to Pushkin*. The dream also constitutes a 'counter-encounter' to her meeting with Pushkin's granddaughter: first, in the dream 'someone' introduces Tsvetaeva to the dying Pushkin as 'Marina Tsvetaeva, our best poet', which echoes E. N. Arnold's introduction of her to Elena Pushkina as 'the greatest and most famous woman poet'; second, in reality Elena Pushkina - and it is indeed a Pushkin-like playful irony that his anti-Pushkin granddaughter has the name Helen - Pushkina was the living blood relation who killed Tsvetaeva's dream, while in the dream, Pushkin is dying in order to attain immortality and be with Tsvetaeva in Meudon where she almost lost him. The dream contents raise several interrelated issues that obsessed and mystified Tsvetaeva: 1) Pushkin's dying and fleshly death; 2) Pushkin's direct communication (in the dream, a farewell) with her, 'our best poet'; 3) Identifying Pushkin as he really was and is; 4) Pushkin-Genius' attraction to Goncharova-Emptiness.

By seeing Pushkin dying in her dream, Tsvetaeva returns to her earliest childhood and 'the first thing learned about Pushkin ... that he was killed' (5/57). The nursery atmosphere is also conveyed through the childish diminutive that Pushkin calls the adult Tsvetaeva - 'Masetochka'. Although in the dream Pushkin is dying, his eternal life in representation is already underway as the dreamer sees 'Volodia Sosinskii ... doing a sketch'. At first, the dreamer wonders how she will know Pushkin, but after she meets him, she realizes that it is '*he* ... as he actually was ... *His* brow, hair, sidewhiskers. *His* mouth. From which portrait - I don't know, *not* a photo of a portrait, a composite - of them all' (8/451).

As already noted, Tsvetaeva adamantly rejected any desire for a romantic or amorous connection with Pushkin. Her dream relationship with him bears out her lack of erotic interest. He lies, dying, on a bed - a bed in a dream foretells a journey - in the middle of a hospital room; the other bed to the left of his is empty. 'Masetochka' stands on her knees, a pose traditionally signifying piety or humility, between the two beds. Physical contact between Pushkin and Tsvetaeva is limited to his offering, and her taking, his hand. This may be a symbolic acting out of Pushkin giving the last line 'from his hand' to Tsvetaeva.

She commented to Pasternak that Pushkin's last bit of writing *was* addressed to her - '"That is the way history should be written'" (8/443).

The intercourse Tsvetaeva has with Pushkin in her dream is marked by a quality of non-erotic bedroom intimacy. The dream realizes Tsvetaeva's longstanding wish to be intimate with Pushkin, loving him without being his female lover. Simultaneously, the configuration of two beds, one full with Pushkin and the other empty, strikes one as a symbolic representation of Pushkin-Goncharova, fullness married to nullity. Since seeing a death in a dream traditionally can be read as a predictor of a marriage-to-be, Tsvetaeva's dream suggests a future marriage of true minds between two Russian genius-poets and the two, often competitive, Russian capitals they represent, a harmonizing union between 'our [- the future's -] best poet' from Moscow and our - Russia's - immortal poet from St Petersburg. This marriage without impediment will replace in perpetuity the fatal earthly and sexual marriage of genius and beauty.

Tsvetaeva's first thought about her dream refers to the women Pushkin loved: 'I would not have wanted to be Kern, or Riznich, or even Mariia Raevskaia' (8/452). As if to confirm the *non-love* bedroom connection that she, as a woman, wants with Pushkin, Tsvetaeva rejects any identification with women he loved passionately or romantically - before his marriage - and chooses his 'дряхлая подруга (*frail friend*'), Arina Rodionovna instead, 'for he never wrote to anyone, to anyone, with such wrenching tenderness' (8/452) as he did to her. In reasoning thus, Tsvetaeva attributes to Pushkin her own devaluation of sexual love (and the lovers who evoked it) and, possibly, her own masculinist - and Pushkin's masculine - misogyny (contempt for the women s/he loved). She marries her pure self to Pushkin's immortal self, becoming one with him in gender as she has already merged with him in genius.

But who was Tsvetaeva's Doña Anna and who - her Goncharova? Her twofold identification with Pushkin prepares the way for her own final 'important' insight into Pushkin and her dream about him. This insight enables her to uncover a deep-lying memory, a secret *fact* of her own biography that answers her question about Pushkin - and ours:

> Yes, something important: When, in answer to my own question: how could Pushkin love Goncharova - *the doll*, I recall how I, at 14 years of age in Von Dervise's *pension*, loved Margarita Watson (the only beauty I have ever met in my whole life - (I confirm this in 1938)), how not merely hopelessly, but without even conceiving of hope for what? reciprocity? as if there is such a thing as that in the face of longing the way I did) - how clearsightedly, fatefully, I loved Margarita Watson - - I cease to understand my own question (8/452-3).

Margarita Watson - Tsvetaeva's answer to Doña Anna and Goncharova, 'Pushkin's fateful wife'. 'Proud, closed, intelligent, cold-hearted Margarita

Watson', recalls Sofia Liperovskaia, a schoolmate of Tsvetaeva's.[3] Margarita Watson was one of two heroines of a novella Tsvetaeva began at Von Dervise's Pension, but did not finish, or return to. In acknowledging more than 20 years later her secret fateful love for Margarita Watson, a secret of being different, of hopeless longing for her native sky, not of Africa, but of Lesbos, Tsvetaeva allows her self complete, threefold identification with her poetic godhead, Pushkin, and realizes a solution, from life, to the last remaining mystery of the Original Russian Poet.

NOTES

1. All quotations are from Marina Tsvetaeva, *Sobranie sochinenii v 8-i tomakh*, Ellis Lak, Moscow, 1995. The first number in parenthesis indicates the volume, the second the page. All translations are by the author of this chapter.
2. D.N. Anuchin, 'A.S. Pushkin (Antropologicheskii eskiz)', in *Russkie Vedomosti*, 1899, p. 44.
3. Sof'ia Liperovskaia, 'Iunye gody' in *Vospominaniia o Marine Tsvetaevoi*, Sovetskii pisatel', Moscow, 1992, pp. 31-40 (p. 34).

Love and Death in Pushkin's *The Stone Guest* and Nabokov's *Death*

by

CHRISTOPH VELDHUES

In this chapter two dramatic texts will be compared: Pushkin's *The Stone Guest* (*Каменный гость*, 1830)[1] and Nabokov's *Death* (*Смерть*, 1923).[2] Their juxtaposition certainly has a personal background in Nabokov's distinct admiration for Pushkin.[3] Yet my issue here is neither the problem of authorial influence in general nor the two plays' genetic relationship in particular. The following, then, does not aim at a contribution to literary history, but presents an essay in intertextual interpretation: to understand the meaning of one text, or rather give it a possible reading, via its identification/differentiation with another text (that is, by extension of Lotman's *so-protivopostavlenie* principle of literary criticism from the intra- to the intertextual level).[4]

What makes the two texts comparable from this point of view is the correspondence of their semantic structures; or, to be more concrete, the amazing way they both succeed in 'making strange' a quite traditional love conflict by connecting it with a prominent death motif. Moreover, both dramas have the permanent presence of death within life itself as their constructive principle. Pushkin as well as Nabokov exposes the vagueness of the allegedly firm borderline between these two realms (life and death) and thereby calls into question the security based on the idea of a clear-cut here/beyond difference, which in either cases is replaced by an uncertain, ambiguous this-world/otherworld interference.

It is especially in Nabokov criticism that a good deal of attention has been paid to this writer's very peculiar literary construction of such a this-world/otherworld interference known under the term of *potustoronnost* (which might be translated as 'crossing-to-the-other-side').[5] Therefore I would like to start my essay with an outline of this concept which will help the reader understand the use Nabokov makes of it in his play, and at the same time will serve as a frame of reference for the intertextual juxtaposition to come. It will then be shown how this *potustoronnost* concept is connected with the love and death complex in *Death* (which, moreover, gives me the opportunity to summarize the play for those who happen not to know it).[6] In the main section of the chapter I shall transfer this reading of *Death* on to Pushkin's *Stone Guest* in order to demonstrate, on the one hand, the two texts' structural correspondence, and, on the other hand, the functional difference in the use they make of the love and death complex, which - whether by authorial intention or not - lets Nabokov's drama appear the very semantic inversion of its Pushkinian intertext.

Nabokov, with a striking recurrence, tells variants of one and the same story, in which he lets the hero cross into a fantastic parallel reality and look upon the world he left from that other side, to wit, from the *potustoronnost* position. This narrative scheme is based on a particular cosmological construction (bearing some traits of platonic dualism): namely, the assumed coexistence of two independent worlds, the known 'here' and an unknown 'there'. They are, however, supposed not as a temporal sequence - of, for instance, two principally excluding each other *aeons* as in the apocalyptic cosmology -, but as a synchrony of two contiguous spaces (that is, a conception of transcendence opposed to this world's immanence as an 'otherworld' and not as a 'hereafter'). For Nabokov's protagonist who is always desperately looking for what is essential, namely, for sense, this situation calls into question which of the two worlds he should take for the 'real' one, the one he can rely on, the one that matters: the world he lives in or that other one - the *Terra incognita* - that he alone can imagine and longs for because of his extraordinary, literally æsthetic sensibility. An answer to this crucial question is to be expected only by crossing the border between the two worlds, and that means death. Death alone can reveal the 'real reality' of existence, its very mystery, the understanding of which, however, from a logical point of view will always come too late for this hero, as the crossing of the ultimate border - to die - already implies that he has taken the irrevocable decision for one of the two worlds, namely the beyond (there is simply no way back from death into life ...).

As a literary construction, however, *potustoronnost* suspends this binary logic, defers the otherwise clear decision for this life or the beyond by extending the point of the two worlds' contact death - to an ambiguous 'twilight zone', which enables the hero not only to experience his own physical death, but also to live it as a sort of metaphysical continuation in the here and there simultaneously. This paradoxical double existence of a posthumous and therefore essentially unconcerned participant in worldly matters procures him the desired access to the mystery, discharges the promise of an absolute understanding by furnishing him with the most extreme form of human self-experience: to face oneself as 'self' and 'other' simultaneously. It is this (to a certain extend schizophrenic) dissociation, or doubling, of the character's experience that the *potustoronnost* mystery at least formally seems to consist in.[7] Its substance, however, - what *is* the 'other' of one's 'self' - is always being revealed to the protagonist alone and remains inaccessible to the reader, because, as an utmost, that is, 'gnostic'[8] knowledge (the *Ultima Thule*), it can in no way be put into words.[9]

(The paradoxical here-and-there existence, the self-and-other experience of the literary hero in the *potustoronnost* situation lets this construction, now on the metaliterary level, become an allegory of the fictional ontology in general: of literature's singular privilege to create - and, in a way, to 'live' - an autonomous parallel reality, namely the textual world of fictional characters and events that, although obviously connected with the extratextual world, yet does not submit to its conditions. This exclusive licence brings both the authors and readers of literature close to what Nabokov suspects to be the very mystery of life. However, this poetological implication of *potustoronnost*, clearly a focus of Nabokov criticism, remains marginal in *Death* and therefore does not need further examination in this chapter.)

The protagonist will reach this state of being and achieve the mystery only if he dies. This *sine qua non* condition makes death the central event of any *potustoronnost* plot and, technically, its starting point (that is, the semantic border that, according to Lotman's narratology, must be crossed in order to make the story run). The form of death Nabokov's hero mostly chooses is suicide. Such (proto-) typical *potustoronnost* texts as, for example, the short novel *The Eye* (*Соглядатай*, 1930) as well as *Death*, however, leave open whether he actually dies or, after an unsuccessful would-be suicide, in fact remains alive, merely believing himself to be dead and thus taking his continuing life to be a posthumous experience.

This textual ambiguity leaves the decision to the reader, who either votes for a realistic interpretation (death as a non-factual pseudoevent: *potustoronnost* as a schizophrenic delusion of a living person) or a fantastic interpretation (death as a factual event: *potustoronnost* as the metaphysical experience of an 'un-dead' person).

In Nabokov's rather idiosyncratic literary construction the hero's continuing consciousness after death is, however, limited to a temporary transition phase only, with the specific *potustoronnost* situation being explained as a mental process driven by its own inertia for some time, but gradually slowing down to an inevitable finish (which lets it somehow resemble Dostoevskii's short story *Bobok*, 1873). The duration of this strange period of indecision is related to the intensity of the hero's worldly life, it depends on the *mémoire*, on the ability of this life to be recollected in the beyond. But whilst, for example, in *The Eye* this period is measured according to how deeply someone is mourned by others - he 'lives on' as long as he is kept in their minds - in *Death* it is the protagonist's own memories of his life before death that, as a sort of mental echo, at least temporarily keep running through his mind after death. Thus, the *potustoronnost* passage - and with it the power of absolute understanding - will come to an end anyway: either (in the case of a realistic reading) when the hero 'awakes' to a life which he had already believed to have left behind; or (if one chooses a fantastic reading) at the moment in which his consciousness finally extinguishes and lets him fall into the abyss of an ultimate non-existence.

What does Nabokov make of this *potustoronnost* construction in *Death*? The place is Cambridge, the year given as 1806.[10] The first act starts with a monologue of master Gonville contemplating an experiment he seems to be conducting at the moment the goal of which is 'to take possession of another person's mind' (*Sm* I, 1 ff.). Into the scholar's study runs his student Edmond, who has just got the news of Stella's death, that is of Gonville's young wife and Edmond's secret and unannounced love. The ensuing conversation exhibits the sober, even cold-hearted Gonville's ability to face her death in a very self-controlled way, while it greatly upsets young Edmond. Soon Gonville's only intention becomes clear: to interrogate the student, whom he suspects of being his wife's lover, about their assumed affair (*Sm* I, 119 ff., 154, 174 ff.). So it turns out to be precisely Edmond's mind the jealous husband wants to intrude into by means of some as yet unknown experiment.

Edmond, however, knows but one subject: his own despair, defined as a romantic soul's total loss of orientation within the 'brain-like, twisted labyrinth' of modernity (*Sm* I, 54 ff.). He suffers from what he considers the modern lack of sense, resulting from an enlightenment that abolished its transcendent guarantee - God - only to replace Him by a mere immanent substitute - Reason -, as personified by scholars like Gonville: 'Science / told me: "This is the world" / ... /And life, from this simplicity, / became even more difficult to understand' (*Sm* I, 76f., 81 ff.).

A world reduced to the rational principle can offer Edmond nothing but one-sided, namely 'this-sided' explanations which, because of this limitation, are unacceptable to him. What they fail to procure for him is an unlimited, mysterious 'understanding-all' that alone will make sense for him, as it covers both the here and there:

> All secret knowledge of the world, / both ancient and new, about its destination, / about its very sense - all, all has vanished / in the face of your incontestable argument: / there is no destination, no sense is left; and yet / I secretly know that they do exist! (*Sm* I, 83 ff.)

Edmond does not find any support in this world (*Sm* I, 61 ff.); again and again he confesses his 'fear of life' (*Sm* I, 58, 106 ff., 171) and, consequently, his longing for death: 'Gonville, / I decided to die'. (*Sm* I, 110 ff.) Into the 'unknown realm' of death (*Sm* I, 172) he is determined to escape; he believes the crossing of this ultimate border the one and 'last effort' that divides him from absolute understanding ('вот еще усилье – / и все пойму я ...'; *Sm* I, 99 ff.). It is exactly this desire that lets Edmond ask his teacher for poison (*Sm* I, 113); which, in turn, means that his beloved Stella's death is only the inducement and definitely not the reason for his committing suicide (as is stated by Boyd, op. cit., p. 204, according to whom Edmond kills himself 'since existence without her has lost its meaning'). Gonville agrees to give him the poison only on the condition that it will be taken at once, with him as an eye-witness (*Sm* I, 144 ff.): this 'perfect scholar' (*Sm* I, 48 ff.) presenting himself to Edmond as an unconcerned observer of a scientific experiment, and yet with more than a little voyeuristic interest in his student's death.

When the curtain rises for the second act, Edmond has taken the poison (if it was poison at all) and now finds, or believes, himself awaking in the beyond. At first glance he is irritated by the unchanged sensation of his surroundings. But soon he learns, from Gonville's words, that this state is only an unstable 'sham world' ('мнимый мир': *Sm* II, 60) made of his own memories and imagination still working for a time. To explain this neither-life-nor-death situation to Edmond, Gonville repeats an image he introduced already in the first act, and calls human life the ride of an 'insane horseman' who, all of a sudden, is confronted with the 'unexpected and unthinkable abyss' of death (*Sm* II, 36 ff.; cf. I, 26 ff.) The conscious state of *potustoronnost*, then, corresponds precisely with the very moment of the rider's leap into this precipice:

> He, from the edge, / leaps into the void. / ... / He's in the empty space now, / above the precipice, - but yet there is no falling / no abyss! / ... / This is the moment, you understand, / *the very moment*. It marks the border / of the confined earthly life. (*Sm* II, 38 ff., 47 ff.: Nabokov's emphasis).

Although objectively it takes only a single moment's time, this leap - the passage from life to death -, from the subject's perspective will last in accordance with the life one has lived: 'the richer the life, / the stronger the horse' (*Sm* II, 52 ff.). There can, however, be no doubt about the end: 'Your falling is inevitable' (*Sm* II, 57).

Gonville is eager to bring back their conversation to the only subject he is really interested in (and in which a realistic interpretation will perceive the very motive for this experiment, namely, the staging of Edmond's 'passage into the beyond'). Insistently he enquires about Edmond's relationship with Stella (*Sm* II, 113, 221 ff.) to learn at last that in fact it did not exceed the student's one-sided admiration for his teacher's wife; and that they came into a sort of contact only the night before, when both, for a few seconds and in total silence, happened to stand side by side at the open window looking into the starry night, and Stella suddenly gave him a momentary glance - 'one single glance' ('один лишь взгляд'; *Sm* II, 251, 253) which romantic Edmond took as a sign of mystic union between them ('we did unite just for one moment' ['сошлись на миг']; *Sm* II, 242), as a getting in touch with 'eternity at its purest' ('вечность обнаженная'; *Sm* II, 236), only to flee from Gonville's house immediately afterwards.

Unconcerned with these somewhat obscure considerations, Gonville has found out what he wants to know and decides to cease his experiment. He announces the poison a harmless drink and, consequently, Edmond's suicide to be a fake only (*Sm* II, 261 ff.). But Edmond refuses to accept that he is alive; he insists on having in fact died: 'It's me alone / who is inventing this / ... / Enough, don't try: / You cannot prove to me / that I'm not dead' (*Sm* II, 272 ff., 316 ff.). He prefers the dubious reality of the inner world which his own mind creates - imaginative, but independent as it is (that is, the traits it shares with fictional literature) - to the limitations of an undoubted outer world's reality to which he is not willing to return.

Gonville, however, is going to abolish just this comfortable ambiguity of Edmond's *potustoronnost* position between life and death at the end of the drama. He calls for Stella, thus forcing the decision Edmond is eager to evade: for either (within the framework of a fantastic reading) the appearance of the really dead Stella will bring upon the 'un-dead' Edmond definite extinction, the death that she herself quite obviously personifies for him; or (in accordance with a realistic reading) the appearance of the living Stella will prove to the only supposedly dead Edmond the continuation of his own unbearable life. Thus, he must fear both of these options, and therefore tries to prevent Gonville from calling Stella in (*Sm* II, 327 ff.). It is precisely from her intrusion that he expects his complete destruction, the final 'fall into the abyss': 'This is the end ... I am falling / Stella!' ('ведь это есть конец ... паденье .../ Стелла!'; *Sm* II, 335). This is the play's last line. Curtain. We do not see whether Stella actually appears on stage, a lack of information which keeps open both the solution (is Edmond dead or not?) and Stella's own state (is she dead or not?).

What makes this last line especially interesting is the fact that it echoes the last line of another play at the end of which somebody falls into or, strictly speaking, is absorbed into the 'abyss of death', thereby pronouncing his last words: 'I am perishing - it is finished - o Doña Anna!' ('Я гибну - кончено - о Дона Анна!': *KG* IV, 139). This is, of course, from Pushkin's *Stone Guest*. Both textual endings, both Don Juan's and Edmond's desperate cries are remarkably similar semantically as well as syntactically; not to speak of their metrical conformity, as both dramas are written in unrhymed iambic pentameter (that is, blank verse). This precise correspondence indicates, as I see it, a much more extensive correlation between Pushkin's 'little tragedy' and Nabokov's two-act play. And yet the distinct use they make of the intertextually recurrent structural elements leads to a totally different impact of their respective textual 'messages', first of all due to an exactly inverted semantic conception of the two protagonists and their attitudes towards this world and the 'otherworld'.

Both stories expose, to begin with, similar triangular constellations on the character level: the rational, very detached, apparently not too exciting husband (the commander Don Alvaro whom Pushkin, against the Don Juan tradition, so significantly changes from Doña Anna's father into her husband, and Gonville who is said to be cold 'as if made of marble' - what the 'Stone Guest', of course, really is);[11] his beautiful, young wife (Doña Anna and Stella);[12] and finally her romantic lover (Don Juan and Edmond), strictly speaking a would-be lover, as adultery is committed in neither of the two cases.

Their semantic relations are 'forbidden love' with respect to the lover/wife axis, and 'jealousy' on the husband/lover axis, resulting in a deadly 'hatred' at least on the part of the two husbands. Both playwrights, however, deviate from this otherwise quite conventional character constellation and the somewhat trivial erotic conflict it contains by presenting one of the spouses - the husband (Don Alvaro) or the wife (Stella) respectively - as already deceased before the dramatic events start, and thus manage to introduce a 'taste of death' from the very beginning.

A closer look at the plot, however, will show the distinctly opposite semantic directions into which the two heroes (Don Juan and Edmond) develop from the first event (that is, the crossing of the story's central life/death borderline) to the last one, in which - together with the erotic conflict - the hero's problematic life/death position is resolved.

The first event in *The Stone Guest*, as well as the play's textual beginning, is Don Juan's venturing into night-time Madrid, by which he moves across not only a spatial, but at the same time two semantic boundaries. First, he returns to the capital defying the King's injunction (he was banned for killing Don Alvaro). Second, he returns to life after having, as he asserts, 'almost died' during his banishment - namely, 'died of boredom' ('я едва, едва / Не умер там со скуки'; *KG* I, 25 ff.), as all the 'beautiful women there' (he explicitly calls them 'тамошние красавицы'; *KG* I, 31), that is in that 'otherworld' of his northern banishment, soon appeared to him like 'lifeless waxworks' ('В них жизни нет, все куклы восковые'; *KG* I, 37). Moreover, in these verses Don Juan elaborates the same topological metaphor for the life/death opposition as Doña Laura will later on when she, in an argument with Don Carlos, contrasts her own 'southern-vital' (serene, bright, etc.) orientation on life to this character's 'northern-morbid' (gloomy, foggy, etc.) orientation on death (*KG* II, 65 ff.). Whilst Don Juan's first movement, at least in this figurative sense, thus is from death to life,[13] the *potustoronnost* plot (though not the text) of *Death* has Edmond's suicide, that is his passage from life to death, as its first and central event - no matter that, for the sake of suspense, it is omitted in the drama itself, namely placed between the two acts and thus completely left to the spectators' imagination.

At the end of both stories the jealous husbands take unexpected revenge on their wives' lovers. The dead Don Alvaro pulls Don Juan down into death; the living Gonville draws, as I see it, Edmond back to life. The two protagonists' complete semantic movement, then, is from death to life to death in Don Juan's case, while Edmond goes from life to death to life. At this point, however, I entirely agree with Akhmatova's opinion that the bold Don Juan is not, as his last words seem to signify, horrified by this sudden and fatal intrusion from the beyond as such. What, instead, really destroys him, he who does love Doña Anna, is that death comes upon him at the very moment when he - according to his own words, for the first time - has found, what he had always been seeking, namely, the 'happiness of life' which her true love provides him with: 'Only since then [that is, when he fell in love with her] I know the value / of this moment's life, only since then / I understand the meaning of the word Happiness' (*KG* III, 87 ff).[14] Edmond, on the contrary, is 'cheated out of death' ('и смерть - обман'; *Sm* II, 305) by Gonville's intrusion *into* his post-mortem *potustoronnost* 'freedom' (*Sm* I, 159), for him a most satisfying state of being - 'Yes, I am at ease ... I feel so calm. Now, / at least one thing I know for sure: I know / that I am not.' (Sm II, 84 ff.) - which he, as weary of life as he is, was always longing for and which his romantic fancy depicts as a mysterious 'fairy tale [land]' (*Sm* I, 136) and, again and again, as an enchanting, 'colourful' otherness (*Sm* I, 117, 136 ff.; II, 2, 275).

Thus, death in *The Stone Guest* and life in *Death* are two forms of ultimate punishment. Both heroes are forced to give up what they desire most of all; and the tragic irony implied in these corresponding solutions is that they are to give it up just at the moment when they seem to have got hold of it at last. The really striking intertextual inversion lies in the fact that in these dramas the semantic opposites life/death turn out to be functional equivalents.

I wish to draw attention to this particular contrast between the two solutions (punishment by death v. punishment by life) for it rather contradicts the profoundly original semantic conception Pushkin attaches to his own version of the Don Juan character - namely, his remarkable affinity with, and attraction by death; a trait which, in line with the intertextual juxtaposition, is likely to let him appear similar to Nabokov's Edmond. In *The Stone Guest* this arch-lover's fixation on death competes with his only allegedly single obsession with love. Within Pushkin's Don Juan the two basic drives, *eros* and *thanatos*, seem to be merged into one; indeed, as has often been noted, every aspect of his erotic behaviour implies a morbid dimension.[15]

Thus, from the very beginning Pushkin succeeds in evoking an atmosphere that can be associated with death, when he makes his Don Juan a 'creature of the night' (with 'Let's wait here for the night' as his and the text's first line; and all further appearances of the hero take place at night); or else he depicts him in what might be taken for a vampire's pose, dressed in a waving cape as he is when preparing to 'fly through the streets' ('полечу по улицам'; *KG* I, 3) of night-time Madrid. Like such an 'un-dead' being, Don Juan considers himself 'sentenced to life' (*KG* III, 96 ff.) and declares the very desire to live a madness: 'Or is to wish the end, o Doña Anna, a sign of madness? / If I was mad I'd rather like to stay alive'. (*KG* III, 70 ff.).

This night/death complex, then, becomes linked to Don Juan's erotic affairs in a very peculiar way. He was in love with the terminally ill Doña Ines (*KG* I, 45 ff.). Their nightly rendezvous frequently took place in the very churchyard of St Antony's monastery (as is explicitly mentioned in the manuscript version: *KG* p. 308). What had fascinated him about this, as he recalls, not really beautiful woman (*KG* I, 54 ff.) was her especially strange, that is moribund charm: 'I used to find a curious pleasure in her sad gaze and her bloodless lips [помертвелые губы] ... And her voice was soft and weak, like that of someone ill'. (*KG* I, 50 ff.). Don Juan and Doña Laura literally make love beside Don Carlos's corpse whom the protagonist has just killed in a duel. Although Doña Laura hints at this outrageous situation - 'Wait ... before the corpse!' (*KG* II, 110) - she soon, being the true female double of Don Juan, finds pleasure in this rather macabre and therefore deeply exciting ambience, and without hesitation accepts his plain invitation: 'let's talk afterwards' (*KG* II, 123).

When this 'necro-erotician' first catches sight of the widow Doña Anna, dressed in black as she is, she has an extremely stimulating effect on him. Her 'black hair on the pale marble' (*KG* III, 38) provokes a sort of aesthetic delight even intensified by the fact that this 'marble' is just the tombstone in which her husband lies. Doña Anna, too, pretends (?) to be shocked by his impudence at courting her in this very place - 'before this tombstone!' (*KG* III, 56) -, but it does not stop her from inviting the young stranger into her home for the next night. There it is she who dissipates his misgivings as to whether he has the right to love her; and by the way manages to ask him, most innocently, whether he is 'bound' to other women (*KG* IV, 39 ff.). A psychologically convincing motivation for Doña Anna's undoubtedly actual falling in love with the man who is allegedly Don Diego is given in her merely functional marriage to the rich Don Alvaro (*KG* IV, 14 ff.). Hence her rather abstract hatred for his murderer which is based on a sense of 'duty of honour' ('По долгу чести': *KG* IV, 66) alone, just as it is for this single reason that she goes on mourning her husband: 'a widow must [должна] be faithful even to the [husband's] coffin' (*KG* IV, 30). Even her repeated allusions to the late Don Alvaro's affection for her (*KG* IV, 11 ff., 31 ff.) only seem to serve the widow as a means to foster, and not without success, her living lover's jealousy of the dead husband.

When Don Juan at last discloses himself as her husband's murderer, the widow attends to her duty and faints (the manuscript version [*KG* p. 314] shows him [is it a trace of necrophilia?], enchanted by the beauty lying as if dead, and lets him seize the opportunity to kiss her - of course! - pale - lips for the first time). Then, however, Doña Anna - *nota bene* - now with the definite knowledge of his being the man who killed her husband - turns out to be most fascinated by this 'cunning seducer', 'wicked corrupter', the 'demon himself' (*KG* IV, 102 ff.); and I am not so sure whether these words are meant as reproaches or rather as a sort of (verbal) caress. At least her otherwise slightly enigmatic remark 'So, this is Don Juan ...' (*KG* IV, 89) indicates that she is deeply interested in, or rather, that she is in love with Don Juan *as* Don Juan. Finally, Doña Anna not only agrees to meet him again, but shows herself concerned about this 'careless man's' escape (*KG* IV, 117 ff.) and does not at all reject his parting-kiss (*KG* IV, 129).

Death is the permanent semantic companion of their talk about love. Already when they meet for the first time - at her husband's grave - Don Juan's reply to Doña Anna's question 'What is your demand?' is: 'Death. / O let me die now at your feet!' (*KG* III, 60 ff.); only to expound at length on the idea of his own being mourned by her, of his tombstone being touched by her 'light foot' (this author's most prominent erotic fetish: *KG* III, 66 ff.); in short, on his replacing the 'мертвый счастливец', the 'dead and happy man' Don Alvaro (KG IV, 9), whom he envies for the widow's devoted love. Later on, at Doña Anna's home, the hero explicitly links a new declaration of love with his confession to be her husband's murderer (*KG* IV, 75 ff.); which, however, in the particularly pointed wording of the early text version almost sounds as if it was precisely this identity that entitles him to love her: 'I am the murderer of Don Alvaro / I'm Don Juan and I'm in love with you' ('Я убийца Дон Альвара / Я Дон Гуан и я тебя люблю'; *KG* 314). Afterwards he asks her twice more to take his life in order to gain her love (*KG* IV, 72, 88).

Here it becomes quite clear that Don Juan's speech behaviour, as well as the idea it contains, has to be regarded within the framework of romantically conventionalized discourse patterns. He makes use of death first of all as a most intensive verbal image of the utmost love.[16] For him the equation 'love = death' is a rhetorical device only, an oxymoron metaphor (which, however, clearly against his own expectation comes to be realized in the dramatic solution) perfectly in line with the fashionable Byronistic cliché of morbid love and an erotically charged weariness-of-life-and-longing-for-death complex.[17] It is precisely the stupendously theatrical way in which Pushkin lets his hero submit to this conception of love, his obviously melodramatic exaggeration, that reveals Don Juan's coquetry with death as nothing other than a deliberately chosen pose.[18] The emphasis he lays on his orientation towards the beyond is but surface spleen like the *strannosti*, the strange traits he finds so attractive in women (*KG* I, 50, 92). Seemingly it gives his love life an additional erotic kick and might as well be a means to the success of this seducer, who 'knows how to use life and death to serve the ends of love'.[19]

There cannot be any doubt that Don Juan's true desire is directed towards living in this world: 'Here - not there' ('Здесь - не там': *KG* IV, 8 ff.), that is, it is not at the grave of Don Alvaro that he wants to be together with Doña Anna. His idea of happiness is as worldly as can be; it is to be found in the vivid love of this woman that makes him 'happy as a child' and 'ready to embrace the whole world' (*KG* III, 120; 126 ff.). It is in this vital impulse (*zhizneradost*) that we should see the hero's main characteristic: 'Le Don Juan de Pouchkine est un Don Juan vital, "cavalier insolent" qui risque tout et ose tout au nom de la vie'.[20]

This impulse is disclosed even in the play's beginning, when Don Juan, as mentioned above, frankly declares his preference for a 'southern-vital' way of life - with love being but life's epitome - to that other one which the 'northern-morbid' banishment forced him to live (*KG* I, 25 ff.). Indeed, he is prepared to give his life for this great and overwhelming love: 'What, then, is death? For a sweet moment of our being together / I'd give my life without a word.' (*KG* IV, 116 ff.). But this again makes love - and not death - the real end of Don Juan's life.

With Nabokov's protagonist the situation is reversed. Don Juan's exclusive orientation towards this world matches a total orientation towards the beyond with Edmond; the pseudo-longing of Pushkin's hero for death is in stark contrast to his pseudo-longing for love.

Edmond, in fact, is not in love with Stella, but with the death she personifies for him (quite in accordance with the traditional literary motif of a young woman representing a 'she-death', as is supported by the feminine gender of death in Russian [смерть] as well as in Latin [*mors*]).[21] Her image becomes blurred with Edmond's idea of death,[22] when for him the very name of Stella announces that she herself is the starry night, the 'starry madness' ('звездное безумие': *Sm* II, 147) that had always provoked both Edmond's horror and desire, for he 'can lose himself in it' (*Sm* I, 96 ff.). He remembers in particular her starry eyes, which his imagination likens to an abyss (the 'abyss of death', of course) and thus takes for the 'gateway' to the promised absolute understanding:

> Tormented was my soul: / there precipices opened like her eyes ... / Unbearably sweet and frightened / I felt with her, and Stella knew it. / How to explain my horror and the vision? / I heard the noise of uncountable worlds / in her casual rustling. I smelt / the breath of vague mysteries in her words (*Sm* II, 199 ff.).

For Edmond, then, her momentary glance - and this is what their entire relationship actually consists of! - anticipates precisely the one moment it takes to pass into the beyond, that is, the moment of death; at which, as he had said before,'the bright windows of eternity' shall open (*Sm* I, 117) and to which his whole life is therefore directed. Now, when he experiences Stella's glance, standing by the window, he at last looks into the 'eyes of eternity' itself: 'Wild and aerial / her eyes looked into mine - no, / I don't know whether these were her eyes / or eternity at its purest ...' ('не ведаю, - глаза ли это были / иль вечность обнаженная': *Sm* II, 233 ff.).

Edmond's idea of condensing love, like death, into a single moment's glance from his beloved may also be taken as another reference to the Pushkinian intertext to be found in Nabokov's text. It corresponds to Don Juan's sensation of his love for Doña Ines encapsulated in one glance: 'Her eyes, / just her eyes. And their expression ... such a look / as I've never met with since.' (*KG* I, 55 ff.); or his being prepared 'to give up everything ... for just one kind look' from Doña Anna's eyes (*KG* IV, 21 ff.). In both texts the union of love, or death, takes but one moment respectively (cf. 'Сладкий миг свиданья' [*KG* IV, 116]; 'сошлись на миг' [*Sm* II, 242]).

It is, in short, his looking into Stella's starry eyes that finally brings Edmond into the (longed for and feared) contact with the beyond. Don Juan - who frequently talks about death without taking it seriously at all - realizes its very existence for the first time, when he invites the dead commander's statue to witness his rendezvous with Doña Anna: and the statue nods as a sign of acceptance (*KG* III, 154 ff.). Stella's glance and the statue's nod, therefore, turn out to be functional equivalents. Both indicate intrusions of the transcendent beyond into this world's immanence, they serve as evidence for the permanent presence of death within life. This seems to be the basic conflict dealt with in these two texts (and, moreover, throughout most of Nabokov's fiction in general as well as in a considerable part of Pushkin's later work):[23] the suspension of the borderline between life and death which had been considered so solid, their mutual penetration and the profound existential uncertainty following from it.

Whilst Edmond, after this sudden insight into 'the other side' that Stella gives to him, is now attracted by death even more, Don Juan - being in an exalted state of mind because of his love for Doña Anna (with whom, to repeat, he wants to live!) - suppresses this understanding at once. That is why death can surprise him when it grasps the hero with a 'hand of the grave' 'not from this world' (cf. the textual variants 'Могильное пожатие руки' [*KG* p. 316] and 'Не здешнего холодное пожатье!' [*KG* IV, 138]) and pulls him down with all the power it possesses over life; a power that finds its metaphor in the Herculean dimensions of the commander's statue which, as Don Juan notices in astonishment, by far exceeds the stature of the living original (*KG* III, 14 ff.). It is only now that he comes to learn that the 'Stone Guest' personifies death, as does Stella in the intertext. He is the hidden, but omnipresent central character of this tragedy, as its very title indicates (which Pushkin promotes against most of the other dramatizations of the Don Juan story); this, in turn, makes the titles of the two plays - *Death* and *The Stone Guest* - synonymous.[24]

Thus, an at least possible reading of *The Stone Guest* may consider the 'Stone Guest' an allegory of death which, out of envy, cannot accept the happiness with which love provides the living (including the fact that love lets them forget about the omnipresence of death). Yet, from the intertextual perspective, the comparison with *Death* offers an additional line of interpretation for the very peculiar ontological state of the commander whom Don Juan has killed. It is, namely, in perfect accordance with Nabokov's conception of *potustoronnost* as outlined at the beginning of this chapter.

The fantastic textual situation of *The Stone Guest* makes Don Alvaro an absent-present, 'undead' being that has to watch how his murderer courts his widow, and obviously with success. One can imagine that such an observation would please no husband (no matter whether alive or dead). But for this particular husband, if we take Nabokov's *potustoronnost* construction as a frame of reference for Pushkin's drama, it concerns his very existence, since the transition phase between life and death that he apparently holds will continue only as long as he is remembered; and only as long as his own wife will remember him by honouring his grave which, not without reason, is referred to as a 'memorial' ('памятник': *KG* I, 89) In line with this reading it is perfectly clear, why this widow's 'remembrance / faith-beyond-death' aspect is made a recurrent and prominent topic in the text (*KG* I, 89 ff.; IV, 4, 30 ff.); or why, in Doña Anna's words, 'a widow must be faithful even to the [husband's] coffin' (*KG* IV, 30). It is for the simple reason that her betrayal, her forgetting him and falling in love with Don Juan must inevitably lead to Don Alvaro's 'fall into the abyss', his final non-existence; and this is precisely what threatens him from the two lovers' first encounter onwards.

Pushkin once more deviates from the textual tradition and even carries to extremes this situation by having his Don Juan summon the statue to witness a rendezvous in Doña Anna's very home in order to give her husband a practical demonstration of her adultery and, consequently, his extinction from her memory: 'Commander, I beg you to come / to your widow, where tomorrow I will be, / and keep watch at the door.' (*KG* III, 154 ff.) In other words, Don Juan is going to turn the dead husband (Don Alvaro) from a mere observer into a voyeur of his rival's vivid love. In comparison we can consider the constellation in *Death* - Edmond admits the living husband (Gonville) as an observer and voyeur of his death - to be its exact inversion. The challenged commander, however, does not restrict himself to the role of spectator. He interferes from the beyond into this world when he literally 'takes a hand in' and pulls Don Juan down into the abyss.

NOTES

1. Quoted as *KG* (+ scene, line) from Alexandr Pushkin, *Polnoe sobranie sochinenii*, Akademiia Nauk SSSR, Moscow and Leningrad, 1948, VII, pp. 135-71 (variants pp. 307-16).
2. Quoted as *Sm* (+ act, line) from Vladimir Nabokov, *P'esy*, Iskusstvo, Moscow, 1990, pp. 43-58.
3. 'Perhaps no one at home or in exile made claim to Pushkin's legacy more faithfully than Vladimir Nabokov. Born in 1899, one hundred years after Pushkin, Nabokov adopted Pushkin as his personal muse and never abandoned that calling': Sergej Davydov, 'Nabokov and Pushkin' in Vladimir E. Alexandrov, ed., *The Garland Companion to Vladimir Nabokov*, Garland, New York and London, 1995, p. 482.
4. For some theoretical remarks on this approach see my essay 'Gleich- und Gegenüberstellung: intratextuelle und intertextuelle Bedeutung in der Literatur', *Zeitschrift für Slawistik*, XL, 3, 1995, pp. 243-67.
5. According to Vera Nabokova, the author's widow, *potustoronnost'* 'saturates everything he has written, it symbolizes, like a watermark, all of his creation' (cited from Davydov, op. cit., p. 483). For a list of studies on Nabokov's *potustoronnost'* construction see Vladimir E. Alexandrov, 'The Otherworld' in Alexandrov, ed., op. cit., p. 571.
6. Apart from a few shallow remarks, *Death* has not been noticed critically up to now. It seems to share the fate of the writer's early dramas in general, which keep being considered 'not yet mature Nabokov', as in, for example, Simon Karlinsky, 'Illusion, Reality and Parody in Nabokov's Plays', *Wisconsin Studies in Contemporary Literature*, VIII, 1967, p. 269.
7. Cf., as a lyrical expression of this *potustoronnost'* state of mind, Nabokov's poem *Fame* (*Slava*, 1942): 'But one day while disrupting the strata of sense / and descending deep down to my wellspring / I, like in a mirror, saw the world and me / and the other, other, other' (cited after Vladimir E. Alexandrov, *Nabokov's Otherworld*, Princeton University Press, Princeton, 1991, p. 2).
8. Cf. D. Barton Johnson, *Worlds in Regression: Some Novels of Vladimir Nabokov*, Ardis, Ann Arbor, 1985, pp. 185-223 ('Nabokov as a Gnostic Seeker').
9. 'That main secret tra-tá-ta tra-tá-ta tra-tá / but I must not be overexplicit' ('Эта тайна та-та, та-та-та-та, та-та / а точнее сказать я не вправе'; from Nabokov, *Fame*, loc. cit.).
10. This setting bears a clear romantic connotation and, moreover, might include an association with Byron. Yet I must admit that I do not catch a concrete textual meaning from it and therefore can only agree with Boyd, who calls *Death* 'a romantic, slightly Faustian closet drama set in Byron's Cambridge, but with Byron a fleeting shadow for no more than a vivid line or two' (Brian Boyd, *Vladimir Nabokov. The Russian Years*, Chatto and Windus London, 1990, p. 204).
11. Don Juan characterizes the man Don Alvaro metonymically by repeatedly laying the emphasis on the material, that is, the marble his effigy is made of (*KG* III, 38, 43; IV, 11). Edmond, in turn, uses the same marble semantics metaphorically when he charges Gonville with a lack of human emotions in view of his wife's death: 'You are as if made of marble: / a solemn white suffering ...' (*Sm* I, 39).
12. I consider Doña Anna the central female character in *The Stone Guest* since it is she alone to whom the hero's desire is directed in the text (that is, they complement each other as the story's narrative subject and object). In contrast, both Doña Ines and Doña Laura first of all function as personified reflections of the two main components of Don Juan's love conception before he meets Doña Anna: namely, erotic morbidity and sexual spontaneity, that is, promiscuity.
13. 'Don Juan n'est qu'une ombre, un revenant qui sort du royaume des morts. Il ne rentre peut-être à Madrid que pour mettre en scène une mort qui a déjà eu lieu.' (Hélène Henry, 'Portrait du

poète en chevalier masqué: l'unité des *Petites tragédies*', *Revue des études slaves*, LIX, 1, 1987, p. 232).

14. Cf. Anna A. Akhmatova, '*Kamennyi gost'* Pushkina', *Pushkin. Issledovaniia I materialy*, II, 1958, pp. 190 ff.

15. 'Some Russian critics have called Don Juan a deliberate study in sexual morbidity' (John Bayley, *Pushkin. A Comparative Study*, Cambridge University Press, Cambridge, 1971, p. 201). His 'sexual morbidity' is considered the key to Pushkin's Don Juan, for instance, by Dmitrii S. Darskii, *Malen'kie tragedii Pushkina*, Moscow, 1915, p. 60; Dmitrii D. Blagoi, *Sotsiologiia tvorchestva Pushkina. Etiudy*, Federatsiia, Moscow, 1929, p. 219; Vikentii V.Veresaev, 'Vtoroklassnyi Don-Zhuan' [1937] in his *Zagadochnii Pushkin*, Respublika, Moscow, 1996, p. 352; and, to refer to at least one non-Russian critic, by Barbara Heldt Monter, 'Love and Death in Pushkin's *Little Tragedies*' [1972/73] in Harold Bloom, ed., *Alexander Pushkin. Modern Critical Views*, Chelsea House, New York, 1987, p. 69: 'Sexuality, traditionally associated with Don Juan's vigor and love of life, is here specifically connected with death. ... Don Juan is different with different women, but one thing remains constant: with all his women he seeks the morbid'.

16. Cf., as but one example for an analogous usage of horror as a paraphrase for sexual lust, of death as a metaphor for climactic love, Pushkin's own lyrical fragment 'Kak shchastliv ia ...' (1826): 'A moment's chill, like horror, is passing / by my head, and the heart is beating aloud, / while dying of a most tormenting love. / And at this very moment [!] I would happily lose my life, / I wish to groan and drink her kisses ...' (Aleksandr Pushkin, *Polnoe sobranie sochinenii*, Akademiia Nauk SSSR, Moscow and Leningrad, 1948, III, pp. 36 ff.).

17. In his seminal study on romantic 'decadent' eroticism *La carne, la morte e il diavolo nella letteratura romantica* (1930), Mario Praz gives a concise historical survey of this so-called 'beauty of Medusa' conception (see *Liebe, Tod und Teufel. Die schwarze Romantik*, DTV, München, 4th edition, 1994, pp. 43 ff.), which he traces back to Tasso ('where beauty and death are blurred. ... The approaching death seems to provide love with a new incitement'; ibid., p. 51) and sees it taken to perfection in Byron, until it 'will reappear at the end of the [19th] century' (ibid., p. 65). It certainly plays a prominent role in Pushkin's work, too. Cf., for instance, his *Rusalka* fragment (1829-32), featuring the hero's fatal love for a drowned woman; the inevitable death serves as a stimulus for love in *The Feast in Time of Plague* (1830); death is the prize readily paid for a night's love in the *Kleopatra* poem (1824/28) as well as in its prose version *Egyptian Nights* (1835). Already in the three longer 'Southern Poems' (1820-24) it is death that ultimately substitutes for love.

18. Cf. Bayley, op. cit., p. 202.

19. Monter, op. cit., p. 69.

20. Henry, op. cit., p. 232.

21. Cf. Blok's highly stylized play *The Fair Show Booth* (*Balaganchik*, 1906) as one of the more prominent examples of a modernist usage of this motif. In its heroine, however, it is already laid bare as a literary cliché.

22. Apart from Edmond's subjective identification, the equivalence Stella/death is indicated by the fact that she is of Italian origin (*Sm* I, 133 ff.), as is the poison that is to bring Edmond death: a 'grey glowing fire / like a morning in Florence' (*Sm* I, 164 ff.). This poison, that is, a metonymy of death, is said 'to be as sweet / and to take effect as momentarily [!] as love' (*Sm* I, 168 ff.).

23. See, for instance, Iuri M. Lotman, 'Pushkin. Ocherk tvorchestva' [1989] in his *Pushkin*, Iskusstvo-SPB, St Petersburg, 1995, pp. 208 ff.

24. Moreover, Nabokov seems to quote this very Pushkinian title paragrammatically, when he has Edmond, during his talk with Gonville and rather unmotivated by the context, describe a party among his friends, where they not only drink Spanish wine, but, strangely enough, remember

their playing ball against a '*stone* wall' (*Sm* II, 125; my emphasis) and then, in one of the next lines, welcome a 'third *guest*' (*Sm* II, 129; my emphasis).

The Pushkin Contexts of Georgii Ivanov's
Disintegration of the Atom

by

JUSTIN DOHERTY

My aim in this chapter is to examine the Russian émigré poet Georgii Ivanov's well-known (and somewhat notorious) 1937 prose work *Disintegration of the Atom* (*Распад атома*) from the perspective of a system of intertextual references around which the work is organized, and at the centre of which stands the figure of Pushkin. I will examine its underlying structural and thematic dependence on Pushkin, and on one key text in particular, the elegiac lyric poem of 1829

> На холмах Грузии лежит ночная мгла;
> Шумит Арагва предо мною.
> Мне грустно и легко; печаль моя светла;
> Печаль моя полна тобою.
> Тобой, одной тобой ... Унынья моего
> Ничто не мучит, не тревожит,
> И сердце вновь горит и любит - оттого,
> Что не любить она не может.[1]

> (On the hills of Georgia nocturnal darkness lies,
> Before me the Aragva roars.
> I am both gay and sad: my sorrow - luminous,
> My sorrow filled by you.
> By you, by you alone ... And my despondency
> Nothing troubles, nothing alarms,
> And once more my heart burns and loves -
> For it is unable not to love.)

Before enlarging upon Ivanov's uses of Pushkin and this text in particular, it is worth dwelling briefly on Pushkin's poem itself. This poem is probably one of the most widely anthologized of all of Pushkin's love-lyrics: written in 1829, it was composed during Pushkin's journey to the Caucasus and Turkey, and forms part of what has become known as the 'Caucasian cycle' of some seven or eight poems inspired by Pushkin's impressions and feelings during his travels. The poem is often cited as an exemplary indication of the creative direction taken by the 'mature' Pushkin later on in the 1830s, revealing as it does, according to Blagoi, the quintessential qualities of brevity (it is only eight lines long, having existed in an earlier version of 16 lines or four stanzas) and concreteness (it contains very few poetic figures and almost no extravagant 'poetic' language).² However, even a cursory reading of the text reveals a number of vital residual features entirely characteristic of literary Romanticism: it has an exotic setting (Georgia, mountains, the river Aragva); its temporal setting is the liminal zone of dusk;³ and, not least importantly, its poetic message rests on the rhetorical device of oxymoron or contradiction.

Specifically, Pushkin's poem exhibits oxymoronic features at both a local and a global level: locally in terms of phraseological units ('мне грустно и легко' ['I feel sad and easy'], 'печаль моя светла' ['my sorrow is luminous']),⁴ globally in terms of an underlying structural organization around contradictory perceptions or feelings (sadness, melancholy and darkness on the one hand, love ['сердце ... горит' ('my heart ... is on fire')] illumination ['светла' ('luminous')], even happiness ['мне ... легко' ('I feel ... easy')] on the other). Anthropomorphic imagery underscores the oxymoron: darkness in the surrounding world ('ночная мгла' ['nocturnal darkness']) stands in opposition to inner illumination ('печаль моя светла' ['my sorrow is luminous']). Here the structural unity is emphasized by Pushkin's rhyme structure: in the first quatrain 'мгла' ('darkness') rhymes with its semantic opposite, 'светла' ('luminous'), while 'мною' ('me') rhymes with the subject's 'other', 'тобою' ('you').

The reason why I draw attention to these features of Pushkin's text should become apparent when we turn to Ivanov's work. 'На холмах Грузии ...' ('On the hills of Georgia ...') seems to have exerted a particular fascination over Ivanov: not only does he cite it repeatedly in *Disintegration of the Atom*, it also makes an appearance in the earlier memoir work *Petersburg Winters* (1928).⁵ Why this particular poem, aside from its general familiarity? I believe that important features of Ivanov's poetic system, thematic and structural, can be seen to be prefigured in Pushkin's poem, and indeed that certain attributes of Pushkin himself, as what it has become current to term a 'cultural myth',⁶ are equally germane to much of Ivanov's work, lyric poetry (which dominates his output) as much as *Disintegration of the Atom* itself.⁷

Much of Ivanov's literary output from the early 1930s onwards seems to be founded upon the principle of contradiction, and thus to be heavily dependent on the rhetorical figure of oxymoron. A typical example is the poem beginning 'Все неизменно, и все изменилось ...' ('All is unchanging and all has changed ...), first published in 1949:⁸

> Все неизменно, и все изменилось
> В утреннем холоде странной свободы.
> Долгие годы мне многое снилось,
> Вот я проснулся — и где эти годы!
>
> Вот я иду по осеннему полю,
> Все, как всегда, и другое, чем прежде:

Точно меня отпустили на волю
И отказали в последней надежде.

(All in unchanging and all has changed
In the morning cold of a strange freedom.
Over long years I dreamed of much,
Now I have woken — and where are those years!

Now as I walk across an autumn field,
All is as it was, and other than before:
As if I had been set free
And refused my last hope.)

While many similar examples could be used to illustrate this point, the key one to be made here is that oxymoron serves not simply as an external decorative feature within Ivanov's poetic system, but functions (in the same manner which was evident in Pushkin's poem 'On the hills of Georgia ...') at a deeper structural level and plays a vital role within that poetic system. Thus, as with Pushkin's lyric poem, Ivanov's text exhibits oxymoron or contradiction at both a local, phraseological level and at a global level. At the beginning of each stanza, Ivanov states his main theme through similar constructions built around an oxymoron and whose subject is the word 'все' ('all'): in stanza one, line one: 'Все неизменно и все изменилось' ('All is unchanging and all has changed'), and in stanza two, line two: 'Все, как всегда, и другое, чем прежде' ('All is as it was, and other than before']). This type of parallelism[9] is replicated in the second half of each stanza, where we once more find a contradiction or antithesis (stanza one, lines 3-4: 'Долгие годы ... и где эти годы!' ['Over long years ... and where are those years!']; stanza two, lines 3-4: 'отпустили на волю ... отказали в последней надежде' ['set free ... refused my last hope']).

On another level, Ivanov's rhyme structure indicates how oxymoron is embedded in the poem's global construction. In stanza one, the rhyme words demonstrate a semantic constrast: 'изменилось' ('has changed', line 1), associated with the negative idea of a changed present, rhymes with 'снилось' ('dreamed', line 3), which connects with the (for Ivanov typically) positively nuanced idea of memory and dreams; in the even lines 'свободы' ('freedom', line 2), here at best semantically ambivalent, rhymes with 'годы' ('years', line 4) which, while positively connected with memory, are also semantically negative here as they are years which are now lost. In stanza two, Ivanov shifts to a scheme where the rhyme words also 'rhyme' semantically, while the element of opposition is now situated in the conflict between each rhyming pair. In lines 1 and 3, where 'полю' ('field') rhymes with 'волю' ('freedom'),[10] both words are associated with emancipation or freedom of movement, and thus at first glance positively nuanced. Both are, however, undermined by what follows:

'прежде' ('before', line 2) and 'надежде' ('hope', line 4), while both associated directly with a positive idea (memory of the past and hope for the future), both are in fact negated here - the past has changed and hope is refused. It is worth noting also that in both stanzas Ivanov uses the rhyme structure to negate or devalue the idea of freedom in the conventional sense (both 'воля' and 'свобода' serve as rhyme words),[11] replacing it with a kind of existentialist recognition of freedom as a stripping away of comforting illusions.

It is arguable that *Disintegration of the Atom* itself provides the most sustained instance of Ivanov's dependence on oxymoron or contradiction. A typical example is the passage below, which consists of an ironic meditation on the resolution of opposites or contradictions through the sexual act:

> Женщина. Плоть. Инструмент, из которого извлекает человек ту единственную ноту из божественной гаммы, которую ему дано слышать. Лампочка горит под потолком. Лицо откинуто на подушке. Можно думать, что это моя невеста. Можно думать, что я подпоил девчонку и воровски, впопыхах насилую ее. Можно ничего не думать, содрогаясь, вслушиваясь, слыша удивительные вещи, ожидая наступления минуты, когда горе и счастье, добро и зло, жизнь и смерть скрестятся как во время затмения на своих орбитах, готовые соединиться в одно, когда жуткий, зеленоватый свет жизни-смерти, счастья-мученья хлынет, из погибшего прошлого, из твоих погасших зрачков.

> (Woman. Flesh. The instrument out of which man elicits the sole note from the divine scale which it is given to him to hear. A light bulb glows under the ceiling. Her face is thrown back on the pillow. It is possible to think that she is my fiancée. It is possible to think that I have made a girl drunk and furtively, hurriedly I am raping her. It is possible to think nothing, trembling, listening, hearing astonishing things, awaiting the arrival of the minute when grief and happiness, good and evil, life and death will intersect as during an eclipse in their orbits, ready to join together as one, when the terrible greenish light of life-death, happiness-suffering will well up, from the dead past, from your extinguished eyes.[12])

As is made explicit at certain points in the narrative itself, the 'atom' of the work's title is itself a figure for the unstable unity of opposites represented by the contemporary individual, Ivanov's I-narrator in the first instance, but equally 'man' in the broadest sense.[13] This modern 'I' is seen to exist under the unbearable pressure of contradictory forces: on the one hand, the 'positive' ideal of art or culture, order and harmony, love and human intimacy; and on the other, the antithetical realities of isolation and suffering, philistinism, chaos and disharmony, which serve to negate any positive ideal.

In this respect, Pushkin and his poem may be seen to serve primarily as an embodiment of Ivanov's (apparently self-deluding) positive ideal; and yet at another level it may be that Pushkin's own ability to create harmony out of contradiction can serve as a model for a resolution of the fissuring of the modern psyche which Ivanov's prose poem so effectively articulates. Ivanov's text situates the opposing forces of culture and philistinism within two distinct intertextual centres: the world of culture is centred on Pushkin, and particularly on his poem 'On the hills of Georgia ...'; philistinism is embodied in the fictional world of Gogol, and specifically in the figure of Akakii Akakievich from Gogol's Petersburg story *The Overcoat*. Pushkin's poetry represents beauty, purity and lucidy; Gogol's story of the 'poor clerk' Akakii Akakievich (or 'ink rat',[14] as Ivanov describes him), on the other hand, is employed by Ivanov to suggest spiritual and aesthetic impoverishment, sterility and self-delusion. It is out of the clash between these two opposite cultural forces, linked by Ivanov explicitly on the one hand to Russia's aristocratic pre-revolutionary 'high culture', and on the other to 'democratic', plebeian forces which have reshaped Ivanov's homeland, that the climax of *Disintegration of the Atom* is wrought.

The central position of Pushkin in Ivanov's text is hardly accidental. *Disintegration of the Atom* is dated 24 February 1937, that is, only days after the official commemoration of the centenary of Pushkin's death. Frequent references to Pushkin within *Disintegration of the Atom*, especially towards the end, and in particular two references specifically to Pushkin's death,[15] would seem to reinforce the impression that this work is both an anti-commemoration of the Pushkin centenary, and equally a fraught meditation on Pushkin's culturological significance.

If we return to Ivanov's treatment of Pushkin's poem 'On the hills of Georgia ...', one thing which is immediately striking about Ivanov's use of it is the fact that the first line of the poem is *misquoted* in *Disintegration of the Atom*. In a predicatably cold review of *Disintegration of the Atom* published in *Vozrozhdenie* (28 January, 1938), Vladislav Khodasevich criticized Ivanov for this misquotation (in *Disintegration of the Atom*, the first line is given as 'На холм*ы* Грузии *легла* ночная мгла ...' ['Upon the hills of Georgia nocturnal darkness *lay*']: my emphasis); Khodasevich remarks:

> У Пушкина этой безвкусицы, этого «легла мгла», нет, Пушкин не мог ее написать, - а герой Иванова ее твердит как ни в чем не бывало - он даже *повторить* не умеет того, что Пушкин умел *написать*, потому что у него уши заложены, потому что поэзия ему была и есть глубоко, органически чужда.[16]

> (In Pushkin there is none of this tastelessness, this 'legla mgla' ['darkness lay'], Pushkin could not have written it, yet Ivanov's hero repeats it as if nothing were wrong - he cannot even *repeat* what Pushkin was able to *write*, because his ears are blocked up, because poetry was, and is, organically foreign to him [emphasis in original].)

Here, Khodasevich is partly right, in attributing Ivanov's misquoting of Pushkin to his narrator-hero's bad taste and ignorance, but he fails to see that the misquotation might be meaningful in its own right. This poem turns out to be a key text in highlighting the characteristic metaphor of Pushkin's eclipse and of the darkness of the post-Pushkinian age (signalled by Khodasevich himself, incidentally, in his famous 1921 Pushkin speech 'The Shaken Tripod',[17] and featured in several poems by Mandelshtam also written around that time, most notably 'В Петербурге мы сойдемся снова ...' ['In Petersburg we shall meet again ...'].)[18] It is worth noting in passing, indeed, that Ivanov himself uses the imagery of darkness falling and of eclipse in *Disintegration of the Atom* and elsewhere in an almost obsessive manner - for example, in the late memoir essay 'Sunset over Petersburg'.[19]

In Pushkin's poem, 'ночная мгла' ('nocturnal darkness') should probably be read as a combination of, first, Romantic scene-setting (the privileged moment of darkness falling presaging artistic revelation), and secondly, as a source of contrast, equally Romantic, between outer darkness and the poet's inner sense of illumination which emerges later in the poem ('Печаль моя *светла*' ['My darkness is *luminous*']); in other words, there is no sense in Pushkin of the apocalyptic thematics characteristic of such imagery in Russian Modernism. In Pushkin, 'darkness' ('мгла'), whether inner or outer, is opposed and overcome by the poet's dominant emotion of love, and the luminous joy it brings to him. By contrast, in Ivanov's recontextualization of Pushkin's imagery darkness (as a metaphor for emptiness - 'пустота' - or non-being, the equivalent of the existentialist 'Néant') has triumphed over a love which has been tragically curtailed for Ivanov's narrator: consequently, Ivanov's substitution of the past tense verb 'легла' ('lay') suggests a permanent and irremediable state of darkness rather than a transient one which can be overcome. The use of the past tense may also be read as an attempt by Ivanov to underscore the historical separation of his narrative from Pushkin's text: what in 1829 is represented by Pushkin in the process of happening has become an irreversible fact, had passed into historical time, by 1937.

As well as misquoting Pushkin, Ivanov's text also subjects Pushkin's poem to a process of desacralization. The clearest example of this occurs when Ivanov once more misquotes the opening line of Pushkin's poem, and goes on to develop a debased analogy with the second line of Pushkin's text ('Шумит Арагва предо мною' ['Before me the Aragva roars']): '"На холмы Грузии легла ночная мгла". И вот она так же ложится на холм Монмартра. На крыши, на перекресток, на вывеску кафе, на полукруг писуара, где с тревожным шумом, совсем, как в Арагве, шумит вода.'[20] ('"Upon the hills of Georgia nocturnal darkness lay". And here in the same way it is falling upon the hill of Montmartre. Upon the rooftops, upon the crossroads, upon the café sign, upon the semicircle of a pissoir, where, with a fearsome din, just as in the Aragva, the water roars').

However, it is important to note that, despite this 'desacralization' of Pushkin, there is another aspect to Ivanov's (or rather, Ivanov's narrator's) appropriation of this poem in particular, namely, the fact that it (and Pushkin) are very often placed in opposition to some literary context which is represented as 'more' degenerate. For instance, when the poem 'On the hills of Georgia ...' is first cited in *Disintegration of the Atom*, it is immediately contrasted with the famous *zaum* poem by Aleksei Kruchenykh beginning 'Дыр бул щыл / убеш щурь' ('Dyr bul shchyl / ubesh shchur'; characteristically, this text is also misquoted: it is cited as 'Дыр бу щыл убещурь' ['dyr bu shchyl ubeshchur']).[21]

Let us examine the context of this textual collision more carefully. Ivanov's narrator first refers to Pushkin's poem as he attempts to invoke a higher metaphysical reality ('Я хотел бы выйти на берег моря, лечь на песок, закрыть глаза, ощутить дыхание Бога на своем лице' ['I would like to walk out to the beach, lie down on the sand, close my eyes, feel the breath of God on my face'];[22] here, the spatial setting clearly parallels the subject's attempt to move beyond 'mundane' urban reality and attain a higher spiritual realm). Pushkin's language is posited as the means to achieve communication with this higher realm: '"На холмы Грузии легла ночная мгла",- такими приблизительно словами я хотел бы говорить с жизнью' ('"Upon the hills of Georgia nocturnal darkness lay",- it is more or less with these words that I would like to speak with life').[23] However, the paragraph which follows this asserts the impossibility for the narrator of making the connection, of sharing in what is termed Pushkin's 'harmony' (aesthetic and spiritual): 'Жизнь больше не понимает этого языка. Душа еще не научилась другому. Так болезненно отмирает в душе гармония.'[24] ('Life no longer understands this language. The soul has not yet learned another. Thus harmony painfully dies away within the soul').

This disjunction between Pushkin's language and aesthetic and the present is then reinforced by Ivanov's reference to Kruchenykh, whose *zaum* verse stands for precisely this loss of the modern subject's capacity to perceive and communicate beauty, harmony, and spirituality (it is interesting that this is once again expressed through an oxymoron):

'На холмы Грузии легла ночная мгла' - хочет [душа] звонко, торжественно произнести, славя Творца и себя. И, с отвращением, похожим на наслаждение бормочет матерную брань с метафизического забора, какое-то «дыр бу щыл убещур».²⁵

('Upon the hills of Georgia nocturnal darkness lay' - [the soul] wishes resoundingly, triumphantly to pronounce, giving praise to the Creator and to itself. And yet, with a disgust very like enjoyment, it mutters some obscene filth scrawled on the metaphysical fence, some 'dyr bu shchyl ubeschur'.)

Consequently, it is not the fault of Pushkin's text but of Ivanov's narrator if its language and reality are no longer seen to be accessible; indeed, Ivanov's narrator models the (albeit chiefly rhetorical) 'rejection' of Pushkin declared by Russian Futurism. The dialectical clash between Pushkin and Kruchenykh is then recreated elsewhere in the text of *Disintegration of the Atom* in the crucial opposition between Pushkin and Gogol's Akakii Akakievich, who comes to stand for the anti-cultural, utopian and revolutionary strand in Russian literary history, and which Ivanov connects with the disastrous event of the 1917 Bolshevik Revolution.

In this respect, there is one further connection between *Disintegration of the Atom* and Pushkin which needs to be pointed out. Towards the end of the work, Ivanov introduces another Pushkinian text, *The Bronze Horseman*, incorporating the opening line of the final section of Pushkin's paean of praise to the city of Petersburg in the poem's 'Introduction', 'Красуйся, град Петров, и стой ...' ('Stand beautiful, Peter's city, and remain ...'). On the surface of things this is a recapitulation of the opposition Ivanov has developed between Pushkin and Gogol's Akakii: to Pushkin's self-assertion as a cultural monument, however, Ivanov's Akakii/Gogol figure cannot even replicate the challenge to the statue of Peter by Pushkin's Evgenii in *The Bronze Horseman* ('Ужо тебе!' ['Just you wait!']), pathetically responding 'Ничего, ничего, молчание' ('Nothing, nothing, silence').

In a similar way, the arrogant self-assertion of Pushkin's 'Don Juan list' is contrasted with the negativity of Akakii/Gogol's self-abuse.²⁶ However, on another level, this Pushkin reference introduces a theme which emerges as a counter to the prevailing images of fissuring and destruction in *Disintegration of the Atom*, that of the permanence of art in the face of the evanescence of human life. This is, moreover, a 'classical' theme repeatedly explored by Pushkin himself (most characteristically in the poem *Exegi monumentum* of 1836, but equally in a lengthy chain of 'statue' or 'monument' poems).²⁷

This paradoxical theme is also characteristic for Ivanov in his later period, in association specifically with the city of St Petersburg. I would like to refer as an example of this to the following poem of 1955:

Ты не расслышала, а я не повторил.
Был Петербург, апрель, закатный час,
Сиянье, волны, каменные львы ...
И ветерок с Невы
Договорил за нас.

Ты улыбалась. Ты не поняла,
Что будет с нами, что нас ждет.
Черемуха в твоих руках цвела ...
Вот наша жизнь прошла,
А это не пройдет.[28]

(You did not catch my words, I didn't repeat them.
It was Petersburg, April, the hour of sunset,
Luminescence, waves, lions of stone ...
And the breeze from the Neva
Completed our unfinished words.

You smiled. You did not understand
What would happen to us, what awaited us.
In your hands the cherry-blossom flowered ...
Thus has our life passed,
But this will never fade.)

Here, what are in certain contexts figured as oppositional forces are resolved into some kind of unity: transient elements of life and the natural cycle ('апрель' ['April'], 'волны' ['waves'], 'закатный час' ['hour of sunset'], 'ветерок' ['breeze'], 'черемуха ... цвела' ['the cherry-blossom ... flowered']) merge with the physical reality of Petersburg, linked here with its literary representation (and indeed with Pushkin) via the figure of the stone lions (an echo of *The Bronze Horseman*). Once again, the liminal zone of dusk ('закатный час') is introduced; and again, in a further echo of Pushkin's poem 'On the hills of Georgia ...', darkness is paradoxically connected to light or illumination (in Pushkin, 'ночная мгла' ['nocturnal darkness'] v. 'светла' ['luminous'], in Ivanov, 'закатный час' ['hour of sunset'] vs 'сиянье' ['luminescence']).[29] The potential collision between the 'Город пышный' ('city of splendour')[30] and the human is resolved by the transformation of both into art: as Ivanov asserts in maximally simple terms, 'Вот наша жизнь прошла, / А это не пройдет' ('Thus has our life passed, / But this will never fade'), the contrast maximized by the repetition of the same Russian verb ('пройти' ['to pass, go past']) but transformed from perfective past to future perfective. This poem seems to me particularly significant for Ivanov's later period in that it also seems to effect a resolution between what is generally taken to be Ivanov's later philosophy, that is, a type of existentialist refusal of value or comprehension in life and/or art (here, in the phrase 'Ты не поняла' ['You did not understand']), and certain elements of Ivanov's earlier Acmeist outlook (specifically, the metaphor of stone as an index for art's enduring value, preeminently in the context of St Petersburg, and the motif of flowering which Nikolai Gumilev associated with the idea of 'Acme').[31]

Returning to *Disintegration of the Atom*, the question arises as to whether any such recuperative reading is possible here in the face of what might appear to be an unrelentingly negative or even nihilistic message. I believe that such a reading is possible and necessary, and that the figure of Pushkin in once more central to it. In *Disintegration of the Atom*, there is a persistent association between the work's deep-rooted nihilism and the 'Akakiis' of Russian culture, but this 'myth of the clerk in his garret' ('чердачный канцелярский миф') of the plebeian philistine nevertheless stands opposed by counter-myth of 'Pushkinian lucidity' (just as, earlier, the language of Pushkin's poetry is seen to resist the destructiveness of the *zaum* of Kruchenykh):

> Закат давно погас. Служба давно кончилась. На чердаке у Обухова моста булькает теплое пиво, клубится табачный дым. «Он был титулярный советник, она генеральская дочь»[32] - вкрадчиво, нежно, бархатно вздыхает гитара. Расцветает чердачный канцелярский миф — миф самозащита и противовес ледяному мифу пушкинской ясности. Миф серная кислота, тайная мечта — который эту ясность обезобразит, разъест, растлит.[33]

(The sunset has long since died away. His work is long since finished. In a garret by the Obukhov bridge warm beer gurgles, tobacco smoke swirls. 'He was a Titular Counsellor, and she a general's daughter' - sigh the ingratiating, tender, velvety notes of a guitar. Here flowers the myth of the clerk in his garrett - a myth which serves as self-defence and as a counter-weight to the myth of Pushkinian lucidity. This myth is sulphuric acid, a secret dream - which will disfigure, will corrode, will corrupt this lucidity.)

It should be pointed out that the 'destructiveness' of the Akakii-type of Russian utopian dreamer here stands for the destructiveness, for Ivanov, of the 1917 October Revolution. In this context, Pushkin and his legacy stand as a superior reality partly beyond the grasp of Ivanov's narrator (hence his inability to quote Pushkin correctly), but glimpsed dimly as a possible way out of the auto-destructive and sterile world of 'Akakii'. This sense of a superior vision reinscribed at the end point of a process of disintegretion and collapse is certainly present, for example, in the culmination of the 'spiral' passage near the end of *Disintegration of the Atom*, in the teleological orientation of the whole passage (and possibly the entire text) towards the ultimate vision of 'твое лицо' ('your face').

If we turn to the title of Ivanov's work itself, in the gulf between the 'disintegration' or fissuring of alienated contemporary man and the 'Stand beautiful ... and remain' of Pushkin's legacy, we see encapsulated the fundamental dilemma of Ivanov in the émigré period. Yet the legacy of Pushkin, in the obsessively returning lines from 'On the hills of Georgia ...', hints also, for Ivanov, at a possible way out of the dilemma. The modern 'human condition' may be problematic and uncomfortable (and Akakii-like romantic self-delusion easier and more reassuring), but it must be confronted. In this sense Pushkin should no longer be seen as a refuge for those seeking to escape into the realms of aesthetic pleasure, but rather (and this is surely the key to Ivanov's meditations on Pushkin) as providing a model ('Pushkinian *lucidity*') for precisely such an unyielding confrontation of the 'modern' human condition. Returning to the Pushkin poem which provides the anchor for this vision in *Disintegration of the Atom*, we find that Ivanov's message is actually pre-inscribed in Pushkin's text: in the face of darkness, we are presented with a paradoxical vision of hope in which 'sadness is luminous' and where the poet 'cannot *not* love'. Even in the face of universal negation, life, and hope, must continue.

NOTES

1. Alexandr Pushkin, *Polnoe sobranie sochinenii v desiati tomakh*, III, Izdatel'stvo akademii nauk SSSR, Moscow, 1963, p. 114. For an earlier version of the poem see ibid., p. 462.
2. See D. Blagoi, *Tvorcheskii put' Pushkina*, Sovietskii pisatel', Moscow, 1967, p. 463.
3. This is particularly emphasized in the earlier redaction of the text: see the opening lines, 'Все тихо - на Кавказ идет ночная мгла, / Восходят звезды надо мною -' ('All is quiet - on to the Caucasus comes nocturnal darkness, / The stars are rising above me'): see *Polnoe sobranie sochinenii v desiati tomakh*, III, p. 462.
4. It is important to note that there seems to be a persistent association for Pushkin between the adjective *svetlyi* ('light' or 'bright') and the river Aragva: see Pushkin's *Journey to Arzrum* (my emphasis):

   The sudden passage from the fearsome Caucasus to comely Georgia is delightful. The air of the South suddenly begins to waft over the traveller. From the height of Gutgora one sees the Kashaurskaia valley open up, with its inhabited crags, with its *bright Aragva* (*svetloi Aragvoi*), twisting and turning like a silver ribbon ...

   Polnoe sobranie sochinenii v desiati tomakh, VI, Moscow, 1964, pp. 655-6.
5. Ivanov, *Peterburgskie zimy*, La Source, Paris, 1928. The poem is mentioned in a passage in chapter 12 of Ivanov's memoir, where he describes the Acmeist poet Vladimir Narbut. The poem's romantic aura is debunked by Narbut thus:

   On the hills of Georgia nocturnal darkness lies,
   Before me the Aragva roars ...

   I can't even think calmly about these verses, straight away my heart starts thumping. When I was in the Caucasus, I made a special trip to take a look at this Aragva. It's a grotty, muddy little stream, by the way ... (Ivanov, *Sobranie sochinenii v trekh tomakh*, III, 'Soglasie', Moscow, 1994, p. 114).

   It is worth noting that here Ivanov correctly quotes Pushkin, which supports my contention above that the misquotation of these lines in *Disintegration of the Atom* is deliberate.
6. For the application of this term to Pushkin see several of the contributions in Boris Gasparov, Robert P. Hughes, Irina Paperno, eds, *Cultural Mythologies of Russian Modernism. From the Golden Age to the Silver Age*, University of California Press, Berkeley, 1992.
7. For examples of poems by Ivanov which invoke Pushkin, see the following (page references are to volume I of Ivanov, *Sobranie sochinenii v trekh tomakh*, 'Soglasie', Moscow, 1994): 'Through the wide windows a rural scene ...', ('V shirokikh oknakh sel'skii vid ...', p. 107); 'Aleksandr Sergeevich, I miss you ...', ('Aleksandr Sergeevich, ia o vas skuchaiu ...', p. 553). For further 'quotation' of Pushkin's poem 'Na kholmakh Gruzii ...' see, for example, 'A half-tone of rowan-berry and raspberry ...' ('Polutona riabiny i maliny ...', p. 378).
8. For this poem see Ivanov, *Sobranie sochinenii*, I, p. 320 (612-13); see also Irina Agushi, 'The Poetry of Georgij Ivanov', *Harvard Slavic Studies*, V, 1970, pp. 145-8, who tends to categorize such instances as 'semantic antithesis' rather than strict oxymoron.
9. For some brief but illuminating comments on Ivanov's use of symmetrical structures, see Iu. I. Levin, 'Simmetriia i otkloneniia ot nee v postroenii liricheskogo stikhotvoreniia', in Eric de Haard, Thomas Langerak, Willem G. Weststeijn, eds, *Semantic Analysis of Literary Texts: To Honour Jan van der Eng on the Occasion of his 65 [th] Birthday*, Elsevier, Amsterdam, 1990, pp. 377-83.
10. I give 'voliu' here literally as 'freedom', while earlier translating the phrase 'otpustili na voliu' as 'set free', since its literal meaning, 'released into freedom', cannot really be rendered idiomatically into English.

The Pushkin Contexts of *Disintegration of the Atom* 133

11. Compare Ivanov's poem with Pushkin's 1823 lyric, 'A Little Bird' ('Ptichka'), where Pushkin uses both the common Russian words for 'freedom', 'volia' and 'svoboda', and in which the idea of exile ('v chuzhbine') is central. In particular, Ivanov seems to echo line 3 of Pushkin's poem ('Na voliu ptichku vypuskaiu' ['I set a little bird free']) in his line 'Tochno menia otpustili na voliu' ('As if I had been set free'), though with an interesting twist: while Pushkin's '*vy*puskaiu' evokes the phrase 'vypustit' iz tiur'my', 'to release from prison', Ivanov's '*ot*pustili' (related to 'otpusk', 'leave') suggests only temporary release. I am grateful to J. Douglas Clayton for indicating the possible parallel between Ivanov's poem and Pushkin's.

12. Russian text in Ivanov, *Sobranie sochinenii*, II, p. 15. Note the 'Dostoevskian' detail of the young girl made drunk and taken advantage of, reminiscent of the scene in *Crime and Punishment*, part I, chapter four, where Raskolnikov confronts a 'gentleman' who has been following an inebriated girl with dubious intentions, and shouts at him 'Svidrigailov'. 'Dostoevskian' colouring of scenes dealing with sexuality is widespread in *Disintegration of the Atom*.

13. See for example, pp. 10-11 in Ivanov, *Sobranie sochinenii*, II, especially the following: 'an immense spiritual life grows up and is consumed in the atom, in a man who is outwardly in no way extraordinary, but is chosen, exceptional, unique'.

14. The 'rat' image is an echo of a desription earlier in *Disintegration of the Atom* of a waste bucket in which, amongst other detritus, a dead rat floats (see Ivanov, *Sobranie sochinenii*, II, p. 11).

15. Ivanov, *Sobranie sochinenii*, II, p. 27: 'Sunsets, thousands of sunsets. Over Russia, over America, over the future, over past centuries. The wounded Pushkin leans on his elbow in the snow and onto his face streams the red sunset ...'; and ibid., p. 31: 'D'Anthès will kill Pushkin and then Ivan Sergeevich Turgenev will most politely shake his hand and it will be fine, his hand won't shrivel up ...'.

16. Vladislav Khodasevich, *Sobranie sochinenii*, II, 'Soglasie', Moscow, 1996, p. 418. The 'tastelessness' of Ivanov's misquotation of Pushkin is chiefly phonetic: 'legla mgla' ('darkness lay') sounds ugly, as it repeats the same sound cluster (Khodasevich exaggerates this effect by placing the two words side by side, which is in effect a distortion of Ivanov's distortion). For this reason I have kept the Russian original in my translation.

17. Khodasevich, *Sobranie sochinenii*, II, pp. 77-85. Khodasevich gave this speech at an evening in honour of Pushkin organized by the Petrograd 'Dom literatorov' on 14 February, 1921.

18. See Osip Mandelshtam, *Sobranie sochinenii v trekh tomakh*, I, Inter-Language Literary Associates, Washington, D. C., 1967, pp. 85-6.

19. See also Vadim Kreid, *Peterburgskii period Georgiia Ivanova*, Hermitage, Tenafly, N. J., 1989, where it is demonstrated that the image of 'zakat' is of equally central importance in Ivanov's pre-exile poetry.

20. Note the association between this text and the dying Pushkin - doubly suggestive of darkness having irrevocably fallen - in *Disintegration of the Atom* (Ivanov, *Sobranie sochinenii*, II, p. 27): 'Perhaps his (that is, the old man's) deaf-mute soul is struggling to blurt out in its own fashion - "On the hills of Georgia ...". Sunsets, thousands of sunsets. Over Russia, over America, over the future, over past centuries. The wounded Pushkin leans on his elbow in the snow and onto his face streams the red sunset ...' Note also that this description reproduces in words the famous picture of the dying Pushkin by Naumov; compare Marina Tsvetaeva's explicit treatment of Naumov's painting in her *Moi Pushkin*: - on this see especially Alexandra Smith, *The Song of the Mocking Bird: Pushkin in the Work of Marina Tsvetaeva*, Peter Lang, Berne, 1994, pp. 108-17.

21. First published in Aleksei Kruchenykh, *Pomada*, Moscow, 1913. As the poem has no denotative meaning but rather consists of invented words belonging to 'the poet's own language' (see Kruchenykh's prefatory comments to this poem and two others which

accompany it in *Pomada*), I have simply transliterated the Cyrillic text of Kruchenykh's poem here.
22. Ivanov, *Sobranie sochinenii*, II, p. 18.
23. Loc. cit.
24. Loc. cit.
25. Loc. cit. One might note in passing that, despite dismissing Khruchenykh's text as something resembling obscene graffiti, Ivanov must have been aware of the polemical context surrounding Kruchenykh's poem when it first appeared in print, and particularly that it was explicitly compared to Pushkin in one of the key Futurist manifestoes, 'Slovo kak takovoe': 'incidentally in this five-line verse there is more that is national and Russian than in the entire poetry of Pushkin' - in Vladimir Markov, ed., *Manifesty i programmy russkikh futuristov*, Fink, Munich, 1967, p. 55.
26. Ivanov, *Sobranie sochinenii*, II, p. 30.
27. On this subject see Roman Jakobson, *Pushkin and his Sculptural Myth*, Mouton, The Hague, 1975.
28. Ivanov, *Sobranie sochinenii*, I, p. 438.
29. Note the extremely widespread occurrence of this oxymoronic image in Ivanov's poetry: see, for example, the poem of 1926, 'Siiaet noch', i parus golubeet...' ('The shining night, and pale-blue sail...'), in Ivanov, *Sobranie sochinenii*, I, p. 508 (626).
30. See Pushkin's poem 'Gorod pyshnyi, gorod bednyi ...' of 1828, in Pushkin, *Polnoe sobranie sochinenii v desiati tomakh*, III, p. 79.
31. See Ivanov, *Sobranie sochinenii*, I, for frequent references to what is claimed to be Ivanov's later 'rejection' of Acmeist value in the editors' commentary on the poems, for example, p. 612 (notes to the poem 'Chto-to sbudetsia, chto-to ne sbudetsia ...' ['Something will be, or something will not be ...']), or p. 620 (notes to the poem 'Ia liubliu beznadezhnyi pokoi ...' ['I love the hopeless peace ...']), etc. For Gumilev's formulation of the meaning of 'Acme', see 'Nasledie simvolizma i akmeizm', in *Apollon*, I, 1913, pp. 42-5.
32. The first line of a poem by P. I. Veinberg, which in the latter part of the nineteenth century became popular in a musical setting (see Ivanov, *Sobranie sochinenii*, II, p. 446). The rank of 'Titular Counsellor' was the rank held by Gogol's Akakii Akakievich in the story *The Overcoat*; the ninth rank in the 'table of ranks' created by Peter the Great, it was the highest grade which did not confer hereditary noble status on its holder (hence the 'eternal Titular Counsellor', destined never to rise to true noble status).
33. Ivanov, *Sobranie Sochinenii*, II, p. 28.

Dovlatov's *Sanctuary* and Pushkin

by

JEKATERINA YOUNG

Sergei Dovlatov's[1] story *The Sanctuary* (*Заповедник*) is loosely based upon the author's own experiences during a period spent working in the 'Pushkin Hills' museum at Mikhailovskoe. It was not unusual for members of the Moscow and Leningrad intelligentsia to work as guides at the museum, and when Dovlatov's life in Estonia became unbearable and he could neither find employment in Leningrad nor persuade publishers there to accept his work, he took a job in Mikhailovskoe as a way of earning a living. It is clear from a letter to Liudmila Shtern that he actually worked there in the mid-1970s;[2] the action of the story, however, is attributed to a slightly later time, no earlier than 1978, since mention is made Likhonosov's novel *When Shall We Meet?* (*Когда же мы встретимся?*) which was published in that year. Dovlatov wrote the story in 1982, and it was published in America in 1983.

The museum is known as 'Пушкинский заповедник' ('The Pushkin Sanctuary'), a name which has connotations of 'nature reserve', or 'bird sanctuary', a place for the preservation of rare and exotic species, but which also has reverberations akin to the modern English 'theme park'. It is a kind of Pushkinland. That is to say, Dovlatov presents it not merely as a museum, a legitimate preservation in the present of something valuable from the past, but as a fictionalized past, a wilfully manipulated version of the past designed to fulfil a specific function in the present.

Paul Debreczeny has discussed in his recent book, *Social Functions of Literature. Alexander Pushkin and Russian Culture*, how the cult of Pushkin has evolved through the last two centuries: 'There have been other poets in history whose cult was engendered as much by personal myth as by poetic works. What makes Pushkin unique is an unprecedented reinforcement of literary achievement by social circumstance and the need for a national myth.'[3] Through the centuries there were different reasons for Pushkin's elevation to sainthood; one of the compelling reasons for this in post-revolutionary Russia, when the myth of Lenin was a more logical choice, is explained by Debreczeny:

> If the official version of Lenin's personality presented to the public for adoration lacked the complexities of a human being, Pushkin's image was not flattened out and thus provided an opportunity for vicarious enjoyment of vivid images in the midst of grey Soviet reality. Needless to say, his colourful literary texts continually reinforced the text of his life.[4]

It also needs to be added that the reading and studying of Pushkin mainly in hagiographic terms was encouraged by the Soviet authorities with a particular aim in mind. He was used to manipulate society, to deflect interest from real issues, but at the same time to allow some safe topics for public discussion. No diversion from ready-made clichés about Pushkin was possible. This is one aspect of Dovlatov's story *The Sanctuary*.

Dovlatov was not alone at this time in re-evaluating his attitude to Pushkin. From the late 1960s onwards the Soviet intelligentsia began to approach Pushkin with light-hearted irreverence (Andrei Siniavskii's *Strolls with Pushkin* [*Прогулки с Пушкиным*] written around the mid-seventies is perhaps the most famous example), and to establish distance from official writing on Pushkin. This state of affairs is illustrated in the story, when the narrator is examined on Pushkin and tries to express his own opinion of the poet's achievement, saying that Pushkin's writing goes beyond Russian tradition, that Pushkin is not such a typical Russian writer, and concluding that 'Pushkin is our belated Renaissance'.[5] The reaction to such a non-standard answer (however banal it may seem) is complete bafflement and hostility: 'What has Goethe to do with it? Not to mention the Renaissance!' (SD: 1993, I, 340). Dovlatov shows that this culture of false enlightenment has become the dominant culture of the Sanctuary/Soviet Union.

Siniavskii's *Strolls with Pushkin* provoked outrage and fierce polemics in the émigré press and when it eventually reached the Soviet Union during perestroika. Rodnianskaia, in *The Liberated Captive ...* (*Освобожденный пленник*...), points out that the polemics about Pushkin go back a long way and cites an earlier exchange between Rozanov and Solovev. What is the key to Tertz-Siniavskii's book? Why do writers, Dovlatov included, in the seventies turn to a re-evaluation of Pushkin? Rodnianskaia convincingly shows how Pushkin was manipulated to serve the totalitarian state. Just as Schiller in Nazi Germany was proclaimed 'Hitler's comrade in arms', so Stalin exploited Pushkin particularly in the ambitious 1937 celebrations of the centenary of the poet's death. However, what Siniavskii and others saw in Pushkin was freedom, and they rebelled against this political usurpation of a writer's personality: 'Broadly speaking the point is freedom, an island of freedom, which the author of the book seeks to secure amidst the ocean of miscellaneous restrictions. [...] I will say straightaway - it is the freedom of art.'[6] This island of freedom is also important for Dovlatov and his contemporaries. As Siniavskii wrote in response to the hostile émigré community: '... I wrote *Strolls with Pushkin*, ... as a continuation of my concluding speech at the trial - in defence of free art.'[7]

Writing about Bitov's *Pushkin House* (*Пушкинский дом*, 1978), Susanne Fusso describes the position of the Soviet postmodernist writer, as 'alienated from the history of culture, which has been preserved and petrified by hegemonic forces. Culture is a museum, not a living presence'.[8] This is exactly the situation that Dovlatov depicts in Pushkinland.

The sanctuary is a microcosm of Soviet reality (as, indeed, could be said of Dovlatov's earlier work, *The Zone* (Зона). At the forefront of the author's attention is the double life of the sanctuary (the Soviet Union) which reveals the prevalent underlying hypocrisy. Pushkin is the great national treasure. He is in the hands of the authorities and becomes an instrument of propaganda. Crowds of tourists flock to this national park. Some come here because they have received travel vouchers from the trade union, some because they are compelled to take part in cultural and educational programmes. Some come here seeking adventure: 'Tatusia, can you hear? Stay at home ... The weather is lousy ... But the main thing is - there aren't any fellers there at all ... Hello! Can you hear? Lots of girls come away without getting a proper holiday'(SD: 1993, I, 405), records the narrator of *The Sanctuary*. On the whole the tourists (the term preferred by the staff of the Sanctuary is 'pilgrims') are indifferent to poetry and if instead of Pushkin a few lines of Esenin are read to them, nobody even notices. 'Поэт то и дело обращался к няне в стихах. Всем известны такие, например, задушевные строки ... [...] Ты еще жива, моя старушка, / Жив и я, привет тебе, привет! / Пусть струится над твоей избушкой ... ' (SD: 1993, I, 352) ('The poet constantly addressed his nanny in his poetry. Everyone is familiar with such heart-warming lines as: 'Are you still alive, old woman? / So am I. I send my love. / May there flow over your little house ...')[9] For most tourists who come the mere fact that they are there is important, because they know that Pushkin is the symbol of culture. However, the visitors' level of ignorance about Pushkin is illustrated in Dovlatov's letter to Liudmila Shtern:[10] 'The tourists ask weird questions: 1. Was Anna Karenina Esenin's mistress? 2. Who was Boris Godunov? 3. Why did Pushkin and Lermontov fight a duel?'

This ignorance on the part of the tourists is matched by the wilful falsity of much of the information purveyed. When the narrator indicates that he wants to become a guide in the Sanctuary he is told that he needs to train: 'Study the instructions. In Pushkin's life there is so much that is still not researched. One or two things have changed since last year ... "In Pushkin's life"? - I exclaimed' (SD: 1993, I, 332). There is no portrait of Pushkin's ancestors available, so a substitute is found: a white, sunburned (because he fought in Asia) general:

> Well, what's the difference, Hannibal or Zakomelskii ... The tourists want to see Hannibal. That's what they pay the money for. They don't give a toss for Zakomelskii?! So, our director put Hannibal up ... To be precise, he put Zakomelskii up to stand for Hannibal. (SD: 1993, I, 332)

Dovlatov is not concerned to contrast with this falsehood and ignorance some notional 'truth' about Pushkin. Nevertheless, it can be seen that in *The Sanctuary* he is pursuing the process of recuperating the cultural legacy of the Pushkin period in his own way. This chapter will argue that Dovlatov's account of his semi-fictitious narrator's experience in Pushkinland is at the same time an exploration of parallels between the literary scene in Pushkin's time and his own, raising questions of style and narration, and of parallels in the relationship between the artist and the state in those two periods.

The Sanctuary is framed by the journeys of the narrator (called Boris Alikhanov, a name Dovlatov used for the narrator of *The Zone*) from Leningrad to Pushkinskie Gory at the beginning, and back again at the end, some two or three months later. Arrival and departure are marked by bouts of heavy drinking. On his journey to the Sanctuary, the narrator hints at his inebriated (post-binge) state: 'My hands were trembling terribly.' (SD: 1993, I, 327) 'I paused, wondering whether to have another drink' (SD: 193, I, 329). At the end of the story the narrator is alone in his Leningrad flat: 'On the eleventh day hallucinations began' (SD: 1993, I, 414). The climax of the story is the visit by the narrator's wife to the Sanctuary, which is their last meeting before her impending emigration with their child. Their dialogue on this occasion picks up themes from earlier conversations between them that have been given in flashback.

The story's closed structure emphasizes the sense of a dead-end experienced by the narrator, which is intimated on the journey out: 'I tried to dispel the feeling of catastrophe and dead-end' (SD: 1993, I, 335) and fully realized at the end, as he returns to his empty Leningrad flat. His wife and child are far away, he is not sure he will ever see them again, he has no money, has run out of alcohol and finds it difficult to move his limbs (because he is too drunk); he is also on the verge of a psychological breakdown. His flat is under siege by the KGB and the militia. There is a last telephone conversation with his wife, who is calling from Austria. There is no escape: 'I needed to get to sleep in an empty, stifling room ...' (SD: 1993, I, 415) The narrator's last 'optimistic mirage' is the sentence that emerges from his hallucinations: 'Only death is irreparable!' (SD: 1993, I, 415).

Apart from these arrivals and departures there is little in *The Sanctuary* that can be called action. The story is essentially plotless, since, as Lotman argues, the movement of the protagonist within defined boundaries cannot be seen as an event or action.[11] The story's focus of interest lies in the development, largely through dialogue, of various themes, all of which are concerned, in one way or another, with literature. Foremost among these is the exploitation of Pushkin's biography, as revealed in conversations with various guides and administrators. The problem of literary recognition and the difficulty of being published, besides being the primary motivation of the journey, is the subject of discussions between the narrator and his wife, as well as with officers of the KGB. His situation is contrasted with that of Stasik Potoskii, who, having read a dozen contemporary books, decided to become a writer. His trivial, anodyne stories, produced at the rate of one a day, are published with success. 'The most vivid features of his stories were the stylistic flaws and the misprints,' writes Dovlatov. Of his approach to writing, Potoskii says: ' ... I am a writer like Chekhov, sod it. Chekhov was quite right. Stories can be written about anything' (SD: 1993, I, 357).[12]

Dovlatov introduces into the text a direct polemic with Viktor Likhonosov, as a representative of the *derevenshchiki* (village prose writers). The main trends and characteristics of village prose have been extensively studied. Deming Brown describes the main preoccupation of the genre thus:

> Village literature is oriented on peasant families - their antecedents and traditions, their formation and ferment, and often their alienation and break-up. Village writers like to dwell on memories of rural childhood and youth - sometimes idyllically happy, sometimes confused, deprived, and impoverished. The contrast, and frequently the conflict, of generations is emphasised. Particular prominence is given to elderly persons, especially women, who are shown to embody the best elements of peasant culture and serve as the last repositories of ancient Russian spiritual values.
>
> The village writers lovingly describe their own birthplaces and the fields, forests, meadows, rivers, lakes, and living creatures around them. Their characters speak in local dialects; the characters' folk beliefs and their arts and crafts display regional peculiarities. In paying such close attention to ethnic detail, writers are not only attempting to preserve a cultural heritage but also pleading against the obliteration of the culture itself.[13]

Viktor Likhonosov describes in his novels the contradictions between town and country, and the description of bygone life in the village is most nostalgic. In his comments on village prose, Dovlatov's narrator warns against false patriotism, anticipating, perhaps, the movement's later swing to the right-wing chauvinism: 'I think that the love of birch trees triumphs at the expense of love for human beings. It develops as a substitute for patriotism ...' (SD: 1993, I, 331).

The narrator's response to Likhonosov's work subtly indicates a parallel between the official 'culture-as-museum', embodied in Pushkinland, and the village prose writers' attitude to the preservation of the past:[14]

> Of course, he is a good writer. Talented, vivid, supple. He's marvellous at reproducing live speech. (Tolstoi would have loved to hear such a compliment!) And all the same, at bottom - a hopeless, miserable feeling that you can't shake it off. A fleshless, tedious theme: 'Where are you, Russia?! Where has everything disappeared?! Where are the songs, the embroidered towels, the head-dresses? Where is the

> hospitality, the daring and the grand scale? Where are the samovars, the icons, the feats of heroism and the Holy fools? Where are the ordinary horses for God's sake?! Where is the chaste bashfulness of feelings?! They rack their brains over it: Where are you Russia? Where did you disappear? Who disfigured you?! Who! It's obvious who! There is no need to rack your brain over it ... ' (SD: 1993, I, 362).

Dovlatov's description of the village of Sosnovo provides a sharp contrast to the loving descriptions found in village prose:

> I walked through the village hoping to meet someone. The grey unpainted houses looked miserable. The stakes of the ramshackle fences were crowned with earthenware pots. Chicks were fussing around in pens covered with sheets of plastic. Chickens strutted out with a nervy, cartoon-like step. Squat, shaggy-haired dogs were yapping loudly (SD: 1993, I, 342).

Dovlatov takes an ironic view of the use of 'local dialects' by the inhabitants of Sosnovo. This is how he characterizes the speech of Mikhail Ivanych[15] from whom the narrator rents a room in the village: 'His speech was akin to classical music, abstract painting or the singing of a goldfinch. Emotion clearly took precedence over meaning. ... Misha's utterances reminded one of the sound patterning of the Remizov school,' (SD: 1993, I, 363).

Mikhail Ivanych is, according to Dovlatov, a typical representative of the village folk and the narrator has only seen him sober twice during the whole summer. His character is a combination of cruelty and unexpected consideration, and is implicitly compared with the blacksmith Arkhip in Pushkin's *Dubrovskii*. Dovlatov introduces *Dubrovskii*[16] into the story through an anecdote about the informer, Lenia Gurianov's student days. In *Dubrovskii* Arkhip is watching a burning house in which people are trapped:

> In a moment the flames engulfed the whole house. Red smoke swirled above the roof. The windows cracked and shattered, burning beams began to fall and plaintive wailing and cries could be heard: 'We're burning, help us, help us.'
> 'Not likely,' said Arkhip who was watching the blaze with a malicious smile.[17]

However, when Arkhip notices a cat on the roof of the burning house, he risks his own life to save it: '"What are you laughing at, you little devils," the blacksmith said to them angrily. "You don't fear God: God's creature is perishing, and you're pleased about it, you little fools," and placing a ladder against the burning roof, he clambered after the cat'.[18]

As with Arkhip, it is difficult to understand Mikhail Ivanych's mentality. Mikhail has not himself burned anybody alive, but approves of Germans killing Jews and Gypsies. These are not the humane and ethical values that village writers were so keen to promote, but for Pushkin and Dovlatov it showed the narrow line dividing good and evil in the human personality.

> I never did understand what sort of a person he was. On the surface he was ridiculous, kind, muddle-headed. Once he hanged two cats on the rowan-tree. He made the noose out of fishing line.
> 'They multiply everywhere,' he said, 'the bastards ...'
> Once I inadvertently bolted the door from inside and he sat on the porch the whole night, not wanting to wake me ... (SD: 1993, I, 363).

The ethical ambiguity which Dovlatov show in Mikhail Ivanych is a topic that runs through some other stories, notably *The Zone*. What fascinated Dovlatov in Pushkin was Pushkin's ability to rise above moral judgements, above the antagonism of good and evil: 'Подобно луне, которая освещает дорогу и хищнику и жертве' ('Like the moon which lights the way to predator and victim alike', SD: 1993, I, 361). He echoes the sentence in *The Captain's Daughter* that struck him by its apparent indifference: 'Ночь была тихая и морозная. Месяц и звезды ярко сияли, освещая площадь и виселицу.' ('The night was quiet and cold. The moon and the stars shone brightly, lighting the square and the gallows').[19]

Igor Sukhikh considers that in *The Sanctuary* Dovlatov is presenting a portrait of an unsuccessful contemporary writer, shown in contrast with Pushkin: 'He shows a portrait of an unsuccessful writer contrasted with Pushkin. With Pushkin from the Pushkin Sanctuary and his attendants (who are also partly portraits)'.[20] I would argue that it is not so much a question of using Pushkin as a background, but rather of Dovlatov drawing a comparison of the restrictions under which Russian writers lived in the past and the present. Informers, denunciation and betrayal have long held a fascination for Russian writers not only in the Soviet period. Pushkin's works contain references to an earlier antecedent, the novelist, critic and informer of the Third Department, Faddei Bulgarin, with whom he came into conflict. Bulgarin was a prolific and successful writer, whose novel *Ivan Vyzhigin* was a sell-out, while Pushkin's work was not a commercial success. Bulgarin was also a publisher, editor of *The Northern Bee*, in which capacity he manipulated the Third Department and used it to destroy competition and other talented writers.

The theme of censorship and surveillance is introduced by Dovlatov not only as a contemporary feature, but also as a parallel with Pushkin's times. It gives him the opportunity to look at the eternal Russian question of the relationship of the intelligentsia and the Establishment from a different historical angle. The theme of creativity and conflict with the State runs through the whole story and it is interesting to follow its escalation, with the State's inevitable victory.

The first meeting with the informer in the story is at the beginning, when the narrator arrives in the Sanctuary:

> 'Everything here lives and breathes Pushkin,' said Galia, 'literally every branch, every blade of grass. You keep expecting to seen him coming round the corner ... Top-hat, cloak, the familiar profile ...' But round the corner came Lenia Gurianov, the police informer from university days (SD: 1993, I, 333).

This omnipresence of the informer mirrors the omnipresence of Faddei Bulgarin in Pushkin's life.[21] The narrator in *The Sanctuary* is also under constant police surveillance (of course Pushkin was under surveillance in Mikhailovskoe). 'I knew you were coming' (SD: 1993, I, 334), the university informer Gurianov greets him; and the local KGB man at an informal gathering volunteers information about the narrator: 'The security agent concentrated his attention on the braised duck. Then he raised his head and briefly spoke his mind: "There is evidence that he is coming to Pushkinskie Gory ..."' (SD: 1993, I, 334).

Eventually, when at the end of the story the narrator's wife and daughter receive their visa to emigrate, it is clear that the local KGB man Beliaev has been informed about it first, but that he also knows about the narrator's every step. It is not surprising that the narrator has excuses ready: 'Rumours were reaching us about publications in the West. I tried not to think about it. After all, it does not concern me what goes on in the other world. That's just what I'll say if I am questioned' (SD: 1993, I, 365).

The reaction of the bleached blonde Galia to the departure of Alikhanov's wife is typical. The narrator wants to borrow some money to return to Leningrad and say farewell to his family, but does not want to tell her. However, she knows already: 'I know anyway. Your wife has betrayed our Motherland' (SD: 1993, I, 404) says Galia.

The narrator is summoned to the KGB whose duty (like the Third Department's in the nineteenth century) it is to educate citizens who go astray. At the KGB offices the narrator again bumps into Gurianov:

> 'Oh, hello ... Beliaev is expecting you ...' ... He wanted to show that everything was all right. As if we had bumped into each other in the doctor's surgery and not in the Gestapo headquarters.
> I asked him: 'Is he your superior?'
> 'Who?'
> 'Beliaev. Or is he your subordinate?'
> 'Don't make fun', said Gurianov.
> His voice acquired a strict managerial tone.

'And remember. The KGB is currently the most progressive organization. It's the only real force in the state. And, by the way, the most humane. If only you knew those people! ...' (SD: 1993, I, 406).

The 'humaneness' of the KGB consisted in the fact that in the late seventies they did not on the whole imprison writers simply for their writing, particularly the ones who had publications abroad, but 'humanely' hounded them out of the country. Only a few years before the events in the story Solzhenitsyn was similarly 'humanely' transported abroad. The KGB officer Beliaev who significantly now has a portrait of Makarenko above his desk rather than Dzerzhinskii, tries to educate and influence the narrator.[22] The essence of suppression and its manifestations for Pushkin and Dovlatov were barely distinguishable.[23] However, these considerations were common in the lives of most Russian writers through the centuries.

Just before his death Dovlatov gave an interview to John Glad in which he discussed Russian traditions of story-telling. At their basis is Pushkin's refined and laconic prose,[24] but according to Dovlatov this tradition was interrupted and in spite of the brilliance of Tolstoi, Dostoevskii, Turgenev and many others, and the respect and admiration that their prose commands, the style of writing that they developed in the decades following Pushkin's death cannot be called laconic. However, such a tradition in Russia does continue to exist.

From time to time we can see sparks of Pushkinian refinement and Pushkinian laconism (laconism and refinement are almost synonyms, because one can do something faultlessly only by sweeping aside all that is redundant). In many ways, 'laconic' does not mean just using few words ... There were flashes of the Pushkin tradition in the person of Zoshchenko, who wrote very concisely and clearly.[25]

Among writers continuing the Pushkin tradition, apart from Zoshchenko, Dovlatov singles out Venedikt Erofeev, Fazil Iskander, and Georgii Vladimov in *Faithful Ruslan* (Верный Руслан). To write concise and laconic Russian, following the criteria established by Pushkin, was the task Dovlatov set himself in *The Sanctuary*.

Pushkin's dissatisfaction with state of contemporary prose is well known. He found it flowery, poeticized and affected. He demanded that prose should be clear, precise, laconic, but not without ideas: 'Precision and brevity are the two foremost merits of prose. It requires ideas and more ideas. Without ideas brilliant expressions serve no purpose'.[26] Pushkin's writings about the style of prose fiction are often perceived as symptomatic of his tendency towards realism. In equal measure though they can be seen as an attempt to create a specific poetics of prose fiction.

Obviously Pushkin was not alone in this preoccupation. Russian prose generally was tending towards the creation of a new poetics in this sense. But

Pushkin seems to have been more consistent than others. He sensed the necessity of establishing prose as an independent genre alongside poetry.

Lotman draws attention to the specific literary circumstances in which this process took place. In that period the dominance of poetry was overwhelming. This demonstrated itself among other things in the poeticization of prose. It was in opposition to this that the poetics of *Tales of Belkin* became so clearly defined: '... the aesthetic perception of prose becomes possible only against the background of poetic culture'.[27]

A parallel can be drawn here with the romanticism of the 1960s, the prevalence of poetry over prose, and the search for a new idiom. Apart from 'official' poets such as Evtushenko, Voznesenskii and Akhmadulina who filled sports stadiums with listeners to their poetry, the 1960s saw an incredible flourishing of guitar poetry and underground alternative poetry. In terms of prose, the most popular writers were Aksenov and Gladilin, who were the idols for the younger generations of writers.[28] There were, of course, other writers, such as Siniavskii and Solzhenitsyn. Nevertheless, it was the 'romantic' quality that appealed in Aksenov's and Gladilin's writing. So an atmosphere of romantic prose and the dominance of poetry were also typical of the sixties and seventies.

The description of scenery is considered by Lezhnev a touchstone of a writer's stylistic skill. He shows that Pushkin distances himself from the prevailing description tradition of Russian prose of the time. In Dovlatov's writing we will look in vain for verbose and extensive description of landscape or detailed description of surroundings and interiors. And if in Dostoevskii we just note the absence of nature descriptions, then Pushkin and, following in his footsteps, Dovlatov puts scenery in a subordinate position, reducing its function and extent. There is no need to quote the well-known passage with the terse, laconic description of the onset of the blizzard in *The Captain's Daughter*. The smells and sounds of a summer's day are outlined by Dovlatov in short, minimalist strokes:

> В детстве лето было озвучено гудками паровозов. Пригородные дачи ... Запах вокзальной гари и нагретого песка ... настольный теннис под ветками ... Тугой и звонкий стук мяча ...
> Выжженый солнцем пляж ... Жесткая осока ... Длинные трусы и следы резинок на икрах ... Набившийся в сандалии песок ...
>
> (Summer in childhood had a soundtrack of train whistles. Holiday houses ... The smell of soot in the station and warm sand ... table tennis under the trees ... the taut, resonant tapping of the ball.
> The sunscorched beach ... Spiky sedge-grass ... Long swimming trunks, and elastic marks on your calves ... Shoes full of sand ... : SD: 1993, I, 337).

Distinctive characteristics of Pushkin's style find a continuation in Dovlatov's work. 'He uses short, firm, swift phrases, and prefers to avoid subordinate clauses.'[29] Just such an alteration of short, energetic phrases creates the swift pace of Dovlatov's prose. This deliberate restraint became his hallmark. Dovlatov's conscious continuation of Pushkin's style is expressed in a number of stylistic devices. Lezhnev notes how the sparing uses of epithets in Pushkin's prose combines with a great wealth and variety of verbs. He observes that an over-abundance of epithets slows the phrase down and makes it static. The use of verbs, on the other hand, adds liveliness and intensity. The absolute limit Pushkin is aiming for is described as: '... it is a noun plus verb, the naked phrase without adornments'.[30] Dovlatov's own expressiveness is likewise achieved by a predominant emphasis on the verb over all other parts of speech. Like Pushkin he reduces his sentences to a bare expressive minimum, using noun plus verb constructions: 'Я пересек деревню, вернулся. Помедлил возле одного из домов. Хлопнула дверь.' ('I walked across the village, then returned. I lingered by one of the houses. A door banged': SD: 1993, I, 342). Or take the following description of the narrator's day: 'Дни мои *проходили* однообразно. Экскурсии *заканчивались* в два. Я *обедал* в Лукоморье и *шел* домой. Несколько раз Митрофан с Потоцким *звали* выпить. Я *отказывался*...' ('My days *passed* monotonously. The tours usually *finished* around two. I *had lunch* in the Lukomore and *went* home. Mitrofanov and Pototskii *asked* me out for a drink a few times. I *refused* ...': SD: 1993, I, 362: my emphasis). This stylistic feature even attracts an admiring comment from the narrator when it is observed in his semi-literate landlord: 'Misha only uttered nouns and verbs' (SD: 1993, I, 363).

It was illustrated by Lezhnev that 'In Pushkin's prose the metaphor is strictly subordinate and establishes a particular feature of the object.'[31] Dovlatov's metaphors and comparisons are similarly specific:

> Я направился в Сосново. Дорога тянулась к вершине холма, огибая унылое поле. По краям его бесформенными грудами темнели валуны. Слева зиял поросший кустами овраг. Спускаясь под гору, я увидел несколько изб, окруженных березами. В стороне бродили одноцветные коровы, плоские, как театральные декорации. Грязные овцы с декадентскими физиономиями вяло щипали траву. Над крышами летали галки.

> (I headed for Sosnovo. The road led to the summit of a hill, curving round a dejected field. Dark boulders lay in shapeless heaps around its edges. On the left gaped a ravine, overgrown with bushes. As I went down the hill I caught sight of a few huts surrounded by birch trees. Some monochrome cows, two-dimensional like stage scenery, were ambling round nearby. Dirty sheep with decadent physiognomies were

languidly nibbling the grass. Jackdaws were flying around over the roofs : SD: 1993, I, 342).

The means of depiction convey the essential qualities of the landscape: its static nature, the squalor of the village and the surrounding field. The sobriety of description is emphasized by 'prosaic' details 'Я увидел несколько изб' ('I caught sight of a few huts'); and almost ironic comparisons: 'плоские, как театральные декорации' ('two-dimensional like stage scenery').

The breakthrough Pushkin made in adapting the Russian language by combining its different layers into a single literary language is well documented. Beyond this, however, his particular achievement was in the creation of lively dialogues and the conversational intonation of much of his prose. Dovlatov's stories are similarly written in an everyday language. Their ordinariness is such that many perceive his writing as made up of direct quotations or verbatim renderings of actual conversations, rather than fiction. But just like Pushkin's dialogue, Dovlatov's has a descriptive function as well as a function in the plot. This, too, is brought out clearly in *The Sanctuary*. Pushkin made a point of using simple, 'democratic' language. He distanced himself from Karamzin's abstractness of expression and, more importantly, from Dal's stylized naturalism.[32] In this respect, too, Dovlatov differs from his contemporaries. The discussion of village prose, introduced into *The Sanctuary*, is a pointer to Dovlatov's rejection not only of its ideological stance, but also of the idea of the artificial conservation of language.[33]

Stylistic reorientation of such a kind requires a simultaneous re-assessment of the persona of the narrators. The moralizing tone that Pushkin ridiculed in Bulgarin has its parallel in the didacticism of much poetry and prose in the 1960s, such as the rhymed journalism of Evtushenko, or (at an entirely different level of seriousness) the much-quoted conclusion of Solzhenitsyn's *Matriona's House*, from which village prose is often thought to stem. Both Pushkin and Dovlatov avoid cautionary tales and allegories, never allowing their narrators to utter *obiter dicta* of a moral nature. The place of moralizing is taken by irony.

V.V. Vinogradov remarked that 'Pushkin's contemporaries were struck by the author's intention of making the image of the storyteller (*povestvovatel*) the constructive and stylistic centre of *The Tales of Belkin*'.[34] The text of *Belkin* is divided between several types of narrators. Pushkin went out of his way to prove the 'authenticity' of the narrators and place the image of the storyteller to the forefront of *Belkin*. 'Pushkin leaves the dividing line between author and characters flexible ... He does not become one of them and does not dissolve the characters in the author's voice.'[35] The consciousness of the 'publisher' constantly merges with Belkin's. The relationship of Belkin and the narrators is similar. The texts of the 'original' stories are oral: each story bears Belkin's inscription 'heard by me from such and such a person'.[36]

It could equally be said of the relationship between Dovlatov's semi-fictitious narrator, Alikhanov, and the biographical author that the boundary between the two is unstable. The narrator is not distanced from the author by the kind of complicated mechanism we have seen in the case of Belkin, and it is often impossible to tell for certain which voice is the bearer of a particular utterance. That is why a number of scholars have been inclined to read his prose as purely autobiographical. However, Pushkin in *Belkin* and Dovlatov in *The Sanctuary* share the crucial feature of ironically subverting a tradition of naive, romantic sentimentality.

Writing later in the USA, Dovlatov admitted that he would not have written such a work as *The Sanctuary* in emigration: 'In 1982 I wrote *The Sanctuary* and many people consider that this is the most tolerable of my books. Now I would not have written *The Sanctuary*. It is a typically Russian story and the chances of successful publication in English are minimal' (SD: 1993, I, 345).

In this chapter I have attempted to show how Dovlatov exploited the almost anecdotal episode of his sojourn in Pushkinland to develop a number of related topics, each of which displays a particular aspect of that 'typically Russian story', which he felt would not be appreciated in the West. On the level of the action, perhaps the most 'typically Russian', and in that sense untransportable, aspect of the story is the unchanging relationship between the writer and the state. Both Pushkin in the 1820s and Dovlatov in the 1970s were under police surveillance at Mikhailovskoe, suspected of seditious intentions and a wish to leave the country. The state organizations of both periods used other writers to assist in that ignoble task, creating divisions between writers and offering opportunities to the unscrupulous.

There is a continuity in Russian life and culture revealed here which is at variance with the relationship of past and present as embodied in the theme park itself, where, for ideological reasons, a distorted and fictionalized version of the past is casually retailed to a largely indifferent public. This is parallelled in the work of the *derevenshchiki*, the village writers who bewail the passing of a rural Russia, embellished in their imagination, which can be used as a stick with which to beat the present. I have suggested that behind the text itself stand also the typical literary modes of the 1960s, the flamboyant prose of Aksenov and the rhetorical poetry of Evtushenko. Alikhanov/Dovlatov, the narrator/author of *The Sanctuary,* stands aloof from all of these tendencies. His open polemic with the *derevenshchiki,* and his implicit rejection of the 1960s, have much in common with Pushkin's opposition to the archaicizing tendencies of his own time. In his quest for the narrative manner appropriate to his own purpose it is to Pushkin that Dovlatov turns, finding in Pushkin's prose both a style of writing and an approach to the persona of the narrator that serve him well.

Lotman wrote of the Pushkin period:

> The Pushkin period, as the initial period, was marked by considerable internal contradiction, which allows us to see in it both the origins of Tolstoi and the roots of Dostoevskii. At the same time there is no doubt that this period is not exhausted by those two tendencies, which came to occupy such a dominant role in Russian literature. The richness of this period [the Pushkin period] consists in the depiction of potential, hitherto unrealized models, which are perhaps still waiting to reveal themselves in the future.[37]

It seems to me that in writing *The Sanctuary* Dovlatov recuperated the Pushkin tradition for his own time in just such a way as to create one of those 'hitherto unrealized models' of which Lotman spoke.

NOTES

An earlier version of this chapter appeared in *Slavica*, XXX, Debrecen, 2000, pp. 133-51.

1. As early as 1962 Dovlatov wrote to his father saying that he had composed a jocular poem about Pushkin's duel with D'Anthès. In this poem Dovlatov 'defends' D'Anthès. See *Armeiskie pis'ma k ottsu* (*Army Letters to his Father*), published by Ksenia Mechik-Blank, *Zvezda*, V, 1998, p. 125.
2. In a letter to Liudmila Shtern dated 7 December 1976 he writes: 'It was wonderful in the Pushkin Hills.': in Ar'ev, A., ed., *Maloizvestnyi Dovlatov,* Limbus Press, St Peterburg, 1995, pp. 301-2.
3. Paul Debreczeny, *Social Functions of Literature. Alexander Pushkin and Russian Culture* , Stanford University Press, Stanford, California, 1997, p. 219.
4. Ibid., p. 244.
5. Sergei Dovlatov, *Sobranie prozy v trekh tomakh* , Limbus Press, St Petersburg, 1993, I, p. 340. (All further references to this work are inserted in the text, on the following model: SD: 1993, I, 340. All translations are by the author of this chapter.)
6. Irina Rodnianskaia, *Literaturnoe semiletie (1987-1994)* , Izdatel'stvo 'Knizhnyi sad', Moscow, 1995, pp. 264-72. 'Vzoshla zaria. Tropoi dalekoi / *Osvobozhdennyi plennik shel ...* ' ('Dawn broke. His distant path / *the liberated captive walked ...*'). This quotation from Pushkin's *The Caucasian Captive* Rodnianskaia considers the key to understanding Siniavskii's notion of freedom.
7. 'I wrote *Strolls with Pushkin* in conditions of extreme censorship. I wrote it in 1966-8, as a continuation of my final statement at the trial (only in a different style), - in defence of free creativity ... And in no way is it "criticism", and Solzhenitsyn has no reason to call me a "critic". It is a piece of lyrical prose by the writer Abram Tertz, in which I attempt in my own way to declare my love for Pushkin and express my gratitude to his shade, which saved me in the camps.' Andrei Siniavskii, 'Chtenie v serdtsakh, *Sintaksis*, XVII, 1987, pp. 191-206.
8. Susanne Fusso, 'The Romantic Tradition', in Malcolm V. Jones and Robin Feuer Miller, eds., *The Cambridge Companion to the Classic Russian Novel* , Cambridge University Press, Cambridge, 1998, p. 185.
9. Ibid., p. 352. This event is recorded as a true story by Evgenii Rein, *I Miss Dovlatov. Life of Moscow's Bohemia*, Limbus Press, St Petersburg, 1997. The guide has confused Pushkin's poem *Winter Evening* addressed to his old nurse, with Esenin's poem to his mother.
10. *Maloizvestnyi Dovlatov,* op. cit., p. 302.
11. Iu.M. Lotman, *Struktura khudozhestvennogo teksta* , Iskusstvo, Moscow, 1970, p. 288: 'Movement of the hero *within* the space allotted to him does not constitute an event.'
12. Dovlatov admitted that he himself wrote very slowly and the writer and translator Boris Rokhlin recalls that Dovlatov used to tell his stories a couple of times to an informal gathering of this friends first and only then put them down on paper. This is perhaps one of the reasons why Dovlatov's style strikes one as confiding and intimate: see Boris Rokhlin, special issue of *Zvezda*, III, 1994 dedicated to Sergei Dovlatov, pp. 132-3.
13. Deming Brown, *The Last Years of Soviet Russian Literature,* Cambridge University Press, Cambridge, 1993, p. 80.
14. Dovlatov was a member of the short lived literary association of Leningrad writers, '*Gorozhane*' ('City dwellers') as opposed to the village, whose founder was Boris Vakhtin. His *Odna absoliutno schastlivaia derevnia* (*One Absolutely Happy Village*), posthumously

published in the Soviet Union only during perestroika in 1986, is a gentle satire on life in the village and describes a peasant woman whose husband perished in the war.

15. It was in the village of Berezino (in the novel Sosnovo) that Dovlatov rented a room from the forester (he died recently), who is the prototype of Mikhail Ivanych in the story. According to Ar'iev, editor of *Zvezda* and Dovlatov's close friend, he was pleased with what Dovlatov wrote about him: 'He says nothing bad about me as a forester'.

16. Professor Bialyi is examining Gur'ianov:

    'Have you read *The Tales of Belkin*?'

    'I haven't got round to it, somehow,' Lenia replied. 'Do you recommend it?'

    'Yes,' Bialyi checked himself. 'I definitely recommend you read this book ...'

    Lenia came back to see Bialyi a month later and said:

    'I've read it. Thanks. There was a lot I liked ...'

    'Ah, what did you like?' Bialyi asked with interest.

    'Lenia made a great effort, remembered and answered:

    'The story *Dombrovskii* ...' (SD: 1993, I, 406).

17. A.S. Pushkin, *Sochineniia v trekh tomakh*, Gosudarstvennoe izdatel'stvo khudozhestvennoi literatury, Moscow, 1985, III, pp. 346-7.

18. Ibid., p. 347

19. Pushkin, op. cit., p. 489.

20. Igor' Sukhikh, *Sergei Dovlatov: vremia, mesto, sud'ba*. Kul'tInform Press, St Petersburg, 1996, p. 154.

21. 1998 saw the publication of Bulgarin's letters and denunciations: A.I Reiblat, ed., *Vidok Figliarin. Pis'ma i agenturnye zapiski Faddeiia Bulgarina v III otdelenie* , Novoe literaturnoe obozrenie, Moscow, 1998. See also, A.G. Altunian, '"Politicheskie mneniia" Faddeiia Bulgarina. Ideino-stilisticheskii analiz zapisok F.V. Bulgarina k Nikolaiu I', *Nezavisimaia gazeta*, 29 October, 1998. Since the fall of the Soviet regime a considerable polemic has arisen in the press about the morality of informing: see *Voprosy literatury*, III, 1990, p. 87, *Novoe literaturnoe obozrenie*, II, 1993, p. 124, *Nezavisimaia gazeta*, 14 January, 1999, p. 12.

22. E.A. Tudorovskaia describes this episode in her article 'Putevoditel'' po *Zapovedniku*', in the special issue of *Zvezda* (III, 1994) dedicated to Sergei Dovlatov. The scene where the narrator is being 'educated' by the KGB reminds Tudorovskaia of A. K. Tolstoi's satirical poem *Popov's Dream* (*Son Popova*). For detailed analysis see pp. 197-8. The objectives of the Third Department are in no way different from those of the KGB as Tudorovskaia indicates.

23. Pushkin, as his letters to A.N. Vul'f (of August 1825 and 10 October 1825 from Mikhailovskoe) testify, was hoping to travel abroad either illegally or under a pretext of an operation abroad. Pushkin was advised to have his operation on aneurysm in Pskov, which he declined. In *Perepiska A.S. Pushkina v dvukh tomakh*, Khudozhestvenaia literatura, Moscow, 1982, II, pp. 180, 181.

24. Pushkin is often considered by many critics as the founder of Russian prose. However, there were also reservations expressed about Pushkin's prose. This is discussed in R. Clegg, 'Pushkin's Novelistic Prose: A Dead End?', *Slavic Review*, LVII, 1, Spring, 1998, pp. 1-27.

25. 'Pisat' ob absurde iz liubvi k garmonii. Interv'iu Dzhona Gleda s Sergeem Dovlatovym', *Vremia i my*, New York, CX, 1990, pp. 159-73.

26. A.S. Pushkin, *Polnoe sobranie sochinenii*, Izdatel'stvo Akademii Nauk SSSR, XI, 1949, p. 19.

27. Iu.M. Lotman, 'Analiz poeticheskogo teksta' in his *O poetakh i poezii*, Iskusstvo, Leningrad, 1972, p. 38.

28. Dovlatov himself confesses to this: 'Their heroes were our contemporaries. I was myself a bit of Viktor Podgurskii. With a tendency to astral journeys'. Sergei Dovlatov, 'Literatura prodolzhaetsia', in special issue of *Zvezda,* dedicated to Sergei Dovlatov, op. cit., p. 117.
29. A. Lezhnev, *Proza Pushkina. Opyt stilevogo issledovaniia*, Izdatel'stvo 'Khudozhestvennaia literatura', Moscow, 1966, p. 30.
30. Ibid., p. 33.
31. Ibid., p. 69.
32. Dal''s *Russkie skazki - piatok pervyi* (1832) are stylized fairy tales and were hailed by many (including Pushkin) for the invention of a folk narrator.
33. The parallel here is with A.S. Shishkov (1754-1841) and his society Beseda Liubitelei Russkogo Slova and Shishkov's defence of the Russian literary language against Westernization.
34. This issue is discussed in detail by S. Schwarzband, *The History of Belkin's Tales,* The Magness Press, The Hebrew University, Jerusalem, 1993.
35. V.V. Vinogradov, *Stil' Pushkina*, Goslitizdatel'stvo Nauka, Moscow, 1941, p. 535.
36. Pushkin, op. cit., III, p. 232.
37. Iu.M. Lotman, *O russkoi literaure. Stat'i i issledovaniia: istoriia russkoi prozy, teoriia literatury*, Iskusstvo, St Petersburg, 1997, p. 601.

Pushkin and Brodsky: the Art of Self-deprecation

by

VALENTINA POLUKHINA

> Поди, и он
> здесь подставлял скулу под аквилон,
> прикидывая, как убраться вон,
> в такую же - кто знает - рань,
> и тоже чувствуя, что дело дрянь,
> куда ни глянь.
> И он, видать,
> здесь ждал того, чего нельзя не ждать
> от жизни: воли.
> Joseph Brodsky [1]

Pushkin had a far larger influence, intellectually and emotionally, on Brodsky than has generally been recognized[2] or as Brodsky himself would like us to think. Although Brodsky wrote little about Pushkin and had a declared preference for Baratynskii he knew his Pushkin by heart: '*The Bronze Horseman* I knew and, I believe, still know to this day by heart'.[3] Pushkin dwells in Brodsky's poetry in the form of well-known quotations; numerous borrowings, citations, reminiscences, allusions, echoes of Pushkinian texts, dissolved as it were, in Brodsky's poetry. Being an unusually well-read man, Brodsky, even when still in Russia, was well acquainted with the literature about Pushkin through Akhmatova and his friend Iakov Gordin. He lived for a long while with the Tomashevskii family and made use of their very large library. He personally knew Iu. M. Lotman and Academician Alekseev and was a regular visitor in the Meilakh household. Brodsky himself gives a much less complicated answer: 'any author who takes up writing in Leningrad ... associates himself in one way or another with the harmonic school of Pushkin'.[4] Any attentive reader of Brodsky soon comes to sense that Brodsky was engaged in a constant, lifelong dialogue with Pushkin. Loseff testifies that 'in the last weeks of his life Brodsky was talking about and re-reading Pushkin' and that he wrote to James Rice, a professor at Oregon State University, sketching an imaginary portrait of Pushkin at work.[5] From interviews and private conversations we know that Brodsky never said Pushkin. It was always Alexander Sergeevich.

In this chapter I will try to demonstrate that Pushkin's place in Brodsky's writing is as significant as it is in that of any other Russian poet. To identify the similarities and dissimilarities between any two poets separated by 150 years, we need to see the larger picture, to convey the full scale of their contribution to Russian poetry, to the Russian poetic language, to Russian intellectual life, and so on. Like Pushkin, Brodsky was engaged in giving the Russian language of his time a perfect poetic form. Both poets were able to immerse themselves in the truly vernacular idiom. Perfecting form, experimenting with diverse poetic genres, they surrendered to the language, their commitment to it being absolute. Brodsky subscribed to Pushkin's sense of harmony. He, too, has created a new kind of harmony, unthinkable or apparently unachievable before him. Finally, these poets possessed an outlook that was both Russian and European. Indeed, they are perhaps Russia's only true Russian Europeans. Hence, their common complaint - 'Бывало, что ни напишу, / Все для иных не Русью пахнет' ('For some, nothing that I write, is Russian enough': *Дельвигу* [*To Delvig*], 1821). It is hard not to think of Brodsky's situation in Russia when one reads these lines of Pushkin. Brodsky has been constantly accused of losing his Russianness and this in spite of the fact that he underlined his Russianness and hoped that in his case 'it's a widening that's taking place, not a narrowing of it'.[6]

  This study will deal with a particular aspect of their poetics. I will attempt to identify certain features of self-portraiture common to both poets. Brodsky's tendency to belittle himself in the scheme of things, to see the worst in himself, echoes Pushkin's practice in some of his own self-portraits. In Pushkin, too, self-depiction is often ironic, anti-romantic, far from flattering and transcending the conventional bounds of the poetic. The external details of their self-descriptions are banal and disparaging. In contrast with the self-admiration often characteristic of work by their contemporaries, both Pushkin and Brodsky cultivated self-denigration and self-abnegation. This may have something to do with their obsession with death. However, both poets appear as figures of intellectual sobriety with a sense of perspective. I am aware that any attempt to select only one aspect, one particular feature out of a complex system of parallels and similarities between Pushkin and Brodsky is to simplify the picture. Hence, I will also have to deal, however briefly, with both the biographical and the typological aspects of their work in order to come to some sort of understanding of the myth of Brodsky as a second Pushkin.

  The coupling of their two names began as a joke which circulated widely in Leningrad when someone dubbed the then eighteen-year-old Brodsky 'the Jewish Pushkin'. The first time that the two names were coupled in the same sentence in all seriousness was when Anatolii Naiman wrote his preface to *Остановка в пустыне* (*A Stop in the Desert*) sometime between 1964-68.[7] After Naiman other Russian poets, Gorbanevskaia, Gordin, Krivulin and Loseff, Brodsky's contemporaries, found both superficial and more fundamental parallels between the lives and works of the two poets.[8]

However, the not infrequent comparisons between Pushkin and Brodsky were limited, as a rule, to biographical parallels: their falling out with their respective regimes, their being shadowed by the Tsarist Okhranka and the Soviet KGB, their exiles, the censoring of their work. As Thomas Venclova has remarked '... the theme of Pushkin's exile is easily projected onto his [Brodsky's] biography. In *Lithuanian Nocturne* Brodsky takes upon himself the role of both Ovid and Pushkin'.[9] Viktor Krivulin is inclined to continue the analogy Brodsky-Pushkin at the personal level: they were both born in May, under the sign of Gemini and they died in January, under Aquarius.[10] He does, it is true, omit to mention that Brodsky lived not 37 years but 55; however, had he remained in Russia he would, affirms Boris Khazanov, have probably died at a much younger age than he did.[11] V.A. Saitanov reminds us of yet another biographical parallel:

> When Pushkin was catapulted to fame in Russia upon the appearance of *Ruslan and Liudmila* he was 21. At 21, in 1961, Brodsky wrote *Christmas Romance* (*Рождественский романс*) which fastened the attention of the entire country upon him .... At 32 Pushkin got married and moved to Petersburg, entered the service of the Tsar, a cushy job, and began to write prose. At the same age Brodsky went off to America and got a cushy job, and began teaching Russian literature and writing prose.[12]

When he wrote that, Saitanov did not know that Brodsky, like Pushkin, would be married to one of the most beautiful women (Brodsky's wife is, in fact, a descendant of Pushkin). Brodsky himself, of course, also did not know about this when he wrote jokingly, in an epistle to a friend long before his marriage: 'Не знаю, есть ли Гончарова, / но сигарета мой Дантес ('I don't know about a Goncharova / but a cigarette is my D'Anthès'). 'Strange coincidences, as if they were both living to the same schema confirmed on high for the both of them,' Saitanov continues.[13]

Towards the end of his life one had the impression that Brodsky's ambition to be a second Pushkin had been heard by somebody up there: the cult of Pushkin throughout the course of the nineties was gradually transformed, in Russia, into a cult of Brodsky - television programmes and films were devoted to him; his plays were put on; his *Collected Works* were published as were some hitherto unknown poems of his (such as, for example, the grandiose *Столетняя война [Hundred Years' War]*); memoirs about him were published by anyone who had even fleetingly glimpsed the idol;[14] international conferences were devoted to his work;[15] the study of Brodsky became so modish, so prestigious in academic circles as to vie for equal prestige with Pushkin studies; finally Brodsky, too, became compulsory in school.

Their relationships with tyrants are no less amusingly a confirmation of how history repeats itself, caricatures itself: Khrushchev and his henchmen staged Brodsky's trial in 1964 and sent him into exile. But it wasn't just the poet himself who was arrested; there was also the first compiler of his works, Vladimir Maramzin and the first person to study them, Mikhail Kheifitz. Brezhnev and Andropov issued him with an invitation to leave the country in 1972. In 1992 Gorbachev paid him a visit in Washington, where Brodsky had his office as US poet laureate, Gorbachev himself having just lost his office in the Kremlin. Yeltsin and Chernomyrdin attempted to correct the image of Russian tyranny by trying to persuade his widow to bury Brodsky in St Petersburg on the basis of the alleged 'literary testament' of the poet himself who wrote in 1962: 'Ни страны, ни погоста /не хочу выбирать. / На Васильевский остров / я приду умирать' ('Neither country nor parish / do I wish to choose / on Vasilevskii Island / I will return to die', I:225). Upon Brodsky's death dozens of contemporary poets committed elegies to paper: in my own archives there are at least a hundred poems dedicated to him.

There is a great temptation to compare the fate, personal and poetic, of the two poets, living at the beginning and the end of their respective centuries in cataclysmic times. However, Lev Loseff has noted that:

> there are at times parallels in the biographies of the two poets [which] only serve to underline that in Brodsky's case he had to deal with a nightmarish or grotesque variant of Pushkin's situation ... The Leningrad party hacks couldn't hold a candle to Benkendorff and Dubelt as educated men ... Pushkin wasn't sent into exile as a convict under armed guard, having gone through the mill of prison cells and mental hospital wards. Being an exiled nobleman on one's own estate at Mikhailovskoe was not the same as being an exiled labourer on a collective farm in Norenskaia.[16]

Their fates have engendered a myth which has been turned into a universal formula.

To reduce their similarities to just those aspects enumerated above would be too banal to warrant attention. This is one case where 'it is impossible to separate the characteristics of the personal temperament from the theoretical position'.[17] It is not so much the biographical similarities as the similarities of personality type and quality of talent, that explain to us similarities in their manner of self-portraiture. Pride and a passionate striving to be the first in everything cohabit with a genuine humility. Pushkin's 'гордый мой рассудок' ('my proud reason', Pushkin, III:178) is echoed by Brodsky's advice to himself: 'Смотри без суеты / вперед. Назад / без ужаса смотри. / Будь прям и горд, / раздроблен изнутри, / на ощупь тверд' ('Look without vanity / before, behind / without horror, look! / Be upright and proud / broken from within / firm to the touch', II:193). But Pushkin also writes about quietness of voice and poverty of talent: 'Конечно, беден гений мой' ('Of course, my gift [genius] is poor', *To My Aristarkh* [*Моему Аристарху*], 1815); 'Мой голос тих' ('My voice is quiet', *Sleep/Dream* [*Сон*], 1816). In Brodsky we find a similar but much more obvious self-deprecatory tone in many of his autobiographical poems: 'Я, певец дребедени, / лишних мыслей, ломаных линий' ('I am a singer of nonsense, / superfluous thoughts, and broken lines', III:44).

What is also characteristic of both poets is their profound desire to retain humility: 'И дух смирения, терпения, любви / и целомудрия мне в сердце ожини' ('And the spirit of humility, of patience, of love / and of chastity revive in my heart', III:421). Brodsky, 'приемыш гордый' ('proud adopted child', III:25), as he called himself, at the end of his life, repeating Pushkin's words 'If God should send me readers ...', said that everyone should be apprentice to such authorial humility.[18] And that despite the fact that both of them were convinced that they 'плетут рифмы' ('wove rhymes', Pushkin, I:18,26) or 'сочиняют стишки' ('compose verselets'), as Brodsky loved to say, better than any of their contemporaries. Of Pushkin's primacy everyone has had their fill. Brodsky's contemporaries testify to his pre-eminence: 'He was the first and paved the way for all the rest to follow,' says writer and historian Mikhail Kheifits in the preface to the *samizdat* collection of Brodsky's poetry that earned him five years, 1974-80, in a prison camp. In his opinion Brodsky uncovered the truths which challenged the catastrophic state of the consciousness of a whole generation.[19] 'The appearance of Brodsky's poetry overturned our own conceptions of ourselves.'[20]

A few words need to be said at this point about the nature of our two poets' cultural endeavours. In Loseff's opinion, both Pushkin and Brodsky,

> in their work, united and brought to perfection all the fundamental trends in literature in their own and in the preceding generation (in Pushkin's case it was Russian neoclassicism and the early Romantic 'school of harmonic exactitude'; in Brodsky's it was Russian modernism from symbolism to Lugovskoi and Slutskii). Both enriched our spiritual world, 'translating into Russian', organically transfusing the Russian mentality with forms of artistic perception, the Russian language with forms of expression alien to it (Pushkin - the Gallic, Brodsky - Anglo-Saxon and Celtic, both of them, the Latin of the classics).[21]

It seems that Brodsky himself realized his leading role in introducing to a Russian audience some notorious icons of world culture. As if fearing that even in his lifetime he would be turned into a monument to his own glory he cultivated, as a form of self-defence, a deliberately disparaging form of self-portraiture: 'я - один из глухих, облысевших, угрюмых послов /

второсортной державы' ('I am one of the deaf, bold, gloomy ambassadors / of a second rate power', II:161). We find something similar in Pushkin: 'Конюший дряхлого Пегаса' ('A decrepit Pegasus's ostler', [*To my Aristarkh*], 1815). Some self-disparaging metaphors of substitution for Brodsky's self are borrowed directly from Pushkin: 'Я, пасынок державы дикой / с разбитой мордой' ('I am a stepson of a savage power / with a bruised face', III:25) refers us to Pushkin's line 'Старым пасынком судьбины' ('Like an old step-child of Fate', (*To Natalia* [*Наталье*], 1813); 'усталый раб - из той породы, / что зрим все чаще' ('a weary slave of that breed / that is seen more and more often', III:27) has its source in 'Давно, усталый раб, замыслил я побег' ('A weary slave, for long I have contemplated my escape', 'It's time, my friend, it's time' ['Пора, мой друг, пора'], 1834).

However, on the personal level, we will note that they are alike both in the nature of their talent and in character: both were 'беспечные обожатели' ('carefree worshippers', *Epistle to Prince A.M. Gorchakov* [*Послание к кн. А.М. Горчакову*], 1819) of female beauty, but were not overly concerned about faithfulness to a particular woman: 'И ты, повеса из повес' ('And you, rake of rakes', *The Carousing Students* [*Пирующие студенты*], 1814); 'Каков я прежде был, таков и ныне я: / Беспечный, влюбчивый. Вы знаете, друзья' ('As I was before so am I now: / carefree, amorous, you know, friends', 1828). Overwhelming personal charm and a great talent for friendship guaranteed both of them the lifelong devotion of their friends and their own equal devotion to them. It is from this, surely, that springs Brodsky's tendency to identify completely with friends who were themselves poets, for example with Thomas Venclova: 'Мы похожи; / мы, в сущности, Томас, одно' ('We are alike. / We, in essence, Tomas, are one', II:325). As ideal doubles Brodsky chose Tsvetaeva and Auden, assimilating many of their poetic traits. Both poets were easily wounded and haughty, short-tempered and absurdly generous. 'The chief thing was that he [Pushkin] lacked what is called tact,' I.I. Pushchin recalled.[22] The same thing could be said of Brodsky; no need to alter a word. Both were well aware of the duality of their nature:[23]

> Порой ленив, порой упрям,
> Порой лукав, порою прям,
> Порой смирен, порой мятежен,
> Порой печален, молчалив,
> Порой сердечно говорлив

('At times lazy, at times obstinate, / At times cunning, at times frank, / At times humble, at times mutinous, / At times sorrowful, at times taciturn, / At times cordially effusive', VI:619.)

Neither their personal appearance nor their origins, it would seem, satisfied either of our poets. Each lavished a great deal of care on his appearance and worried about his physical shortcomings: 'А я, повеса, вечно праздный, / Потомок негров безобразный' ('But I, a rake, ever idle, / ugly progeny of negroes', (*To Iurev* [*Юрьеву*], 1820); 'Я не лейб-кучер, не асессор, / Родов униженных обломок' ('I am no liveried coachman, no assessor, / but a humble fragment of [aristocratic] stock', II:875). A synonym of Pushkin's 'обломок' can be founded in the twelfth of the *Roman Elegies*: 'Я был в Риме. Был залит светом. Так, / как только может мечтать обломок!' ('I was in Rome. I was flooded with light. As / only a fragment can dream of being!' III:48). There are even more unflattering remarks to be found in Brodsky's poems about himself: 'В полости рта не уступит кариес / Греции Древней, по меньшей мере. / Смрадно дыша и треща суставами, / пачкаю зеркало' ('In the mouth's cavity the caries is equivalent / to ancient Greece, at least. / With foul breath, and joints creaking / I stain the mirror', II:290); 'в ломаном «р» еврея' ('in the guttural Jewish "r"', III:43). Such bizarre metaphors are scattered throughout his autobiographical poems: 'отщепенец, стервец, вне закона' ('a renegade, son-of-a-bitch, outlaw', III:8); 'я, прячущий во рту / развалины почище Парфенона, / шпион, лазутчик, пятая колонна / гнилой цивилизации - в быту / профессор красноречья' ('I, who hide in my mouth / ruins comparable with those of the Parthenon, / a spy, a scout, fifth columnist / of a rotten civilization - in everyday life / a professor of rhetoric', II:299).

We must admit that Pushkin is much kinder towards himself in his self-portraiture than Brodsky. Some of Pushkin's self-deprecations ('my genius is poor' or 'my voice is quiet') could be interpreted as a coquettish pose and typical for the romantic tradition (see, for example, Batiushkov's 'мой осиротелый гений' ['my orphaned genius'], *Reminiscences* [*Воспоминания*], 1815, or Baratynskii's 'My gift is scant, my voice is not loud' ['Мой дар убог и голос мой не громок'], 1828). But many other examples in Pushkin indicate an attempt to break with the romantic pose which Russian poets favoured for so long after Pushkin's death. In Brodsky such a persistent tendency in the poet's depiction of his lyrical persona demonstrates his rejection of the time-worn romantic images of the poet: 'I am an epigone and parrot' ('Я эпигон и попугай', I:431); 'Прохожий с мятым / лицом' ('a passer-by with a creased / face', II:320). In Brodsky's interviews we find another explanation for one of his favourite stances when portraying his self - the tendency to self-denigration:

> ... when you write poetry ... you always anticipate that there is some sardonic mind that will laugh at your delights and sorrows. So the idea is to beat that sardonic mind. To steal the chance from him. And the only chance to steal that from him is to laugh at yourself. I've done that for a while.[24]

Discussing their insignificance, their ordinariness our poets often use negative constructions: 'Я не герой, по лаврам не тоскую ... / Я не богач. .. / Я не злодей. ...' ('I am no hero, I do not pine for laurels ... / I am no rich man ... / I am no villain ...', [*Sleep*, 1816]). Pushkin, as a rule, confines himself to enumerative constructions coupled with contrasts: 'Не офицер я, не асессор, / Я по кресту не дворянин, / Не академик, не профессор; / Я просто русский мещанин' ('I am not an officer, nor an assessor, / no oath-taking nobleman, / no academic or professor; / I am a simple Russian petty bourgeois', *My Genealogy* [*Моя родословная*], 1830). This particular grammatical device produces the opposite meaning: Pushkin is saying that he is anything but a petty bourgeois. Brodsky, too, while using Pushkin's formula switches the pluses and the minuses around: 'Пусть Вам напомнит данный томик, / что автор был не жлоб, не гомик, / не трус, не сноб, не либерал, / но - грустных мыслей генерал.'[25] ('Let this little book remind you, / that the author was no miser, no homo, / no coward, no snob, no liberal, / but a general of mournful thoughts.')

Brodsky uses the radical device of the *via negativa*, replacing the lyrical subject, and the contingencies of his existence, with negative pronouns and adverbs: 'совершенный никто, человек в плаще' ('a complete nobody, a man in a raincoat', II:318), 'Нарисуй на бумаге простой кружок. / Это буду я: ничего внутри' ('Draw a plain circle on the paper. / It will be me - nothing inside', III:12); 'Мы с тобой - никто, ничто' ('You and I are nobody, nothing' III:84). A vast array of negative pronouns and adverbs replace the implied lyrical self. Brodsky's ability to look at himself from outside became his second nature: 'Что, в сущности, и есть автопортет. / Шаг в сторону от собственного тела ...' ('This, in essence, is a self-portrait. / A step to one side, out of your own body', [III:92].)

With Brodsky negative tropes of substitution for the self have their origin in the theme of death, a theme far from alien to Pushkin. Besides, being great lovers of life, they both began, very early on, to talk about *old age and death*; Pushkin began writing about old age when he was sixteen: 'Уже я стар ...' ('Already I am old', *To Baroness M.A. Delvig* [*К бар. М.А. Дельвиг*], 1815), 'Печально младость улетит, / Услышу старости угрозы' ('Forlornly youth flies, / I hear the thunderclaps of age' *Elegy* [*Элегия*], 1816). And he wrote about death throughout his life: 'Один с тоской явлюсь я, гость угрюмый, / Явлюсь на час - и одинок умру' ('Alone with my anguish I will appear, a gloomy guest / I will appear at the appointed hour – and alone will I die', *To Prince A.M. Gorchakov* [*Князю А.М. Горчакову*], 1817); 'И сердце медленно хладело, закрывалось' ('And slowly the heart grew cold, closed down', *To Her* [*К ней*], 1817); 'И смерти мысль мила душе моей' ('And the thought of death is sweet to my soul', *Battle is familiar to Me* [*Мне бой знаком*], 1820); 'Умолкну скоро я!' ('I will soon fall silent!', 1821); 'Грядущей смерти годовщину / Меж их стараясь угадать' ('The coming date of my death / amongst them trying to guess', 'Should I wander ...' ['Брожу ли я ...'], 1829).

Brodsky began to croon about old age and death whilst still in his poetic cradle and never abandoned the theme: 'Ничего от смерти не убрать. / Отчего так страшно умирать? (1961, I:129: 'One cannot save anything from death. / Why is it so terrible to die?'). 'Старение! Здравствуй, мое старение! / Крови медленное струение. / ('Growing old! Greetings, my old age! / The slow flow of blood' *1972 god*, II:290-91). Fear of death[26] ('Но не хочу я, други, умирать', ['But, friends, I do not want to die'], *Elegy*, 1830; 'чую дыхание смертной темени / фибрами всеми и жмусь к подстилке' ['I sense the breath of deathly darkness / with every fibre of my being and press myself to the bedding', II:290]), prompted the belief that their poetry, or in Brodsky's words 'россыпь / черного на листе' ('the deposit / of black on the page', II: 458) would outlive them: 'Но что-нибудь останется во мне - / в живущем или мертвом человеке - / и вырвется из мира и извне / расстанется, свободное навеки. ('But something will remain in me - / in the living or in the dead man - / and will break away from the world and from without / will depart, for ever free', 1961, I:51).

Similar ideas are to be found in the young Pushkin: 'Не весь я предан тленью' ('I am not wholly destined to corruption', *A Little Town* [*Городок*], 1815). Thus arises the theme common to both - of the memorial to the self ('памятник самому / себе', I:424).[27] Here are a few examples from Brodsky:

> Я памятник воздвиг себе иной
> [...]
> в стране большой, на радость детворе
> из гипсового бюста во дворе
> сквозь белые незрячие глаза
> струей воды ударю в небеса. ('Я памятник ...' ['I have erected ...'], 1962).

('I have erected a different monument to myself / in a big country, one that will gladden the hearts of children / from a gypsum bust in a courtyard / through white unseeing eyes / like a stream of water I will strike out at the heavens', *Edification* [*Назидание*], p. 12).

> 'Памятник самому / себе, одному, / не всадник с копьем, / не обелиск -'

('A monument to myself, / to myself alone, / no horseman with a spear, / no obelisk', 1965, I:424).

As we see, Brodsky consistently adheres to the poetic tradition, that of Pushkin in particular, in which the poet's image is codified in monumental form.[28] If, in Pushkin's case it expresses his conception of the poet's mission as agent of God's will, in Brodsky's it has more of a tendency to symbolize the poet's triumph as the voice of language transcending Time. Brodsky takes the next logical step, identifying the poet with the word, with the letters of the alphabet, with punctuation marks even: 'я, / бормочущий комок / слов' ('I, / a mumbling heap / of words', II:295); 'я / в глазах твоих - кириллица, названья ...' ('I / in your eyes am the Cyrillic, names', III:148). Such metaphorical substitutions of grammatical categories for the self are not found in Pushkin.

The use of cultural masks is another feature common to Pushkin's and Brodsky's self-portraiture.[29] Both engage in a dialogue with world culture and they keep, in part, the same distinguished company: Horace, Ovid, Dante, Derzhavin. It is possible to regard these shades of the great as dreams of an ideal self: 'И новый Дант склоняется к листу / и на пустое место ставит слово' ('And a new Dante bends over the page / and sets a word in the empty place', II:309). In Iurii Lotman's view, 'Pushkin always made his personal life the life of a poet'.[30] Viktor Krivulin said more or less the same of Brodsky: 'one always feels that no matter what he is doing, in any situation, he acts as a Poet, and all his actions are facts of his biography'.[31] Comparing him with Pushkin, Krivulin points out the 'most radical' similarity: 'The fact is that both Brodsky and Pushkin, recognizing themselves to be unique personalities, were aware of the necessity of somehow hiding that uniqueness, of wearing a mask'.[32]

As we read poem after poem this implicitly critical and ironic depiction comes to form a crucial part of their selves. Both of them possessed many contradictory qualities: intellectual vigour and passion, the fire of creative imagination combined with the coolness of reason; a light touch with breathtaking profundity. Not infrequently, Brodsky has been reproached with making his lyrical poetry too philosophically speculative, too rationalistic. Pushkin, somewhere, remarks that poetry demands thought and then more thought. Brodsky answers that demand in full measure: every time he makes yet one more attempt to solve the evidently insoluble problems of existence and artistic creation - the essence of life and death, of love and faith, the metaphysics of language and poetry, 'turning up his philosophical mode of thought to full power ... he provides fresh answers'.[33] This influenced his mode of self-portraiture: 'Я теперь тоже в профиль, верно, неотличим / от какой-нибудь латки, складки, трико паяца, / долей и величин, следствий или причин - / от того, чего можно не знать, сильно хотеть, бояться' ('In profile I, too, now can hardly be set / apart from some wrinkle, patchwork, domino, / fractions or whole, causes or their effects - / from all that can be ignored, coveted, feared', III:149-50).

Brodsky is a city poet and, essentially, of that one city which he calls Peter and which is ever present, there in the background. Venice, Florence, London, all of them, in his writing, take on that city's traits 'мерзнущего у моря' ('freezing by the sea', III:17). In the character of the exile from the Imperial city we recognize traits of Ovid, of Dante, of Pushkin and of Brodsky himself. Like Pushkin Brodsky was unable to free himself from a lifelong obsession with the magic of that city. In the eyes of many Russian poets Petersburg was the work of Pushkin as much as it was that of Peter. All poets after Pushkin live among the resounding echoes of *The Bronze Horseman*. Brodsky, as noted above, knew the poem by heart.

> It's possible that it's not just this association with the harmonic school of Pushkin but also the very architecture itself, the physical sensation of the city in which is embodied the idea of a certain madness. When you find yourself amidst all these endless, irreproachable vistas, amidst all these colonnades, pilasters and porticoes and so forth, you try, either by choice or involuntarily to transfer them into your poetry.[34]

And, actually, the landscape occupied by Brodsky's lyrical self is, as a rule, an urban landscape.[35] Petersburg also provided both poets with a sense of estrangement: 'the people in Petersburg ... felt that they were indeed on the edge of the empire and in their poetry, they found themselves looking at this empire as if from off to the side. That is, it's precisely this element of estrangement which is necessary for the writer'.[36]

Pushkin, talking about the dreadful events of his own life and of life in Russia, wrote: 'Shall we look at the tragedy through the eyes of Shakespeare' (XIII:259). Brodsky extended that already distanced point-of-view immeasurably: 'С точки зрения времени' ('From the point of view of time', III:61). They don't just see themselves from a detached point of view, they also see themselves through several different sets of eyes. The multiple point-of-view inevitably engenders a multiplicity of self-description. In his manner of self-portraiture these principles are actualized, not just through a system of self-derogation, but also through use of the objective word-image - 'man'. The homeless, nameless 'человек в плаще' ('man in a raincoat' II:318) who appears in *Lagoon* (1973) trails a whole host of lexical doubles: 'Человек размышляет о собственной жизни, как ночь о лампе' ('a man muses on his life like the night on a lamp', II:362). In Pushkin man (человек) is almost invariably rhymed with time ('век') which is another way of viewing a man from the point of view of time: 'Не славь его. В наш гнусный век / Седой Нептун земли союзник. / На всех стихиях человек - / Тиран, предатель или узник. ('Do not praise him. In our vile age / Grey Neptune is the earth's ally. / In all the elements man / Is a tyrant, traitor or prisoner', *To Viazemsky* [К Вяземскому], 1826). To which Brodsky does not fail to answer: 'Как сказано у поэта, "на всех стихиях ...". / Далеко же видел, сидя в своих болотах! / От себя добавлю: на всех широтах. ('As the poet said, "in all the elements ..." / Sitting in his bog, he saw quite far! / And I would add: in all latitudes', *To Evgenii* [Евгению], 1975; II:374).

Brodsky used Pushkin's rhyme in many of his youthful poems: 'он сгорел между полюсами века: / между ненавистью человека / и невежеством человека' ('he burnt up between the poles of the age: / between man's hatred / and man's ignorance, 1959, I:33); 'За веком век, за веком век / ложится в землю любой человек' ('Age after age, age after age / every man lie down in the earth', I:99, 104, 121, 148). Both poets cultivated the theme of the 'little man', which is in keeping with the Christian spirit of their poetry. One could, using different parameters, continue to compare their poetics. The political life of Russia was, to a large extent, bound up with their personal lives. They both responded to the political pressures of the day. Without any love for politics, shunning it even, Brodsky, like Pushkin remained alert to the political problems in Russia: see his poems *A Letter to General Z.* (*Письмо генералу Z.*, 1968), his reaction to the invation of Czechoslovakia; or *Lines on the Winter Campaign of 1980* (*Стихи о зимней кампании 1980 года*) about the war in Afghanistan, the Berlin Wall, the tension in Poland and elsewhere. It is typical of Brodsky to treat politics in terms of the age of Pushkin, even of antiquity: the key words are Empire, Caesar, tyrant, slave and Brodsky includes himself in that set with bitter irony:

> Огрызок цезаря, атлета,
> певца тем паче
> есть вариант автопортрета.
> Скажу иначе:
>
> усталый раб - из той породы,
> что зрим все чаще, -
> под занавес глотнул свободы.
> Она послаще
> любви, привязанности, веры
> (креста, овала),
> поскольку и до нашей эры
> существовала.

('A leftover of Caesar, of an athlete, / furthermore, of a singer / is a version of a self-portrait. / To put it differently: // a weary slave - of that breed / that's seen more often - / tasted freedom before the curtain descended. / It is sweeter / than love, attachment, faith / (the cross, the crescent) / because it existed before / our era', III:27).

As can be seen even in that quotation there are two echoes of Pushkin: 'огрызок цезаря' ('a leftover of Caesar') calls to mind 'родов униженных обломок' ('a humble fragment of [aristocratic] stock', II:875) and 'усталый раб' ('a weary slave') - 'Давно, усталый раб, замыслил я побег' ('A weary slave, for long I have contemplated my escape', ['It is time, my friend, it is time'], 1834).

Discussing Brodsky's cultural endeavours in a Pushkinian context, one cannot ignore his exploration of other cultures. Milosz, having in mind Brodsky's poems about Mexico, about Washington and his Italian cycle, says 'Brodsky really has been a go-getter, conquering America and the West in general; he is also something of a cultural explorer [...] The whole twentieth-century civilisation lives in the imagery of his poetry.'[37] His poems absorb both the texts of past culture and the culture of the present to such an extent that it is simply not possible to separate the warp of his intertextuality from the weft of his own poetic text. Moreover, as Loseff has remarked, there is present in Brodsky an astonishingly Russian note: 'It's what Pushkin and the Pushkin Pléiade did with French poetics ... Brodsky has done exactly the same thing, grafting the great leafy tree of English poetics onto the Soviet wilds.'[38] Both poets, like sponges, absorbed everything they felt they needed (not necessarily the best) from world poetry.

Like Pushkin, Brodsky was engaged in giving the Russian language of his time a perfect poetic form. Both created new genres and variations on old ones: Pushkin created the *poema*, Brodsky the *bolshoe stikhotvorenie*,[39] as in *Petersburg Novel* (Петербургский роман), *Great Elegy to John Donne* (Большая элегия Джону Донну), *Isaak and Abraham* (Исаак и Авраам), *Lullaby of Cape Cod* (Колыбельная Трескового мыса).[40] Brodsky revived such exhausted genres as the ode, the idyll and the eclogue.[41]

It would be timely to compare the extent of their expansion at the level of language, with their introduction of new strata of language into poetry. Pushkin, you will recall, used to stroll around in a red shirt amongst the peasants, 'compensating for the deficits in his accursed education' or he would listen to his nanny's fairy-tales, exclaiming to himself, 'What a delight these tales are!'[42] Instead of a nanny Brodsky first of all had the Leningrad courtyards and streets, then the convicts of the Soviet Gulag carving their nickname (*klikukha*) on a bunk in one of the multitude of barracks scattered around the marshlands of Russia. Brodsky grew up in the lumpen Russia of the camps in the midst of an unprecedentedly vulgar speech. That vulgar and vulgarizing speech, writes Boris Khazanov, he attempted to rehabilitate.[43] If Pushkin 'poeticized' the Russian language, then Brodsky 'prosaicized' it, its syntax and its lexicon. In Pushkin we do not find so many vulgarisms, thieves' slang, bureaucrat-speak, officialese and terms from popular science and technology. The more you look, the deeper the gap yawns between them. For Brodsky language is the building material from which the world is formed; he saw it as an absolute and turned it into a kind of ideal model of the world's existence. Brodsky was convinced that 'only that will survive which brings about improvement, not in society, but in the language'.[44] The perfecting of the language, a harmonious relationship with it is the true task of the poet, on condition that he lives within its orbit and not just on its surface. 'Brodsky's poetic task was to tame the chaos. And this the genuine pathos of his poetry which is embarrassed to be sentimental in any way'.⁴⁵ Brodsky's paganism (his worship of language) is an integral part of his belief that the language is the greatest Russian treasure trove, and it is perhaps more important than its icons or its history.⁴⁶ He felt part of it: its vowels, its consonants, punctuation marks.

In the sphere of poetics, besides the similarities in their mode of self-portraiture, there are other common traits which should be noted. Dmitrii Bavilskii notes that both poets have a predelection for listing, registering the things of this world.⁴⁷ While Belinskii called Pushkin's *Onegin* 'an encyclopaedia of Russian life', Limonov calls Brodsky the 'poet-bookkeeper.'⁴⁸ Bavilskii sees stylistic affinities with the phone book in both poets, giving their poetry an enumerative intonation. In Brodsky's case that intonation, so brilliant in its simplicity, is to be found in many poems where the petty details of everyday life are listed. Its apotheosis may be considered to be *Great Elegy to John Donne* (1963), but Brodsky did not abandon the manner. It remained with him throughout the rest of his life and he even made use of it in his self-characterization: 'здесь и скончаю я дни, теряя / волосы, зубы, глаголы, суффиксы' ('here I will end my days, losing / my hair, my teeth, my verbs and suffixes', *1972 god*, II:292).

In Naiman's opinion, 'they both possess this epigrammatic ease with which they react to events as they happen. This lightness of touch is loaded with meaning'.⁴⁹ Brodsky's wit and talent shine particularly brightly in his occasional pieces. Gordin recounts how they collaborated on a humorous epistle to Kushner on the occasion of his birthday (1969): Gordin improvized the subject matter and Brodsky turned it, at a moment's notice, into poetry:

> Ничем, Певец, твой юбилей
> мы не отметим, кроме лести
> рифмованной, поскольку вместе
> давно не видим двух рублей.
> [...]
> Мы предпочли бы поднести
> перо Монтеня, скальпель Вовси,
> скальп Вознесенского, а вовсе
> не оду, Господи прости.
> [...]
> а ты - ты думаешь сейчас:
>
> спустить бы с лестницы их всех,
> задернуть шторы, снять рубашку,
> достать перо и промокашку,
> расположиться без помех

и так начать без суеты,
не дожидаясь вдохновенья:
"Я помню чудное мгновенье,
передо мной явилась ты."⁵⁰

('Singer, we can celebrate / your birthday only / by rhymed flattery, / because neither of us has seen / a rouble and a rouble together for a long time ... // We would prefer to bring to you / Montaigne's pen, / Vovsi's scalpel, / Voznesenskii's scalp, but certainly / no ode, God forgive us ... // But you - you are now thinking: // I'd rather kick them all downstairs, / draw the curtains, take off my shirt, / get out my pen and blotting paper, / settle myself without hindrance / and start without fuss / not waiting for inspiration, as follows: / "I remember the miraculous moment / when you appeared before me"').

Straightforward references to Pushkin or imitations of his work are to be found in many of Brodsky's humorous poems, for example to *Arion*, in *A Sonnet on the Occasion of Lena Valikhan's and Alik Dobrovolskii's Marriage* (1960): 'Уже сейчас, близки и далеки, / Вы пьете мир из собственной реки. / А я все гимны прежние пою, / Свою одежду ветхую сушу ... ('Already now, close and far / You drink the world from your own river. / But I sing the same old hymns, / Dry my worn out clothes ...'). In this analogy to Pushkin's *Album Verses*, the 'merry Brodsky', as Iakov Gordin calls him, appeared in all his charm.⁵¹

Brodsky often included lines from Pushkin and events in his life in his own poetry as, for example, in *On the Death of a Friend* (*На смерть друга*): 'сочинителю лучших из од / на паденье А.С. в кружева и к ногам Гончаровой' ('to the writer of one of the best odes / on A.S.'s falling into the lace and at the feet of Goncharova', 1973, II:332); as well as Pushkin himself: 'Входит Пушкин в летном шлеме, / в тонких пальцах - папироса' ('Pushkin enters in a pilot's helmet, / in his slender fingers is a cigarette', *A Performance* [*Представление*], 1986, III:114). And without a trace of irony the unnamed Pushkin symbolizes an unfree Russia: 'И отлит был / из их отходов тот, кто не уплыл, / тот, чей, давясь, проговорил / "Прощай свободная стихия" рот, / чтоб раствориться навсегда в тюрьме широт, / где нет ворот' ('And he was cast / out of what is left [after the fetters have been made] he who didn't sail off, / he whose mouth choking, uttered, / "Farewell free element", / so as to dissolve forever in the prison of latitudes / where there are no gates', *At the Pushkin Monument in Odessa* [*Перед памятником Пушкину в Одессе*], 1969-70; IV:9).

Brodsky himself acknowledged that his *Twenty Sonnets to Mary Queen of Scots* 'are largely based on paraphrases of Pushkin ... The beginning of Sonnet 20 is pure Alexander Sergeevich in sound'⁵²: 'Пером простым - не правда, что мятежным! - я пел про встречу в некоем саду ... ('With a simple pen, it is not true that it's rebellious, / I have sung about our meeting in some park', II:345).

His borrowings and quotations from Pushkin, as Tomas Venclova remarks in another context, are sometimes 'parodic and shocking.'[53] It is sufficient to recall Brodsky's explanation of his love for the statue in which he parodies the theme of inseparable love in Pushkin: 'Я вас любил. Любовь еще (возможно, / что просто боль) сверлит мои мозги. / [...] / Я вас любил так сильно, безнадежно, / как дай вам Бог другими - но не даст! ('I loved you. My love (or maybe / it's just a pain) is gnawing my brains ... // I loved you so strongly, so hopelessly / as God grant [you may be] by others - but He won't!' *Twenty Sonnets to Mary Queen of Scots*, II:339); or from *The Prophet*: 'уже ни в ком / не видя места, коего глаголом / коснуться мог бы' ('no longer / seeing a spot where I might touch anyone / with words', *Conversation with a Celestial Being* [*Разговор с небожителем*], II:209) - 'Моих зениц коснулся он' ('he touched my pupils'); 'Не стану жечь / тебя глаголом, исповедью, просьбой, / проклятыми вопросами - той оспой, / которой речь с пелен / заражена' ('I will not burn / you, with words, with a confession, with a supplication, / with the accursed questions - that smallpox / with which speech, / almost from cradle, / is infected', *Conversation*, 1970; II:209) - 'Глаголом жги сердца людей' ('with the word burn the hearts of people'); 'чтоб вложить пальцы в рот - в эту рану Фомы - / и, нащупав язык, на манер серафима / переправить глагол' ('so he might stick his fingers into his mouth, the wound of Thomas, / and feeling his tongue, in the manner of some Seraphim / redirect the word', *Lithuanian Nocturne*, 1973-83; II:325)[54] - 'И шестикрылый серафим / На перепутьи мне явился ... / И он к устам моим приник / И вырвал грешный мой язык' ('and the six-winged Seraphim / appeared to me at the crossroad ... / And he touched my lips / and tore out my sinful tongue'); 'Снайпер, томясь от духовной жажды' ('A sniper, languishing from spiritual thirst', *Letter to General Z.*, II:87) - 'Духовной жаждою томим' ('languishing from spiritual thirst'); 'чтоб пломбы в пасти плавились от жажды / коснуться - "бюст" зачеркиваю - уст' ('so that fillings in the jaws should melt from desire / to touch - I delete 'bust' - your lips', *Twenty Sonnets*, 1974; II:339) - 'И он к устам моим приник' ('and touched my lips').

Deliberate allusion to Pushkin's 'Не дай мне Бог сойти с ума, / Нет, лучше посох и сума' ('God, don't let me go mad, / No, better a staff and a bag', 1833) can be seen at the beginning of Brodsky's poem 'В эту зиму с ума / я опять не сошел, а зима / глядь и кончилась' ('This winter / again I didn't go mad, and in a trice / winter was over', II:257). Paraphrase from Pushkin's 'Again I have visited' ('...Вновь я посетил', 1835) could be found in *From the Margin to the Centre* (*От окраины к центру*, I:217) or Pushkin's 'Здравствуй, племя / Младое, незнакомое!' ('Greeting, tribe, / young, unknown!') is placed in ironic context: 'Здравствуй, младое и незнакомое / племя! Жужжащее, как насекомое, ('Greeting, young and unknown / tribe! The buzzing, insect-like', II:290).

We are presented with a fairly complex network of references to Pushkin texts. Brodsky's 'pushkinisms' can be serious, they can be light-hearted. Pushkin's words 'Страдать есть смертного удел' ('To suffer is the normal lot for mortals') from *Reminiscences in Tsarskoe Selo* (*Воспоминания в Царском селе*, 1814) find a serious echo in Brodsky's view of the world in which, he opines, tragedy is the norm: 'Поскольку боль - не нарушенье правил: / страданье есть / способность тел / и человек есть испытатель боли' ('Inasmuch as pain is not the breaking of the rules / suffering is / the capability of bodies, / and man is the endurer of pain', II:210).

On the other hand, Brodsky, not without a trace of mischief, plays with the tragic Pushkinian situation in the poem *At the Pushkin Monument in Odessa* (IV:7-10):

> там стыл апостол перемены мест
> спиной к отчизне и лицом к тому,
> в чью так и не случилось бахрому
> шагнуть ему.
> [...]
> И я там был, и я там в снег блевал.

('the apostle of changing places froze there / with his back to the fatherland, and facing the fringes [of the sea] / where he never happened to step ... // And I was there, and there I threw up in the snow', IV:8).

The supremely comic lines of *Polonaise: Variation* (*Полонез: Вариация*, III:65): 'И затем, что все на одно лицо, / согрешивши с одним, тридцать трех полюбишь ' ('And because they all look alike, / having sinned with one, you will love all thirty-three') derive from *The Tale of the Dead Tsarevna* (*Сказка о мертвой царевне*). The reader will recognize the source in a poem *Letter to the Academy* (*Письмо в Академию*, IV:17): 'в мои пятьдесят три их клювы / и когти - стершиеся карандаши, а не / угроза печени, а языку - тем паче. / Я - не пророк, они - не серафимы ('In my fifty-three their beaks / and claws - the blunt pencils, and not / a threat to the liver, or what's more the language. / I am no prophet, they are no seraphims').

Just by collecting together all of these references to our first poet one comes to realize how much of Brodsky derives from Pushkin.[55] Brodsky himself has admitted, 'all of us, to some degree and in one way or another, continue writing *Evgenii Onegin*. We do so in part so we can free ourselves from this key.'[56]

In conclusion, I will say that in his relationship to Pushkin Brodsky remained true to himself: on the one hand he followed in his steps, just as he, in general, followed the tradition but, on the other hand, he made a decisive break with tradition and, in many ways, departed from Pushkin's course but only, by doing so, to continue his work. He could be describing his own work when he said about Pushkin, 'he is, to a certain degree, a sort of lens into which the past goes and out of which the future emerges'.[57] At the end of his life Brodsky thought and sometimes sounded like Pushkin, departing from him and looking back at him as if realizing his own metaphor: 'Как тридцать третья буква, / Я пячусь всю жизнь вперед. ('Like the thirty-third letter, / all my life I back away forward', II:457.)

NOTES

1. All references to Brodsky's poetry in this chapter are to *Sochineniia Iosifa Brodskogo*, Pushkinskii Fond, St Petersburg, 1992-99. This quotation is from vol. IV, p. 8: 'Surely, he too / offered a cheekbone here to Aquilon, / figuring out how to get away / at the same ungodly hour perhaps, / and feeling that wherever you look / the game is up. / And apparently here / he waited for what one must expect / from life: liberty'. Translated by Daniel Weissbort. The Pushkin quotations are to be found in the 17 volumes of *Complete Collected Works*, published by the Academy of Sciences, *Polnoe sobranie sochinenii v 17-ti tomakh*, Akademiia nauk SSSR, Moscow, 1937-59. Unless otherwise noted, all translations from Pushkin and Brodsky's originals will be my own. I am grateful to Daniel Weissbort and Chris Jones for helping me with the English literal translations.
2. See the article by D.S. (V.A. Saitanov) 'Pushkin i Brodskii', in L. Losseff, ed., *Poetika Brodskogo*, Hermitage, Tenafly, New Jersey, 1986, pp. 207-18; A. Kalomirov (Viktor Krivulin), 'Iosif Brodskii (mesto)', ibid, pp. 219-29; A. Zholkovskii '"Ia vas liubil ..." Brodskogo: interteksty, invarianty, tematika i struktura', ibid., pp. 38-62; see also 'O Pushkine i ego epokhe', in Lev Loseff and Petr Vail, eds., *Iosif Brodskii: Trudy i dni*, Nezavisimaia gazeta, Moscow, 1998, pp. 13-39.
3. Joseph Brodsky interviewed by Annie Epelboin, July 1981, 'Evropeiskii vozdukh nad Rossiei', *Strannik*, I, 1991, pp. 40-1. In one of his interviews Brodsky said that he began reading Pushkin when he was five years old.
4. Ibid., p. 41.
5. Loseff, 'Introduction' in *Trudy i dni*, op. cit., p. 18.
6. Joseph Brodsky, interviewed by John Glad, *Vremia i my*, XCVII, 1987, p. 137. A similar answer was given when I asked Brodsky during his press conference in Helsinki, in August 1995, 'You have been reproached for losing your Russianness. What do you have to say for yourself?' Brodsky replied, 'Russianness which can be lost is not worth a penny'. For a report on that press conference see, *Sobesednik*, VIII, September 1995, p. 12.
7. N.N. (Anatoly Naiman), 'Zametki dlia pamiati', *A Stop in the Desert* (*Ostanovka v pustyne*), Chekhov Press, New York, 1970, pp. 7-15.
8. See my interviews with these poets in *Brodsky Through the Eyes of his Contemporaries*, Macmillan, Houndmills, 1992, pp. 1-52, 74-93, 176-99. See also the enlarged Russian edition *Brodskii glazami sovremennikov*, Zvezda, St. Petersburg, 1997, pp. 31-74, 87-100, 169-86.
9. Tomas Venclova, 'O stikhotvorenii Iosifa "Litovskii Noktiurn: T.V."', *Novoe literaturnoe obozrenie*, XXXIII, 1998, p. 212. For the English version of this article, see the collection, Lev Loseff and Valentina Polukhina, eds, *Joseph Brodsky: The Art of a Poem*, Macmillan, Houndmills, 1999, pp. 107-49.
10. Employing identical parameters Viktor Krivulin compares Brodsky with Dante: both died in January aged 55 and both were driven out of their native land, that too at the same age (from a talk given at the 'Inter'ernyi teatr' on Nevsky Prospekt, 24 May, 1997).
11. Boris Khazanov, '"S tochki zreniia voron ...": Zametki o Iosife Brodskom v kanun ego rozhdeniia', *Literaturnaia gazeta*, 22 May 1996, p. 6.
12. D.S. (V.A. Saitanov) 'Pushkin i Brodskii' in *Poetika Brodskogo*, p. 207.
13. Ibid.
14. The author of this chapter was present on 26 May 1997, at the soirée 'Peizazh s navodneniem', timed to coincide with the twenty-fifth anniversary of Brodsky's quitting Russia, with reminiscences, music, poetry, organized in Petersburg by Evgenii Belodubrovskii. This event took place in the Pushkin House on the Moika in St Petersburg.

15. The papers from three international conferences are gathered in the collection: Iakov Gordin, ed., *Iosif Brodskii: tvorchestvo, lichnost'*, *sud'ba*, Zvezda, St Petersburg, 1998.
16. 'Introduction' in *Trudy i dni*, op. cit., p. 14.
17. Iu.M. Lotman, *A.S. Pushkin*, Iskusstvo-SPB, St Petersburg, 1997, p. 50.
18. Petr Vail, 'Vsled za Pushkinym', *Trudy i dni*, op. cit., p. 27.
19. Mikhail Kheifits, 'Iosif Brodskii do *Rozhdestvenskogo romansa'*, *Russkaia mysl'*, V-XI, July 1997, p. 13.
20. V.A. Saitanov, 'Pushkin i Brodskii' in *Poetika Brodskogo*, op. cit., p. 218.
21. *Trudy i dni*, op. cit., p. 15.
22. Quoted in Iu.M. Lotman, *A.S. Pushkin*, p. 36.
23. For a more detailed study of the doubles in Brodsky's poetic world see my article 'Metamorfozy "ia" v poezii postmodernizma', *Slavica Helsingiensia*, XVI, 1996, pp. 391-407.
24. Interview with Joseph Brodsky by Eva Burch and David Chin, *Columbia. A Magazine of Poetry and Prose*, IV, Spring/Summer 1980, p. 61. Brodsky expressed a similar idea to his students as early as 1974: 'Poems are a celebration of self-humiliation, not self-indulgence. But one must also remember that a sardonic man will come, and he will laugh at the poet's grief.' See Rosette C. Lammont, 'Joseph Brodsky: A Poet's Classroom', *The Massachusetts Review*, XV, Fall 1974, p. 564.
25. Inscription on the copy of *In the Vicinity of Antlantis* (*V okrestnostiakh Atlantidy*), given to Elena Chernysheva 22 January 1996. Quoted in A. Symerkin's article 'Skorb' i razum', *Russkaia mysl'. Spetsial'noe prilozhenie*, 12-22 May 1996, p. iii.
26. Mikhail Lotman summarizes the interdependence of the theme of death and language in Brodsky in the following way: 'For Brodsky the poet is an organ of language and death is, therefore, in the first place, an assault on language, a narrowing of the sphere of speech and widening of the sphere of silence and emptiness'. M. Iu. Lotman, 'Poet i smert' (iz zametok o poetike Brodskogo)', Lea Pild and Galina Ponomareva, eds, *Blokovskii sbornik*, XIV, Tartu University Press, Tartu, 1998, p. 188.
27. In the opinion of Viktor Iukht, the sculptural myth in Brodsky is directly opposed to the corresponding myth in Pushkin described by Jakobson ('The Statue in Pushkin's Poetic Mythology', in Roman Jakobson, *Language and Literature*, Krystyna Pomorska and Stephen Rudy, eds, Harvard University Press, Cambridge, 1987, pp. 318-67). In Pushkin, maximal semantic tension occurs in those moments when statues (the Commendatore, the Bronze Horseman, the Golden Cockerel) start to move, that is, the dead start to act like the living (static - dynamic). In Brodsky, however, the living being freezes, is petrified, is transformed into a thing (dynamic - static). See Viktor Iukht, 'K probleme genezisa statuarnogo mifa v poezii Brodskogo (1965-1971gg)', *Russian Literature*, XLIV-IV (1998), pp. 409-32.
28. For this theme see my article '*Exegi Monumentum* Iosifa Brodskogo, *Przegląd Rusycystyczny*, XXI, 1998, pp. 69-88. The abridged English version of the article may be found in the collection Lev Loseff and Valentina Polukhina, eds, *Joseph Brodsky: The Art of a Poem*, Macmillan, Houndmills, 1999, pp. 68-91.
29. Iu. M. Lotman writes that 'Pushkin's romantic conduct is distinguished by its peculiarity: it entails not an orientation towards one particular type of behaviour but a whole assortment of different "masks" which the poet varies, changing his types of behaviour.' See Iu.M. Lotman, *A.S. Pushkin*, p. 99. For a study of Brodsky's mask see my article 'Metamorfozy "ia" v poezii postmodernizma', *Slavica Helsingiensia*, op. cit., 1996, pp. 391-407.
30. Ibid., p. 100.
31. Viktor Krivulin, 'Slovo o nobelitete Iosifa Brodskogo', *Russkaia mysl'*, 11 November 1988. Literaturnoe prilozhenie, No. 7, p. ii-iii.

32. Ibid., p. iii.
33. Evgenii Rein, interviewed by the author of this chapter, *Brodskii glazami sovremennikov*, Zvezda, St Petersburg, 1997, p. 21.
34. Brodsky interviewed by Annie Epelboin, p. 36.
35. See my article, 'Landshaft liricheskoi lichnosti v poezii Iosifa Brodskogo' in Valentina Polukhina, Joe Andrew and Robert Reid, eds, *Literary Tradition and Practice in Russian Culture*, Rodopi, Amsterdam, 1993, pp. 229-45.
36. Brodsky interviewed by Annie Epelboin, p. 38.
37. Czesław Milosz, 'A Huge Building of Strange Architecture', in Valentina Polukhina, *Brodsky Through the Eyes of His Contemporaries*, Macmillan, Houndmills, 1992, p. 326.
38. Lev Loseff, 'A New Conception of Poetry', ibid., p. 129.
39. The *poema* is a long narrative poem. The *bol'shoe stikhotvorenie* is an oxymoron, meaning, roughly speaking, 'a long lyric poem'.
40. Some of these poems are discussed in Ia. Gordin's article 'Strannik', *Russian Literature*, XXXVII-II/III, 1995, Special issue: V. Polukhina, ed., 'Joseph Brodsky', pp. 226-45.
41. See my article 'Zhanrovaia klaviatura Brodskogo', ibid., pp. 145-52.
42. Quote from Boris Khazanov, '"S tochki zreniia voron ...": Notes upon Joseph Brodsky on the Eve of His Birthday', *Literaturnaia gazeta*, 22 May 1996, p. 6.
43. Ibid.
44. Brodsky interviewed by John Glad, *Vremia i my*, op. cit., p. 168.
45. Khazanov, op. cit, p. 6.
46. N. Gorbanevskaia's interview with Brodsky, 'Byt' mozhet, samoe sviatoe, chto u nas est' - eto nash iazyk', *Russkaia mysl'*, 3 February 1983, pp. 8-9. Compare Iu.M. Lotman's view that poetry for Pushkin 'was an answer to everything. It became a justification in his own eyes and a promise of immortality'. Iu.M. Lotman, *A.S. Pushkin*, op. cit., p. 37.
47. Pavel Bavil'skii, 'Reestrik bytiia. Ot eposa Pushkina k eposu Brodskogo', *Nezavisimaia gazeta*, 29 September, 1993, p. 7.
48. Eduard Limonov, 'Poet-bukhgalter', *Muleta. Semeinyi al'bom, A-1984*, Paris, 1984, pp. 133-5.
49. Anatoly Naiman, 'Sgustok iazykovoi energii' in Polukhina, *Brodskii glazami sovremennikov*, op. cit., pp. 45-6.
50. Quoted in Ia. Gordin's 'Drugoi Brodskii' in G. Komarov, ed., *Iosif Brodskii razmerom podlinnika*, Tallinn, 1990, pp. 215-21. With additional examples this is reprinted as 'V svoem krugu', *Novoe russkoe slovo*, 20-21 September 1997, p. 39. The quotation 'I remember the miraculous moment' is the beginning of Pushkin's famous poem *To A.P. Kern*, 1825.
51. Ia. Gordin, 'V svoem krugu', op. cit., p. 39.
52. Joseph Brodsky interviewed by Annie Epelboin, p. 41. See also A. Zholkovskii '"Ia vas liubil ..." Brodskogo', in *Poetika Brodskogo*, pp. 38-62; Vladimir Vishniak, *Joseph Brodsky and Mary Stuart*, Alexandr Herzen Centre, Working Paper no. 4: University of Manchester, 1994, and 'Nekotorye nabliudeniia nad strukturoi i kompozitsiei *20 sonetov k Marii Stiuart Iosifa Brodskogo*', *Revue des Etudes Slaves*, LXX, 5, 1998, L'espace poétique: En hommage à Efim Etkind, pp. 705-17.
53. Tomas Venclova, 'O stikhotvorenii Iosifa Brodskogo *Litovskii Noktiurn: T.V.*, op. cit., p. 221.
54. Translated by Tatiana Retivova, in Lev Loseff and Valentina Polukhina, eds, *Joseph Brodsky: The Art of a Poem*, p. 118.
55. There are several articles about reminiscences of Pushkin in Brodsky's poetry, for example, Andrei Ranchin, '"Sluzhen'e muz chego-to tam ne terpit": Iosif Brodskii i poeziia Pushkina', *Strelets*, I, 1999, Paris-Moscow, New-York, pp. 214-34 and 'Ob odnom poeticheskom

treugol'nike: Pushkin - Khodasevich - Brodskii' in A.I. Zhuravleva, ed., *A.S. Pushkin: sbornik statei*, Filologicheskii fakul'tet MGU, Moscow, 1999, pp. 266-75; Irina Kovaleva and Anton Nesterov, 'O nekotorykh pushkinskikh reministsentsiiakh u I.A. Brodskogo', *Vestnik Moskovskogo universiteta*, seriia 9. Filologiia, IV, 1999, pp. 12-17; Natal'ia Galatskii, 'Ia zarazhen normal'nym klassitsizmom' (Pushkin i Brodskii), a paper to 'A.S. Pushkin 2000 Years. The Russian Romantic in a European Context', Uppsala, April 21-25, 1999.

56. Brodsky interviewed by Annie Epelboin., p. 41.
57. Ibid., p. 40. Speaking about his life in exile, Brodsky cited Pushkin:

For a man in exile, there is always the possibility for melodrama, or even drama. But for a poet, the real issue is you versus your language. There is a line in Pushkin that goes, more or less, 'You are a czar, so live alone. Take the free empty world where your free mind leads you to. You will hear the judgement of the simpleton and the roar of the cold crowd, but you ought to remain yourself.' This is the poet's ultimate duty - to write well, to do service to the language, to do what your language dictates to you.

James Atlas, 'The Poetic Triumph', *The New York Times Magazine*, 1980, December 21, p. 40.

Pushkin among Contemporary Poets: Self and Song in Sedakova

by

STEPHANIE SANDLER

Has Pushkin's poetry remained a relevant model for Russian poets in the late twentieth century? Some avant-garde poets have long said no, as they complete the task begun by the Futurists, throwing Pushkin overboard from the ship of modern culture. For them, he represents official, dead culture. At their boldest they even deride myths of Pushkin's death. Dmitrii Aleksandrovich Prigov, for example, gives us a Pushkin as empty as a Soviet leader in *The Captivating Star of Russian Poetry* (*Звезда пленительная русской поэзии*), where he rewrites Pushkin's duel as a parable about enemies of the people.[1] He dismantles the Soviet cult of the hero, and, in the process, takes aim at the holy myth of Pushkin's martyrdom.[2]

When others make mock of the national poet they often separate the myth of the poet from the virtues of his legacy (in this they follow the example not of the Futurists but of Marina Tsvetaeva in her *Poems to Pushkin* (*Стихи к Пушкину*, 1931).[3] A vivid image for this more subtle form of *épatage* appeared on the cover of the early 1990s almanac *Latin Quarter* (*Латинский квартал*): a photograph of the Moscow Pushkin monument encased in scaffolding (Illustration 1). It was a splendid self-image for a culture that saw itself as under repair, and the editors used it to suggest that one might want to improve homage to Pushkin, not tear down monuments to him. In that spirit, Timur Kibirov has successfully used motifs from Pushkin's life and writings in his long poem *To Serezha Gandelevskii* (the full Russian title is *Сереже Ганделевскому. О некоторых аспектах нынешней социокультурной ситуации*, 1990).[4] Kibirov's poem associates Pushkin with official Soviet culture, yet it reaffirms the pleasure and high spirits of Pushkin's own poetry. It is an excellent example of late Soviet poetic responses to Pushkin (the poem well describes the world of late Soviet Russia), and poses the question for us about how, in a period of social and cultural decline, poets made use of Pushkin's legacy. Kibirov's answer is intriguing for its unusual mix of irreverence with imitation. The most extraordinary poems of irreverence are surely those of Joseph Brodsky, written slightly earlier, for example *At the Pushkin Monument in Odessa* (*Перед памятником А. С. Пушкину в Одессе*, 1969 or 1970), 'I loved you' ('Я вас любил', 1974).[5] Brodsky was an important model for Kibirov, as for the poet to whom I now turn.

Latinskii kvartal cover illustration, early 1990s

Olga Sedakova is one of the most interesting poets writing in Russian today.[6] Her poems are an excellent point of departure for a discussion of Pushkin's presence in post-Soviet culture because she has meditated on this theme over a number of years, with essays and self-commentary published as recently as 1999. Sedakova's work bears the impact of many poets and thinkers: Heraclitus, the Bible, Dante, Rilke, Pound, Russian spiritual rhymes (духовные песни), the Bible, eighteenth-century odes, and the poetry of Blok, Mandelshtam, Khlebnikov, and many others. She has written tellingly about the different status accorded to Pushkin. 'Russian thought,' she has observed, 'tries to find itself and its future in its love for Pushkin, as if standing before a fortune-teller's mirror'.[7] Sedakova contrasts this to Pushkin's actual impact as a poet - less, she says, than that of Zhukovskii, Nekrasov, or Blok, which leads her to note the mysterious aspect of Pushkin's fame. Despite attempts to distort or overtake his image, he has remained a 'barrier of protection, often the last such genius-caretaker of a free creative culture ... He unites the "faithful"; hand in hand with him, the encroaching darkness is not frightening'.[8]

All of Sedakova's poetry seeks to stand as a beacon against such 'encroaching darkness', but I want to concentrate here on poems that pick up where Pushkin's poetry has left off. *Ballad of Continuation* (*Баллада продолжения*) and *Old Songs* (*Старые песни*) date to the late Soviet period: the former is from *The Wild Rose* (*Дикий шиповник*, 1978) and the latter appeared in 1990 but is dated 1980-82. Each bears an epigraph from Pushkin's poetry, which marks them strongly because Sedakova rarely uses epigraphs. They are only the top-most layer of Pushkinian thinking in the two poems, which are otherwise quite different. I begin with the earlier poem, *Ballad of Continuation*.

Ballad of Continuation concludes a triptych entitled *Selva selvaggia*, one of Sedakova's early experiments in creating lyric sequences. The title of the triptych, from the opening of Dante's *Inferno*, places the ballad in a dense thicket of repetitions and refrains, all of them musical in origin, as the subtitles of ballad, canzone, ballad suggests. (Music will connect this ballad to *Old Songs*, and to other Sedakova poems as well.)[9] In *Selva selvaggia*, *Ballad of Continuation* is the third and final poem, after *Leavetaking* (*Проводы*) and *Return of the Prodigal Son* (*Возвращение блудного сына*).[10] All three poems describe movement and escape, wandering and return, error and confession. The physical experience of movement through space in search of a discovery rather than in search of a place, and the ethical experience of acknowledging a wrong judgment, combine in what we might call *errancy*, drawing less on the Spenserian and Renaissance tradition of narratives about knights-errant than on biblical tales of wandering in search of God's truth.

Pushkin's inspiration is evident from the first lines of the ballad that opens *Selva selvaggia*, when a crystal sphere reprises Pushkin's 'magic crystal' ('магический кристалл') from the conclusion of *Evgenii Onegin*.[11] Across the entirety of *Selva selvaggia*, Sedakova follows moments of self-contemplation in reflective surfaces made of glass or water, real or imagined, and in this gesture she enacts the divination through mirroring that she has said the entire culture does when it looks at Pushkin. The image returned to the self always includes a remarkable transformation - the Prodigal Son sees himself as Jesus, for example. Self-examination is represented as a form of movement (Sedakova writes, in the canzone, *Return of the Prodigal Son*, that we walk 'like vision, transformed into substance' ['как зренье, сделанное веществом']).[12]

Wandering is pre-eminently important in *Ballad of Continuation*, and in many ways it repeats themes associated with the parable of the Prodigal Son. It ends in a time of celebration, much like the joy that marks the Prodigal Son's return. Paternal or divine reward seems incomprehensible, indeed the Biblical parable (from Luke 15) insists on the value of what is nearly lost (two shorter tales about recovering lost property come before it, and the second brother's angry exchange with his incomprehensibly forgiving and happy father come after it). A more secular and psychological rendition of this tale of loss and recovery (and one equally invested in the music and repetitions of song) would give us a poem like Elizabeth Bishop's fine villanelle *The Art of Losing*, but Sedakova holds fast to the divine meanings of loss and recovery, of celebration and return. These are among her overriding themes across the years of her work, perhaps most beautifully expressed in *Fifth Stanzas* (*Пятые стансы*, 1992), where images of monastic seclusion and ancient pilgrimage emphasize the religious dimensions of her theme.[13]

In *Ballad of Continuation*, however, another narrative of wandering and revelation is evoked, particularly by the three epigraphs (from Pushkin, *Imitations of the Koran* [*Подражания Корану*, 1824], Lermontov, *Three Palms* [*Три пальмы*, 1839], and Pasternak, *The Miracle* [*Чудо*, 1947]). Some commentary on these epigraphs is in order since, against her usual practice, the poet has prefaced a poem with several signposts that create expectations about theme, form, and aesthetic project. Sedakova herself has written an essay that fleshes out these expectations. It treats the Pasternak poem *The Miracle*, the source of her third epigraph, in the context of both Pushkin and Lermontov, presenting a poetic context for Pasternak's parable of the miraculous fig tree. She follows the practice of M. L. Gasparov in describing the semantic aureole attaching to Pushkin's, Lermontov's, and Pasternak's use of amphibraic tetrameter in stanzaic form; the source poem for this sequence, Zhukovskii's *Song of an Arab at the Grave of his Steed* (*Песнь араба над могилою коня*, 1809-10), features motifs which create the semantic aureole used in the later poems: an Arabian desert landscape with its images of heat/thirst and shade/water; the contrast between dynamic motion and stillness; futile attempts at resurrection; and, finally, the theme of immortality and miraculous resurrection.[14] Pushkin, who shortens Zhukovskii's stanzas from eight lines to six, repeats nearly all these motifs; he emphasized the moment when immortality is revealed and the dead are resurrected, which proves crucial for Sedakova.

Only in Pasternak's *The Miracle* do we find a narrative clearly based on the miracle of Jesus causing a fig tree to wither.[15] He adverts to the Bible's importance in the poem's first line, with its movement from Bethany to Jerusalem, and of course in the poem's context among the Biblical poems of the Zhivago cycle. But for Lermontov and Pushkin, as for Zhukovskii, the Bible would seem less important: Pushkin's poem recounts the miracle of a dead palm tree brought back to the beauty of being alive;[16] Lermontov shares this orientation to the East, even subtitling his poem 'An Eastern Tale'; his version is more pessimistic, and it extends Pushkin's theme of human complaint against God.[17] Lermontov's dissonant conclusion to a poem about divine retribution also seems a rebuke to Pushkin's tale of old age transformed to vibrant youth, as Boris Eikhenbaum once observed.[18]

Sedakova's variant on this tale is distinctive in several ways, perhaps best seen, first, by quoting the poem in full.

И путник усталый на бога роптал.
А.С.П.
В пустынных степях аравийской земли ...
М.Ю.Л.
Он шел из Вифании в Иерусалим ...
Б.Л.П.

И страшно и холодно стало в лесу.
Куда он зашел? И зачем на весу
судьбу его держат, короткую воду
в стакане безумном, в стекле из природы,
из слабости: вдруг раскатится, как ртуть.
И шел он, и слезы боялся смахнуть.

И некогда было: еще за ольху -
и вырастет ветер, как город вверху,
и дрогнет душа от собачьего лая.
И слабая жизнь, у стола засыпая,
бренча в угольках, завывая в трубе,
опять, как к ребенку, нагнется к тебе.

Но прежде проснется, кто в доме уснул,
услышит, что голосом сделался гул,
и в окна посмотрит, и встретит у входа
с лицом, говорящим: Я ум и свобода,
я все, чего нет у тебя впереди.
Но хлеба не жалко, и ты заходи.

И долго, пока он еще исчезал,
и знал, что упал, и стакан расплескал,
как этого просит старик, пораженный
худым долголетьем, как хочет влюбленный
его расплескать, оставаясь вдвоем, -
а он не просил, и не помнил о том. -

И долго, пока он еще исчезал,
и мимо него этот сброд проползал,
который и взгляда людского стыдится,
и в дуплях, и в норах, и в щелях плодится -
а здесь проползал, не стыдясь его глаз,
как будто он не жил и не был у нас. -

Так долго, пока он еще исчезал,
твердил он: Ты все, чего я не узнал,
ты ум и свобода, ты полное зренье,
я - обликом ставшее кровотеченье,

И тут раздалось, обрывая его:
- Я ум и свобода, но ты - торжество.[19]

(And the weary traveller grumbled at God ...
A. S. P.
In the desert steppes of the lands of Arabia ...
M. Iu. L.
He went forth from Bethany to Jerusalem ...
B. L. P.

In the forest, all grew frightening and cold.
Where was he? And why, in mid-air,
was his fate held up, like shallow water
in a cup of madness, in the glass of nature,
out of weakness, then suddenly roll off like a ball of mercury?
And he walked on, and feared to wipe away his tears.

And there was no time: just past the alder tree -
and the wind will rise up, like a town up above,
and the soul will shudder at the barking dog.
And weakened life, falling asleep at the table,
strumming in the embers, howling in the chimney,
will bend over you again as if you were a child.

But first, someone asleep in the house will awake,
will hear the rumble turn into voice,
and will look out the windows, and meet at the entrance
with someone, a face, saying, 'I am wisdom and freedom,
I am everything that you will not have.
But there is plenty of bread, so yes, come in.'

And for a long time, while he was still disappearing
and knew he had fallen, had spilled out the cup,
knew how this would be asked by an old man wasted to
thinness by his long years of life, knew how a lover wants
to spill it when left, just the two of them, -
yet he did not ask, and he did not remember it. -

But for a long time, while he was still disappearing,
and this tattered crowd crawled past him,
a crowd ashamed even of the gaze of human eyes,
it multiplies in hollows, in holes, and in little crannies -
even here did it crawl, not ashamed of his glance,
as if he were not alive and was not here with us. -

So, for such a long time, while he was still disappearing,
he said, 'You are everything that I did not come to know,
you are wisdom and freedom, you are vision complete,
and I - have taken on the appearance of flowing blood.'

Then a voice was heard, cutting him off:
'I am wisdom and freedom, but you - are solemn celebration.')[20]

Sedakova's poem would at first seem neither to reinstate the Biblical tale of Pasternak's poem nor the Eastern desert landscape of Pushkin's and Lermontov's poems. Her landscape is a forest, predicted by the title of the cycle (*Selva selvaggia*) and the Dantean forest it suggests. The lexical repetitions of her lines bring an element of song back into the form (recall Pushkin's elimination of Zhukovskii's refrain: Sedakova conveys some of the effects of the lost refrain with her intoned repetitions). Indeed her concluding note of praise well exemplifies the musical celebration heard throughout *Ballad of Continuation*.

What, we might ask, is celebrated here? The implicit narrative across all three parts of *Selva selvaggia* tells of wandering and return, of a spiritual quest that leads back to the discovery of what had seemed abandoned. In the first of the three stanzas in *Ballad of Continuation* that begin 'for such a long time, while he was still disappearing', Sedakova offers us a series of metaphors that link that quest to death and renewal. The cup that spills over is the cup of life itself, but for every old man who will not ask for it to be picked up there is an enthusiastic lover whose passion for time alone with his beloved beautifully models a wish to return to life. Sedakova here introduces the idea of resurrection she had associated with the poems denoted by her epigraphs, one she particularly connected to Pushkin's poem. One might say that, in *Ballad of Continuation*, she effectively returns this kind of poem to one of its Pushkinian premises, this despite her having reversed many of the other motifs, like the desert landscape or the thirst it would engender.

Sedakova also reprises Pushkin's essentially and broadly Biblical language, without relying on the retelling of a specific parable found in Pasternak's *The Miracle*. But Pasternak's poem has a strong presence here, too, for he had repeated Pushkin's celebration of divine power in his own way: 'But a miracle is a miracle, a miracle is God. / When we are confused, in the midst of our straggling, / It overtakes us, and instantly confounds us' ('Но чудо есть чудо, и чудо есть бог. / Когда мы в смятеньи, тогда средь разброда, / Оно настигает мгновенно, врасплох'.)[21] Pasternak's last stanza seeks a minute of freedom among the images of miracle, which in turn grounds the emphasis on freedom ('ум и свобода') in Sedakova's poem.[22]

To comprehend her use of the idea of freedom, however, we need one more subtext: it might well have appeared among the epigraphs to *Ballad of Continuation* since it bears the semantic aureole described in the essay on Pasternak's *The Miracle*; indeed, it is discussed there. The poem is Zabolotskii's 1938 *A Lake in the Forest* (*Лесное озеро*), important not least for its forest setting, which motivates Sedakova's transfer of scene from the Biblical desert (as does the reference to Dante). The lake in Zabolotskii's title is also significant: Sedakova's watery and reflective surfaces owe much to his example, as does her imagery of a cup that spills over with water, including the sexual connotations of that entire passage (Zabolotskii's lake is rightly described by Darra Goldstein as 'the image of a young and beautiful virgin, full of life').[23] In that same passage with the overflowing cup in *Ballad of Continuation*, we encounter the image of an old and ailing man, also found in *A Lake in the Forest*.

Zabolotskii's earthiness grounds Sedakova's descriptions, then, and like him she uses these elements of landscape to create a scene for spiritual quest and possible transcendence. Sedakova has commented on Zabolotskii's pantheistic descriptions of the natural world with this corrective: 'his Muse perhaps also inherited Slavic beliefs that were obscure for the nineteenth century', by which she means 'the prosaic experience of peasants communing with the world'. The dead live on in the clouds, creatures, and foliage of the visible world, she writes, praising Zabolotskii's intense compassion for all living creatures and inanimate objects.[24] In one line of his poem, where the lake is described as 'thinking its own separate thought' ('мыслила мыслью отдельной'),²⁵ he animates a natural object with powers for thought and imagination in a way we often find in Sedakova's poetry.²⁶

Zabolotskii composed *A Lake in the Forest* in a closed freight car while being transported to a forced labour camp in Siberia. That scene of creation inevitably shapes one's reading of his poem, including its first line, 'Once again, there flashed across my mind, fettered with sleep' ('Опять мне блеснула, окована сном'), where the fetters of sleep take on an additional and terribly literal meaning. Sedakova, in a short essay on Zabolotskii, tersely notes that it was written during transport to the camps, without drawing any conclusion from that fact, and certainly one finds in his poem a calmly beautiful scene that seems an escape from closed captivity. But once we realize that the poem is an important source for her images and aspirations in *Ballad of Continuation*, we must consider, too, the possibility that Zabolotskii's experience in creating the poem is also meaningful for her text. One might read the male figure mentioned from the poem's first stanza as Zabolotskii himself, asking as if aloud where he has ended up, feeling the cold fear of a journey that holds his fate in the air before him, and, as the poem continues, hearing the comforting voice of God or nature itself in the forest scene around him. Zabolotskii also becomes the one who disappears, indeed who keeps disappearing for such a long time; he seems a part of a 'tattered crowd' that cannot be looked at directly and that is an emblem of shame; all the time that he is disappearing (that is, that he is hidden away in the camp), he firmly says (by his refusal to mentally collapse at the weight of these experiences) to the natural world that comforts him that he believes in it, and the voice he hears answering him back insists that he is cause for solemn celebration. The title and project of an earlier and very famous Zabolotskii poem, *The Celebration of Agriculture* (*Торжество земледелия*, 1929-1930), further link the celebration that ends this poem back to the fate and poetic achievement of Zabolotskii.

The potency of this biographical allegory does not weaken other philosophical, aesthetic, or religious meanings in the poem; it is characteristic of Sedakova's poetry that meanings exist on many planes, criss-crossing beautifully and distinctively before a reader's eyes, just as the poems draw on a wide multitude of literary and other subtexts that are woven into idiosyncratic and harmonious patterns. But the aspect of the poem that points toward one poet's experience of suffering at the hands of a cruel state, and of surviving to compose poems that celebrate the beauty and imagination of the natural world, is more than one theme or device among many. It shows us that Sedakova also strives to emulate Zabolotskii's insistence on celebration, his firm will to praise beauty even when there is so much ugliness around him. And it shows us that she believes that one task of poems in the present is to include true tales about poems and poets of the past.

We may seem to have strayed far from Pushkin, in a sense exemplifying the dangers of *errancy* Sedakova writes about so often, but in fact we have simply come back to the poem's theme of continuation, affirming Sedakova's success in continuing Zabolotskii's poetic and spiritual quest. She also continues the themes from the first two poems in *Selva selvaggia*, writing of a Dantesque journey that continues. (Sedakova will also, of course, have Pushkin's *Wanderer* [*Странник*, 1836] in mind as well.)[27] By emphasizing continuity, she tells us that the ballad, despite its coming last in a sequence, represents no moment of closure or conclusion. The point is important, given her focus on the *return* of the Prodigal Son in the second poem in *Selva selvaggia*, for she shows us an equal interest in the enduring process of wandering, in the discoveries and self-discoveries of such a quest. In a poem whose epigraphs mix Eastern and Western religious traditions, including an invocation of Eastern quietism, Sedakova's wanderer comes upon a discovery of his own sanctity; the triumphant celebration ('торжество') of the last lines echoes the Prodigal Son's return and the mortal man's revelation of the divine spark he carries in his soul.

Sedakova's poem is a formal continuation as well, particularly of Pushkin's use of ballad form. In drawing her epigraph from the last of his *Imitations of the Koran*, Sedakova points us toward a poem in that cycle that stands out for its use of the ballad tradition within a context that emphasizes religious and philosophical themes.[28] Her own turn to ballad form is thus modeled on Pushkin's, and, like him, she effectively reminds her readers that the ballad form comes down to us (from oral traditions) in several variants, not just the famous romantic form (as in Pushkin's *Black Shawl* [*Черная шаль*, 1820]).[29] Pushkin's imitation from the Koran uses the ballad form associated with hymns and spiritual verse, best documented for the English-speaking world in F. J. Child's monumental *English and Scottish Ballads* (1857-58). The title *Ballad of Continuation*, then, suggests a formal act of continuation as much as a philosophical, spiritual, psychological one: Sedakova continues Pushkin's form, just as she will in her *Old Songs*, to which I am about to turn.

Here our readings must be more cursory, for *Old Songs* fill three large notebooks, 39 poems in all. The second and third notebooks bear dedications to Sedakova's grandmother,[30] but the first notebook has an epigraph, 'What is that turning white on the green hill?' ('Что белеется на горе зеленой?'), from Pushkin's unfinished translation of a Serbian song which is not included in his *Songs of the Western Slavs* (*Песни западных славян*, 1834), but usually printed just after it.[31] Sedakova repeats this formal feature of establishing poems that are connected to, but not a part of, a cycle (his unfinished 'Menko Vuich is writing a letter' ['Менко Вуич грамоту пишет'] also stands just outside his *Songs*): she offers us a deliberate progression through three notebooks in *Old Songs*, each ending with poems that are not included.[32] In *Old Songs*, Sedakova also draws on Pushkin's *Songs* thematically; some of her images can be traced to his songs, and to common sources in the folk tradition.

In one poem, *Consolation* (*Утешенье*), she asks his question, 'What is that turning white on the green hill?', very slightly changing his verb, but she gives a strikingly different answer. In Pushkin's poem, the white motion on the green hill is no natural object (neither snow nor swan), but the tent of Asan-Aga, and the poem ends with the lament of his wife, Asan-Aginitsa. Here is Sedakova's poem:

> Утешенье
> Не гадай о собственной смерти
> и не радуйся, что все пропало,
> не задумывай, как тебя оплачут,
> как замучит их поздняя жалость.
>
> Это все плохое утешенье,
> для земли обидная забава.
>
> Лучше скажи и подумай:
> что белеет на горе зеленой?
>
> На горе зеленой сады играют
> и до самой воды доходят,
> как ягнята с золотыми бубенцами -
> белые ягнята на горе зеленой.
>
> А смерть придет, никого не спросит.[33]
>
> (Consolation
> Do not make guesses about your own death
> and do not feel glad that all is lost,
> do not think that you will be mourned
> or that a belated feeling of pity will trouble them.
>
> All of this is poor consolation,
> for the earth it is an offending amusement.
>
> Better, think and say this:
> what is that turning white on the green hill?
>
> On the green hill gardens sparkle
> and go right up to the water's edge,
> like lambs wearing golden bells -
> white lambs on the green hill.
>
> And death will come, it will ask no one.)

Sedakova reconfigures Pushkin's imagery: the flickers of light on the hill are signs of natural growth and movement ('garden' ['сад'], 'water' ['вода'] frequent words in Sedakova's lexicon) that look like little white lambs. In the word for lambs, 'ягнята/iagniata', she rearranges the sounds of the exotic name found in Pushkin's poem: 'iagniata' is conjured paranomastically from the name Asan-aginitsa. Sedakova also frames Pushkin's natural and domestic scene with gentle if stern imperatives. It is typical of her work, particularly of these songs, for abstract language that invokes spiritual laws to wrap around a narrative or scenic description.

As with *Ballad of Continuation*, questions of formal repetition and embellishment are also important in Sedakova's engagement with Pushkin's poetic legacy in *Old Songs*: she revives his form of the song, a literary imitation of Slavic folk poetry in accentual verse.[34] Pushkin was drawn to this form for its ability to enrich the poetic lexicon of his age; his preface to *Songs of the Western Slavs* quotes a letter from Prosper Mérimée that defends the enterprise for its examples of local colour.[35] He would have appreciated the political value of recreating Slavic folk songs for élite Russian readers, part of the age's larger project of creating a Russian national literature. Can Sedakova, at the end of the Soviet period, be said to be doing anything remotely similar?

A cursory reading of *Old Songs* makes such an argument seem implausible, for the poems' realm is that of the spirit, not of the nation. The actions of the poems involve love, pity, deceit, desire, loss, lament, servitude, divination, and rejoicing. A few include flights of heroic action, although the hero is more likely to be a saint than a soldier (one song from the second notebook, *Marching Song* [*Походная песня*], is about two soldiers). The poems tell of spiritual and psychological quests, and the nouns of these songs tend to be experiences, actions, or concepts (injury, sin, consolation, miracle, mystery), rather than concrete objects or persons. Because the actions of the poems are often performed by abstractions, these deceptively simple songs can be as difficult to interpret as the earlier work in *The Wild Rose* or the later *Iambs* (*Ямбы*), *Elegies* (*Элегии*), or *Poems in the Manner of Alexander Pope* (*Стихи в манере Александра Попа*).[36] Persons do appear: we hear of a wife tested for her unfaithfulness, a fortune-teller urged to announce that she can see nothing, an old woman arguing with a prisoner. All of these figures are symbolic of the values tested in *Old Songs*, for the poet is fascinated by the moments when faith is questioned, truth is divined, argument pursued, and captivity transcended. If the songs lack necessarily the concentration on what I have called errancy in *Selva selvaggia*, still they reprise its themes of error and wandering, for example in the song about the Prodigal Son entitled *A Dream* (*Сон*). The poet broadens the meanings of error by travelling repeatedly down the pathways it traces out: 'In every word there is a road / a mournful and ardent path' ('В каждом слове есть / путь унылый и страстный').[37]

Certainly her poems - all her poems, not just *Old Songs* - are meant as exemplary aesthetic artifacts in a world (the late Soviet world) where poetry was increasingly devalued and where the spiritual revelations and aesthetic pleasures of poetry seemed distant to most Russians. Her project has fewer nationalist overtones than Pushkin's in *Songs of the Western Slavs*, perhaps because the more unsavoury political meanings of nationalism repel her, perhaps because her spiritual motivations usually keep her poems far from politics.[38] Sedakova's idea of genuine poetry makes her doubt the public positions a poet might take,[39] yet as we have seen in *Ballad of Continuation*, she finds ways in even her profoundly spiritual poems to include observations about the fate of the poet in times of political danger. Her allusions to the experience of Nikolai Zabolotskii, encoded in her use of subtexts and of the ballad's semantic aureole, insist that we note this aspect of the poem, even as other subtexts urge us to see the poem's underlying narrative about an errant soul.

Such contextualizing perhaps urges us to interpret the poem's political principles as ethical rather than political in any narrow sense. Sedakova has only rarely undertaken to make the poet's voice more loudly heard in the public realm, and in every instance her statements resound with intonations of modesty and great subtlety.[40] In that quietness of voice, she might seem to differ from Pushkin, whose wish for public esteem has been explored by several scholars and thinkers, most recently David Bethea in *Realizing Metaphors*.[41] But the difference is deceiving. Without seeking any equivalent to Pushkin's position, for example, as a budding historian, Sedakova emulates the fine balance in his work between engagement with contemporary cultural politics and commitment to transcendent aesthetic values. Her Pushkin is very far from the quasi-Decembrist invented during the Soviet period, yet she does not move in the opposite direction advanced in the post-Soviet period by Valentin Nepomniashchii and others who recreate Pushkin as a representative of Orthodoxy.[42] This tangential question, Sedakova's views on religious readings of Pushkin, is complex, and brings us into the more turbulent period of the 1990s: we can say, though, that she has distanced herself from narrowly religious readings, for example in a sly paper she presented before the Moscow Biblical-Theological Institute in 1999 on Pushkin's *gluposti* ('stupidities'). That paper includes the claim that turning to 'the topic of Christianity and "religiosity" in general in Pushkin threatens more than others to cause its proponents to fall into precisely the *gluposti* Pushkin had in mind: immodesty, simplemindedness, and moralizing'.[43] In deftly repudiating the inflated rhetoric of nationalistic religious interpretations of Pushkin, Sedakova comes close to a political stand, of course, but she is motivated, I believe, by aesthetic impulses - by a wish to create for the reading public a Pushkin truer to his full vision of human experience, which is also a wish to preserve historically truer accounts of his work.

Sedakova's sense of that truer Pushkin (she would likely reject the epithet) depends on fresh interpretations of well-canonized, anthology pieces as well as new attention to his little-known jottings and poems. One feels the latter especially in her choice of epigraphs (from *Imitations of The Koran* and *Songs of the Western Slavs*),[44] for these are translations and adaptations, rather than the central achievements of his work. Both are projects in which Pushkin introduced a different point of view or form or intonation into Russian poetry, which means that we hear another voice (including the voice of another culture) in the poems as much as we hear Pushkin's. Sedakova wrote an essay on *The Bronze Horseman*, a structuralist reading of its compositional and plot features,[45] and there are moments when she turns to major and more characteristic works, for example in her essays.[46] Still, it is significant that Sedakova would look to relatively less well-known poems by Pushkin for inspiration; in that impulse she resembles, oddly, Kibirov, who drew on the unfinished prose fragment 'Maria Schoning' for his verse epistle mentioned at the start of this chapter. Such an impulse to look at Pushkin's less famous writings shows us the scholarly side of Sedakova, and it is also her way of circumnavigating the massive myth of Pushkin, indeed of finding her way through the myth back toward the poetic legacy of language, rhythms, and meanings.

If this is a conservative move, then it is so only in a narrow and very specific sense. The poet wishes to keep hold of an idea of poetry from the past, particularly to ensure that less well-known or less well absorbed aspects of the poetry are not forgotten. Sedakova has praised the wish to preserve the past in modernist poetry, and her attention to Pushkin can be read as one instance of preservation in her own work.[47] But the conservatism of this attention should not blind us to its elements of fresh, new thinking: her turn to Pushkin may inspire us toward a more innovative reading of his work, and of her own as well.

I shall make this last point in a cursory way. The most distinctive thing about Sedakova's poetry, I believe, is the way she disperses selfhood in her poems across the objects, ideas, and persons. As she wrote in an afterword to the English edition of *The Wild Rose*:

> If one uses the rather schematic division, proposed by Brodsky, of poetry being either *song* or *confession* (confession of course in the popular sense), then poetry as *song* has always attracted me. In song a person does not engage in self-expression (except unwittingly), rather he wills himself to unite with something essentially other.[48]

A large topic hides here, for Sedakova's songs unquestionably also express a self; to understand the topic, one would need to address the little explored question of how she, like Pasternak and Brodsky, writes poetry that is dense with the logic of philosophy even as it is infused by the beauty of song. But Pushkin's example is also relevant, and in ways that may yield new perspectives on his poetry of self-creation. Monika Greenleaf has provided the best account of Pushkin's elegant patterns of self-description,[49] but Sedakova's songs of the self also lead us toward poems where he seems most absent. Writing of Pushkin, she has exclaimed that no other lyric poet had his capacity to imagine the world without himself in it: 'Pushkin leaves the world free of himself'.[50] New attention to works like *Songs of the Western Slavs* and *Imitations of the Koran* can teach us how poems with few self-referential flourishes also participate in the myths of the poet we inherit from Pushkin. And that topic, in turn, could well circle us back to the contemporary period, when models of poetic self-creation seem to have taken so many new forms.

Stephanie Sandler

NOTES

My thanks to Olga Sedakova for illuminating conversations and for providing me with copies of her published and unpublished writings, and to John Malmstad for very helpful comments on this chapter.

1. Dmitrii Aleksandrovich Prigov, *Napisannoe s 1975 po 1989*, *Novoe literaturnoe obozrenie*, Moscow, 1997, pp. 239-44; Prigov's early poems about Pushkin appear in this volume as well (including pp. 88-91, 96, 107).
2. Also his target in a poem that begins 'Kto vydet skazhet chestno: / Ia Pushkina ubil!' Ibid., p. 88.
3. Prigov daringly suggests that Pushkin's poetry is as tainted as is the myth, as in his poem 'Vnimatel'no kol' prigliadet'sia segodnia', which ends 'A vot by stikhi ia ego unichtozhil - / Ved' obraz oni prinizhaiut ego' (Ibid., p. 90).
4. An excellent discussion of this poem appears in Kevin M. F. Platt, *History in a Grotesque Key: Russian Literature and the Idea of Revolution*, Stanford University Press, Stanford, 1997, pp. 171-82. For the poem, see Timur Kibirov, *Santimenti: Vosem' knig,* Izdatel'stvo 'Risk,' Belgorod, 1994, pp. 297-304; or Platt, pp. 272-85, which includes facing translation into English.
5. The topic of Brodsky and Pushkin is interestingly treated in Valentina Polukhina's contribution to this volume; see also her extensive bibliographical references there. For an instance of pure reverence, see the many Pushkin-inspired poems of Bella Akhmadulina: *Zimniaia zamknutost',* Pushkinskii fond, St Petersburg, 1999, collects her poems and criticism that refer to Pushkin. Another intriguing expression of admiration for Pushkin are the poems that finish his incomplete fragments. For a striking instance, see Genrikh Sapgir, 'Chernoviki Pushkina', *Druzhba narodov*, IV, 1999, pp. 110-15 (the poems were first published in 1992).
6. Even her detractors, like Vladimir Slavetskii, writing in a disdainful *Novyi mir* review essay, praised *Starye pesni*, a focus for the present chapter; see Vladimir Slavetskii, 'Dorogi i tropinka', *Novyi mir,* IV, 1995, pp. 233-7. Similarly hostile is Vladimir Slavianskii, 'Iz polnogo do dna v glubokoe do kraev: O stikhakh Ol'gi Sedakovoi', *Novyi mir,* X, 1995, pp. 224-31. Admiration for *Starye pesni* and some discerning comments about the poetry appear in Mikhail Kopeliovich, 'Iavlenie Sedakovoi', *Znamia*, VIII, 1996, pp. 205-13.
   For admiring responses to *Dikii shipovnik,* see Viacheslav Vs. Ivanov, introduction to Sedakova, 'Solovei, filomela, sud'ba ...', *Druzhba narodov,* X, 1988, pp. 121-5; introduction on p. 121; Sergei Averintsev, 'Gore, polnoe do dna', in Sedakova, *Stikhi,* Gnozis, Moscow, 1994, pp. 358-63; D. S. (= V. A. Saitanov), 'Ol'ga Sedakova: Novyi put''', in Sedakova, *Vrata, okna, arki*, YMCA Press, Paris, 1986, pp. 113-28, which also includes enthusiastic comments about *Starye pesni*.
7. Ol'ga Sedakova, 'Pushkin Akhmatovoi i Tsvetaevoi' (paper presented at the Moscow Tsvetaeva museum, May, 1996).
8. Ibid., p. 2. The 'encroaching darkness' recalls a description in Vladislav Khodasevich's 'Koleblemyi trenozhnik' (1921), in Khodasevich, *Sobranie sochinenii*, Soglasie, Moscow, 1996-97, II, pp. 77-85.
9. Pertinent poems include *Predpesnia, Penie* (both in *Dikii shipovnik,* where two musical interludes also punctuate the volume), and, through its indirect relationship to Wagner's opera, the cycle *Tristan i Izol'da*. See Sedakova, *Stikhi*, op. cit., pp. 30, 43, 100-128.
10. The Prodigal Son tale is extremely important to Sedakova: it is retold in *Pobeg bludnogo syna* (in *Dikii shipovnik*) and invoked in *Stansy pervye*; see Sedakova, *Stikhi,* op. cit., pp. 32-3, 225-8. It is also the subject of one of the *Starye pesni*, mentioned below.
11. Sedakova's *Leavetaking* begins: 'Из тайных слез, из их копилки тайной / как будто шар нам вынули хрустальный - // и человек в одежде поминальной / несет последнюю свечу': see Sedakova, *Stikhi,* op. cit., p. 18.

12. Sedakova, *Stikhi*, op. cit., p. 23.
13. Like *Ballad of Continuation*, *Fifth Stanzas* sustains an aesthetic and self-consciously poetic reading as well. For the text of the poem, see Sedakova, *Stikhi*, pp. 255-8.
14. Sedakova, '*Chudo* Borisa Pasternaka v russkoi poeticheskoi traditsii' in *Pasternakovskie chteniia* 2, Nasledie, Moscow, 1998, pp. 204-14; see pp. 206-7 on Zhukovskii. A slightly different version (with a computer-related garble in the ending) is available on the web at www.rema.ru:8101/komment/vadvad/sedakova/paster.htm.
15. For the Biblical antecedent, see Matthew 21:18-22 and Mark 11:12-14.
16. Yet one should not conclude that Pushkin's poem is in no sense Biblical: as Boris Tomashevskii observed, he drew on a translation of the Koran (by M. Verevkin, 1790) that used the language and style of Church Slavic. See Tomashevskii, *Pushkin. Kniga vtoraia*, Izdatel'stvo AN SSSR, Moscow-Leningrad, 1961, p. 19.
17. Sedakova notes both these points in '*Chudo* Borisa Pasternaka'.
18. B. M. Eikhenbaum, *Stat'i o Lermontove*, Izdatel'stvo AN SSSR, Moscow-Leningrad, 1961, p. 112, quoted in M. Iu. Lermontov, *Sobranie sochinenii*, Khudozhestvennaia literatura, Moscow, 1975, I, pp. 527-8. The commentary for this poem concentrates on its role in a polemic among Granovskii, Belinskii, and later Chernyshevskii; this aspect of the poem's history little interests Sedakova; in fact her realignment of it in a sequence from Pushkin to Pasternak emerges as a corrective to readings that stress political allegory.
19. Sedakova, *Stikhi*, op. cit., pp. 25-6.
20. The translation, as throughout this chapter, is my own, but I have consulted the version in Sedakova, *The Wild Rose*, translated by Richard McKane, Approach, London, 1998, pp. 27-9, and used several of its locutions.
21. Pasternak, *Chudo*, in Pasternak, *Stikhotvoreniia i poemy*, Sovetskii pisatel', Leningrad, 1990, II, pp. 78-80, quotation on p. 80. For a translation of the poem into English, see Pasternak, *Doctor Zhivago*, translated by Max Hayward and Manya Harari, poems translated by Bernard Guilbert Guerney, Ballantine, New York, 1981, pp. 554-5. I have used some locutions from this translation in my more literal version here.
22. I suspect that his poem also provided a stimulus to her *Elegiia smokovnitsy*, in Sedakova, *Stikhi*, op. cit., pp. 306-8.
23. Darra Goldstein, *Nikolai Zabolotsky: Play for Mortal Stakes*, Cambridge University Press, Cambridge, 1993, p. 215.
24. Ol'ga Sedakova, 'O Zabolotskom', *Krug chteniia*, V, 1995, pp. 83-4. Sedakova appended to this brief essay a few of his poems, *Lesnoe ozero* among them.
25. N. A. Zabolotskii, *Stikhotvoreniia i poemy*, Sovetskii pisatel', Moscow-Leningrad, 1965, p. 84. For a good translation of the entire poem, see Goldstein, op. cit., pp. 213-14.
26. This aspect of Zabolotskii's work is well illuminated in Nikita Zabolotskii, '"Prirody ochistitel'naia sila": Sotsial'no-eticheskie elementy naturfilosofskoi poezii Zabolotskogo', *Voprosy literatury*, July-August, 1999, pp. 17-36; *Lesnoe ozero* is briefly discussed in the essay, pp. 26-7. My thanks to Tatiana Babyonysheva for bringing this essay to my attention, and for wonderful conversations about Zabolotskii and Sedakova.
27. For a splendid reading of Pushkin's poem, see Andrew Kahn, 'Pushkin's Wanderer Fantasies', in Stephanie Sandler, ed., *Rereading Russian Poetry*, Yale University Press, New Haven, 1999, pp. 225-47.
28. Other poems in the *Podrazhaniia Koranu* rely more on eighteenth-century Russian philosophical ode, translations of the psalms, or *dukhovnye stikhi*. See Tomashevskii, *Pushkin. Kniga vtoraia*, pp. 25-7, for a concise description of the formal features of *Podrazhaniia Koranu*.
29. In another reading that follows Gasparov's idea of the poem's semantic aureole, Michael Wachtel has written on the many poems shaped by *Chernaia shal'*: see Wachtel, *The Development of Russian Verse: Meter and its Meanings*, Cambridge University Press, Cambridge, 1998, pp. 20-58. Note that the romantic ballad discussed here has the same amphibraic tetrameter found in the poems Sedakova discusses in '*Chudo* Borisa Pasternaka' but with couplet, not stanzaic, form.

30. On Sedakova's dedication of the cycle to her grandmother, see her comments in Sedakova, *The Wild Rose*, op. cit., p. 228.
31. A. S. Pushkin, *Polnoe sobranie sochinenii*, Nauka, Leningrad, 1977-79, III, p. 295, for the entirety of *Pesni zapadnykh slavian*, see vol. III, pp. 263-93.
32. Compare *Dikii Shipovnik*, where musical interludes are placed as pauses in the sequence of poems.
33. Sedakova, *Stikhi*, op. cit., p. 138.
34. Sedakova's reliance on the Pushkinian metrical model has been noted in D. S., op. cit., p. 124. On the metrical features of strict accentual verse, or *taktovik*, see Gasparov, 'Russkii narodnyi stikh i ego literaturnye imitatsii', in Gasparov, *Izbrannye trudy, Iazyki russkoi kul'tury*, Moscow, 1997, III, pp. 54-131; Gasparov, 'Taktovik v poezii XX veka', in Gasparov, *Sovremennyi russkii stikhi: Metrika i ritmika*, Nauka, Moscow, 1974, pp. 294-351; and Barry P. Scherr, *Russian Poetry: Rhythm, Meter, and Rhyme*, University of California Press, Berkeley, 1986, pp. 160-9.
35. For a discussion of Pushkin and Mérimée, see, David Baguley's 'Pushkin and Mérimée, the French Connection: On Hoaxes and Imposters' in Joe Andrew and Robert Reid, eds, *Pushkin's Legacy*, Rodopi, Amsterdam and Atlanta, 2002.
36. One of the most lucid songs, *Nevernaia zhena*, defied the comprehension of Mikhail Kopeliovich in 'Iavlenie Sedakovoi', p. 211 (he calls the poem utterly confusing).
37. Sedakova, *Stikhi*, op. cit., p. 153.
38. Valentina Polukhina, however, rightly notes political impulses in the poem *Elegiia, perekhodiashchaia v rekviem* and in the essay 'Puteshestvie v Briansk': Polukhina, 'Ol'ga Sedakova', in Christine D. Tomei, ed. *Russian Women Writers*, Garland Press, New York, 1999, II, pp. 1445-8; see p. 1446. For the poem and the elegy, respectively, see Sedakova, *Stikhi*, op. cit., pp. 259-68 and *Volga*, V-VI, 1992, pp. 138-57. Sedakova's observations about Soviet commemorations of the Second World War are also pertinent: for these reflections on politically motivated artistic expressions, see her contribution to '"Voiny u nikh v pamiati netu, voina u nikh tol'ko v krovi"', *Znamia*, V, 1995, pp. 183-99; see p. 196.
39. See Sedakova, '"Vakantsiia poeta": k poetologii Pasternaka', '*Byt' znamenitym nekrasivo'*: *Pasternakovskie chteniia*, I, Nasledie, Moscow, 1992, pp. 24-30; translated into English by Vitaly Chernetsky as 'The Vacancy of a Poet: Toward a Poetology of Pasternak', in Sandler, ed., *Rereading Russian Poetry*, op. cit., pp. 71-7.
40. Perhaps the best instance is her work, beginning in 1998-99, on a radio show about poetry. It includes an opportunity for her listeners to call in their questions.
41. Bethea, *Realizing Metaphors: Alexander Pushkin and the Life of the Poet*, University of Wisconsin Press, Madison, 1998. Bethea (in my view) exaggerates Pushkin's wish for public esteem and the role of ambition in his poetic development, but his opinion is shared by others and rightly calls attention to important and complicated aspects of Pushkin's creative psyche.
42. On the creation of an Orthodox Pushkin in the contemporary period, see Brian Horowitz's review of the first four issues of *Moskovskii Pushkinist* and Wendy Slater, 'The Patriots' Pushkin', *Slavic Review*, LVIII, 2, June, 1999, pp. 407-27, 434-9.
43. Sedakova, '"Nesmertnye tainstvennye chuvstva" (o khristianstve A. S. Pushkina)' (presented at the Andreevskie chteniia, Bibleisko-bogoslovskii institut Sv. Apostola Andreiia, December 12-13, 1999, Tsvetaeva museum, Moscow); quotation from p. 3, typescript; an English translation of this paper, in a slightly different version, appears as '"Non-Mortal and Mysterious Feelings": On Pushkin's Christianity' in *Pushkin's Legacy*.
44. There is also a third Pushkin epigraph, used in a journal publication of several poems from *Dikii Shipovnik* but not included in the book: it is a line from Pushkin's translation from André Chénier, 'Bliz mest, gde tsarstvuet Venetsiia zlataia'. The quoted line is the last, 'I tainye stikhi obdumyvat' liubliu ...': see Sedakova, 'Iz knigi "Dikii shipovnik": Legendy i fantazii', *Znamia*, VIII, 1992, pp. 103-10, epigraph on p. 103. That publication includes *Ballada prodolzheniia*, but with no epigraphs.
45. '*Mednyi vsadnik*: Kompozitsiia konflikta', *Rossiia-Russia*, VII, 1991, pp. 39-55.

46. For example, she quotes a landscape description from *Derevnia* (1819) as an instance of something that feels fated in 'Zametki i vospominaniia o raznykh stikhotvoreniiakh, a takzhe POKHVALA POEZII', in Sedakova, *Stikhi*, op. cit., p. 318.
47. Sedakova, 'Uzel zhizni, v kotorom my uznany: Russkaia poeziia 30-40 godov kak dukhovnyi opyt' (unpublished paper, 1999).
48. Sedakova, *The Wild Rose*, op. cit., p. 231. I give my own translation of the Russian original.
49. Monika Greenleaf, *Pushkin and Romantic Fashion: Fragment, Elegy, Orient, Irony,* Stanford University Press, Stanford, 1994.
50. Sedakova, '"Nesmertnye tainstvennye chuvstv"', p. 12 (typescript).

Casting and Recasting the Caucasian Captive

by

HELENA GOSCILO

For Neia Zorkaia, with admiration and sunny memories

Susan Layton's award-winning 1994 survey of nineteenth-century Russia's literary treatment of the Caucasus assigns Pushkin's *Caucasian Captive* watershed status in the historical evolution of that trend. It does so primarily because enthusiastic readers misconstrued Pushkin's first-hand experience as authentication of his verbal paysage-painting. Unlike earlier poets writing about the Caucasus, he had actually visited the area.[1] Accordingly, just as Christ's mythologized birth enables us to tag events as BC or AD, so Pushkin's 1821 *povest* in verse divides Caucasus-focussed texts into BP ('Before-Pushkin') or PP ('Post-Pushkin') eras.

Drawing on such BP works as Gavrila Derzhavin's ode *On Count Zubov's Return from Persia* (На возвращение графа Зубова из Персии, 1804) and Vasilii Zhukovskii's address *To Voeikov* (К Воейкову, 1814), plus Byron's Eastern tales - automatically relegated to the category of precursors by such a model - Pushkin's *Caucasian Captive* precipitated a veritable Caucasian epidemic. The daunting roster of PP authors' names recited by Layton, and, preceding her, Viktor Zhirmunskii, boasts such Lethe-bound epigones as E. Zaitzevskii, Viktor Tepliakov, Aleksei Meisner, Kondratii Ryleev, and Petr Kamenskii, as well as N. N. Muravev, Bestuzhev-Marlinskii, Lermontov (excerpts of whose youthful, derivative *Caucasian Captive* appeared in 1859), and, eventually, Lev Tolstoi.[2] Included in his anti-Romantic *folk stories*, targetting a readership of children and the newly-literate,[3] Tolstoi's historically-grounded *Caucasian Captive* of 1872 served as the basis for Sergei Bodrov's widely acclaimed film by the same title in 1996, approximately when international condemnation of Russia's ill-judged first war in Chechnia reached a sustained crescendo.

Whereas Layton examines only high-culture texts (Literature with a capital L) and, moreover, excludes ballets by C. Cavos, Boris Asafev, and Aram Khachaturian,[4] as well as César Cui's opera,[5] a year later Neia Zorkaia's *Folklore, Lubok, and Screen* widens the critical lens, to embrace mass culture: *lubochnaia literatura*, *lubki*, *balagan*, and film.[6] Layton's analysis mainly addresses issues of empire, the elaboration of Russia's self-identity vis-à-vis

Asia, and the balance between poetic lyricism and ethnographic verisimilitude. By contrast, Zorkaia's focus accentuates the parallels and divergences between élite and popular inscriptions of the Caucasus phenomenon.

Astutely noting that for Pushkin and Lermontov the Caucasus theme served as a laboratory of genres and types that subsequently flourished in mainstream Literature, Zorkaia traces the sustained vitality of kindred 'exotica' for the masses, which dated from 1840: specifically, N. Zriakhov's *Russians' Battle with the Kabardians, or the Beautiful Mahommedan Maiden Dying on Her Husband's Coffin* (Битва русских с кабардинцами[7] или Прекрасная магометанка, умирающая на гробе своего мужа), which by 1899 circulated in 18 different copies. In the meantime, the year 1854 witnessed the publication of the anonymous *Russians' Battle with the Kabardians, or the Beautiful Zemira Dying on Her Husband's Tomb* (Битва русских с кабардинцами, или Прекасная Земира, умирающая на могиле своего мужа), followed by N. Zriakhov's *Russians' Battle with the Kabardians, or the Beautiful Moslem Maiden Dying on Her Friend's Grave* (Битва русских с кабардинцами, или Прекасная мусульманка, умирающая на могиле своего друга), and so on and so forth, in a dizzying flurry of *Battles* and *Beautiful Dying* 'fill in the blank'.

Eleven additional variations on this prose narrative appeared between 1865 and 1909,[8] indexing the irresistible fascination for Russian readers from various social strata of foreign women with lots of dark hair volubly expiring on their beloveds' tombs in sultry heat amidst tall mountains.[9] The distinctive feature of these tales is the indefatigable, largely anonymous reworking of the ready-made - precisely what constitutes anathema for Literature, which, ideally, bears the 'unique creative imprint' of a given author.[10] Chief among the formulas migrating virtually unchanged from one edition to another were the heroic but doomed Russian protagonist and the passionate 'native' beauty, as well as picturesque surroundings, 'ethnic' mores, weaponry, and battles.

Polarization of characters (with enemies as evil incarnate), idealization of the protagonists, patriotism, advocation of fidelity to the grave (indeed, on it), and, in the illustrations accompanying the text, a preoccupation with the decorative garb of the 'exotic' *deva gor* (*maiden of the mountains*) marked practically all versions of this stirring scenario.[11] *Lubki* and *balagan* eventually mined the titillating promise of the verbal text - which dwelled on the heroine's lithe waist and generous breasts - by visually spotlighting the bangles, baubles, pantaloons, veil, and progressively more abbreviated top garment clothing her seductive body: conventional signs of alien mystery and allure later exploited to potent erotic effect by Sergei Diagilev's *Ballets russes*.

My selective examination of contemporary (that is, late twentieth-century) works on the Caucasian theme, condensed here into an outline, cuts across genres and high/low distinctions, to pinpoint the modern revisions wrought upon these two overlapping paradigms from the preceding century. Omitting Bodrov's film, my discussion restricts itself to three highly popular works: Leonid Gaidai's 1966 film, *Kavkazskaia plennitsa*, the unparalleled box office hit of 1967, which drew an astonishing seventy-six-plus million viewers; Tamara Gverdtsiteli's signature song, likewise titled *Kavkazskaia plennitsa*, probably from the 1980s; and Vladimir Makanin's *Kavkazskii plennyi*,[12] which caused a minor sensation among Russian critics, many of whom credited Makanin with prophetic vision: though printed in the April 1995 issue of *Novyi mir*, the story was completed in September 1994, 'anticipating', as it were, Russia's first calamitous war in Chechnia.[13] All three works presume audience familiarity with Pushkin's text while distancing themselves from it, Gaidai through humour that repeatedly slides into slapstick comedy; Gverdtsiteli through a domestication that defuses tragedy; and Makanin through a gender displacement mediated by Dostoevskii that transfigures banality into a dilemma of vital aesthetic and political urgency.

The irreducible components of Pushkin's verse tale arguably amount to (1) an 'exotic' setting; (2) a catalogue of the physical traits and social habits of an alien culture; (3) the nameless, disillusioned, self-absorbed Russian male prisoner; (4) his vaguely beautiful, masochistic, 'ethnic' rescuer; (5) the compressed love plot, culminating with his escape and her death; and (6) in the framing dedication and especially epilogue, the chauvinistic diatribe of militaristic empire that so distressed Viazemskii.[14]

Gaidai's comedy decrowns Pushkin's tragic vision in every conceivable way, starting with the film's trivializing subtitle (*Or the New Adventures of Shurik* [*или новые приключения Шурика*]), and continuing with the coyly self-conscious non-specificity of the locale and the stumbling, good-natured naïveté of the male protagonist, Shurik - a callow ethnographer collecting such folklore material as songs, toasts, and samples of rituals that purportedly reflect national identity. Pushkin's unfathomable beauty metamorphoses into Nina, a perky *komsomolka* athlete on holiday from a pedagogical institute, whom a sleazy local Party boss (the arch-villain of *lubochnaia literatura*, turned buffoon and Stalin clown-clone), seizes for his bride.[15]

The love plot, with its gender-reversed rescue at a river, teems with comic inanities and Three-Stooges gags, and concludes with the happy couple riding off on the donkey that first brought Shurik to the area. Donkeydom rules the film. Devices of repetition and acceleration, as well as the ubiquity of drunkenness, deliberately mistimed or misapplied Soviet clichés (for example, Arkadii Raikin's 'Woman is a friend to mankind'), and ludicrous juxtapositions of elements from incompatible realms thoroughly deromanticize (even carnivalize) the Caucasian theme. Indeed, the locale emerges not as a colourful operatic backdrop for seething passions, but as part of the all too familiar Soviet environment, in which corruption, self-oblivious inebriation, and a time-sanctioned system of mundane quid pro quos thrives unchecked.

If Gaidai's *Kavkazskaia plennitsa* assimilates the Caucasus into the bosom of what Stalin troped as the ideologically-bonded Big Family that was the

Soviet nation, Gverdtsiteli's *Kavkazskaia plennitsa* domesticates the Caucasian scenario through the 'little family' of the individual Soviet citizen, thus scaling down the dimensions of the kidnapped bride motif.[16] Specifically, the song's lyrics unfold the personal story of Gverdtsiteli's biological parents: the Georgian (*not* Russian) prince who, enamoured at first glance of a beautiful princess in Odessa, carries her off to Tbilisi.[17] Through a handful of eloquent details (mist, mountains, sea, and the *lezginka*), the song conveys geographical displacement (now of the female), with the music and the doubling of southern settings operating as signs of 'exoticism'.

Yet the amorous couple normalizes relations, to the extent of marrying and producing a family, as attested by Gverdtsiteli's very existence, which functions as an 'autobiographical' frame, à la Pushkin, for the narrative proper. The other Pushkinian elements of beauty, capture, and intriguingly foreign surroundings are also retained, but their impact and significance modified by the concrete evidence of generational succession, incarnated in the performer/narrator officially recognized as *narodnaia artistka* ('people's artist') - a member, after all, of the Big Family that ostensibly transcends ethnic prejudices and hierarchies, as well as internal imperialism, according to the touted but hollow principle of *druzhba narodov* ('friendship among peoples'). Death and official expansionist ambitions play no role here, and though Gverdtsiteli's remarks preceding her rendition of the song characterize it as 'playful but also sad', gender, not ethnic minority, is the colonized object (a point to which I shall return later).

Particularly when compared to Gaidai's and Gvertsiteli's texts, and, to a lesser extent, Pushkin's, Makanin's revisionary *Kavkazskii plennyi* engages the Caucasus theme within Russian culture in remarkably complex, original, and sophisticated ways. His subtle meditation intertextually summarizes the entire history of that tradition and reconfigures it in an unconventional key. While revisioning its problems, the story preserves virtually all of the major topoi codified by Pushkin: the frame, the 'exotic' locale, the imperialist ideology that fuels military aggression, the 'philosophical' protagonist burdened by memories, the beautiful object of his desire, the death of that object, and the vexed question of who precisely is imprisoned in the Caucasus.

The simple plot recounts the exploits of Rubakhin, a seasoned, thoughtful soldier, and his crude sidekick, the rifleman Vovka, who, broadly speaking, plays Sancho Panza to Rubakhin's Quixote.[18] Indirect, carefully selected indications that the unnamed region is the Caucasus consist of psychologically freighted descriptions of the imposing landscape; a reference to the notorious Aleksei Ermolov, ruthless representative of Russia's political consolidation in the Caucasus during the early nineteenth century; and the use of such words as *aul* ('village'), *kunak* ('blood-brother'), and *churka* - Russians' pejorative slang for a Caucasian or Central Asian.[19] As the soldiers talk, relax, reconnoitre, orchestrate an ambush, and perform other standard military tasks,

Vovka drinks and beds a local woman, while Rubakhin takes prisoner a young man whose dazzling beauty sparks his sexual desire and simultaneously his protective instincts.

Although Makanin refers directly to the hydraulics of male arousal and more discreetly to wet dreams (here called a 'male weakness'), as a writer fiercely independent of literary fads, he never resorts to the shock-seeking strategies of Viktor Erofeev, Igor Iarkevich, and Vladimir Sorokin or the implicit gay-rights advocacy identified with writers contributing to *Risk* and kindred publications. Homoeroticism, while fully acknowledged, serves as a device of estrangement to destabilize timeworn perspectives on the Caucasian theme and recast them, rendering them more intricate. An 'X' rating is not Makanin's goal. Rather, he conceives of the Caucasus from a Russian viewpoint as a mystery, tagged by an 'x' from a different semiotic system.

When Rubakhin, Vovka, and the 'native' prisoner unexpectedly encounter two enemy detachments, Rubakhin strangles/suffocates[20] the young man to prevent him from betraying their unnoticed presence. Haunted in his dreams by memories of the youth's face, he ponders the enigmatic lure of the towering mountains. For the story's central dilemma of beauty, its power and its salvatory potential, Makanin incorporates Dostoevskii into the story's very opening: 'The soldiers, more likely than not, didn't know that *beauty would save the world*, but on the whole both of them knew what beauty is. In the mountains they felt it (a beauty of place) all too well. It frightened them' (p.117).[21]

Via Dostoevskii, the beauty that Pushkin's tale presents mainly as enticing surface becomes an organizing metaphysical conundrum. Dostoevskii's concept of beauty bifurcated into the beauty of Sodom (sensuality, dissonance, formlessness [*bezobrazie*]) and that of the Madonna (spirituality, harmony, unity [the *obraz* that is both form and icon]). In Dmitrii Karamazov's ruminations, the ideal of the latter as a supreme goal degenerates into the former as lived reality ('Man begins with the ideal of the Madonna, yet ends with the ideal of Sodom ... beauty is not only terrible but also a mysterious thing').[22] Inhering in the *perception* of beauty rather than in beauty itself, this dualism is reified in Makanin's young captive (who stimulates sexual appetite/blind, irrational desire) and the mountains (which, in Makanin's scheme of things, awaken memory and, above all, conduce to reflection).[23]

Yet the two forms of beauty, though contrasted through the reactions they elicit, in Makanin are paralled through the shared motifs of silence and speech, most eloquently in the death scene, where the prisoner's struggle - ambiguously presented as an attempt either to breathe or to articulate something - is cut short by Rubakhin's hand. This imposed muteness prefigures the 'mute majesty' of the impressive mountains: 'but what actually did their beauty want to say to him? Why did it call?' (p.154: the text concludes with these words). Rubakhin's curiosity about the mountains' 'message' mirrors his earlier eagerness to hear the captive's voice, and sound first alerts Rubakhin to the youth's presence. By contrasting yet analogizing the beauty of the terrain and its 'native son' ('he [Rubakhin] had no defence against *human* beauty as such [p. 137: emphasis added]'; elsewhere, 'obraz', adverting to the youth's face, carries religious connotations that evoke the Dostoevskian beauty of the Madonna, linked with contemplation: Makanin queries the relationship of one to the other and Russians' perception of both (Russian text, p. 19).

In fact, epistemology here, as in Pushkin, is a key concern,[24] as is the Dostoevskian polarization of essentially religious/spiritual beauty and its sensual, 'demonic' counterpart. If Dmitrii Karamazov perceives a sliding (and descending) scale between the two aesthetic spheres, Makanin intimates the impossibility of distinguishing between and reacting adequately to them. For both Dostoevskii and Makanin, however, beauty belongs to the Feminine, as an attribute either of women or of feminized men (Jesus Christ, Myshkin, Makanin's captive). And while the dilemma is male, its incarnation or symbolization, true to tireless Russian tradition, is female.

Ultimately, the story inscribes Russians' historical relations with the Caucasus as a dire fascination with an enigmatic, seductive culture that may have something to teach an outsider, yet has prompted Russia only to conquer and subjugate. The prisoner is Russia itself, captivated if not captured, as Alibekov makes explicit early in the story (p. 5)[25] and as the final paragraph implies: 'crowding in from the left and right (pressing on his peripheral vision) were those same mountains that surrounded him here and wouldn't let him go' [p.153]). Obsessiveness, invasion, and extermination continue a long-standing national habit, as confirmed in Rubakhin's revealing slip of the tongue: '"How many centuries now!" As if by a slip of the tongue, the words jumped out of a shadow, and in surprise the soldier pondered this quiet thought, which had settled in the depth of his consciousness' (p. 154).[26] Makanin's *Caucasian Captive* echoes Joseph Conrad's *Heart of Darkness*, E.M. Forster's *Passage to India*, and other narratives of colonial dominion where the colonizer in the midst of his alien, 'primitive' surroundings is forced to confront himself, for identity, when all is said and done, defines itself through difference.

Pushkin's *Caucasian Captive*, as Stephanie Sandler and, in her tracks, Luc Beaudoin have argued, projects masculinity as action, decisiveness, militarism, and power, while equating women with nature, silence, and passive submission.[27] His Circassians not only exclude women from communal speech, but arbitrarily determine their fates through exogamy. Their society casts women as captives of male will. After her rebellious liberation of the Russian prisoner, Pushkin's *deva gor* opts for death - the only freedom available to her - rather than marry her father's choice of groom. Women as attractively packaged goods to be traded or seized by force likewise appear, if in less egregious form, in Gaidai and Gverdtsiteli. Makanin deconstructs and problematizes the issue of gender by purposely allotting the only two women in the narrative the stereotypical 'feminine' functions of feeding and providing pleasures of the flesh that Pushkin's poem set firmly in place: Colonel Gurov's wife, Anna Fedorovna, does nothing but make tea and give soldiers food, while the nameless woman parenthetically bedded by Vovka (and reportedly raped earlier by four men) services males sexually. 'She'd like some words of solace, just simple feelings' (p. 125), the narrator observes, but from Vovka she hears, instead, his demand for non-missionary-position intercourse and a bottle of port (Russian text, p. 7).[28]

In short, entrapment in a social pattern of helpless subordination, sexual availability, and psycho-physical victimization are coded as feminine, and Makanin draws attention to that repressive equation through the device of estrangement: he hybridizes the Caucasian prisoner into a beautiful *male* 'native', relentlessly feminized by Rubakhin and his fellow-soldiers precisely because of his physical endowments - the beauty of an oval face, regular features, tender skin, long dark hair, and large dark eyes - evocative of the iconic Madonna, but eliciting 'sodomite'/homoerotic impulses in Rubakhin.[29]

Although men endowed with aesthetic appeal surface in Dostoeskii's texts, true to Russia's unreflexive habit of troping philosophical and political categories as female (wisdom, beauty, nation, etc.), Dostoevskii equated the Christian ideal of beauty with femininity: the passive, self-abnegating, nurturing humility that Village Prose subsequently congealed into the formulaic icon of a timeless, earthbound 'positive womanhood'. In *The Idiot*, that principle of beauty finds unwittingly destructive incarnation in the feminized Prince Myshkin, whose socio-cultural impotence is prefigured in his Swiss-sanatorium retreat from the world and his incapacity throughout the novel to assert the masculine principles so devastatingly enacted by Rogozhin. Myshkin, the 'totally beautiful being', absorbs the feminized traits of epilepsy/hysteria, passivity, prophecy and intuition that Catherine Clément equates with Woman,[30] and at novel's end he retreats into the madness that some feminists identify as unaccommodating woman's sole means of self-expression within a logocentric patriarchy.

Although Makanin codes beauty as feminine - and susceptible to the pseudo-protection of colonialization - he spotlights the self-deluding sexism and bad faith underpinning such predication by transgendering the victim of imperialist desires. Indeed, he pointedly describes Rubakhin's killing of the youth in erotic terms that evoke sexual possession:

> Rubakhin reached his arm back and cautiously touched the body of the prisoner, who trembled slightly, as a woman trembles before an intimate embrace ... Rubakhin slowly drew the youth closer to him ... The youth didn't resist Rubakhin, who, taking him by the shoulder, turned him around toward himself - the youth himself (he was standing slightly below) even drew toward him, pressed closer, sticking his lips below his unshaven chin into the carotid artery.[31] The youth was shaking, not understanding. 'N-n ...,' he weakly breathed out, quite like

a woman who has pronounced her 'no' not as a refusal, but as an expression of modesty, while Rubakhin watched him and waited (guarding against a shriek) ... With his other hand Rubakhin covered both the slighly opened mouth with its beautiful lips and the nose, which was slightly quivering ... His body jerked, legs stiffening, although now unsupported. Rubakhin swept him off the ground. He held him in an embrace to prevent his feet from touching either a sensitive bush or rocks that might stir and make a sound. Blocking any vision, Rubakhin circled his neck with the hand that embraced him. He squeezed; no, beauty didn't manage to save. Several convulsions ... and that was all (pp. 147-8).

Whereas Pushkin's text ends with the self-confident assertion of the Russian male's indifferent - but total - comprehension of the Circassian maiden's death ('he understood everything'), Makanin's concludes with an interrogative confession of bemused bewilderment regarding not only the specific Russian's reaction to the Caucasian, but Russia's prolonged, fatal romance with a region that, judging by today's events in Dagestan and Chechnia, it cannot understand, ignore, or fully appropriate as a jewel for its tarnished crown.

Appendix

Кавказская пленница
Помню в солнечной Одессе
И фонтаны и дома,
Черноморскую принцессу,
Что сводила всех с ума.

Но приехал из Тбилиси
Молодой грузинский князь
И в красавицу влюбился
И решил ее украсть.

И однажды в тумане сиреневом
Он пронзил ее сердцем стрелой.
Моя мама кавказская пленница,
А мой папа то князь удалой.

Ранним утром перегрустном
На тревоге петухи,
А на Малой Арн-амурской
Увидались женихи.

Но зато другим на зависть
В ту далекую весну
В теплой Грузии красавиц
Стало больше на одну.

А на свадьбе шампанское пенится,
Князь танцует лезгинку с женой.
Моя мама кавказская пленница,
А мой папа то князь удалой.

Пусть в Тбилиси нету моря.
А в Одессе нету гор,
Но похож одесский дворик
На тбилисский двор.

Но зато другим на зависть
В ту далекую весну
В теплой Грузии красавиц
Стало больше на одну.

И пока Море Черное пенится
И Арагви окутано мглой
Моя мама кавказская пленница,
А мой папа то князь удалой.

(*The Caucasian Captive*
I remember in sunny Odessa
Both the fountains and the houses
And the Black Sea princess
Who drove everyone mad.

But a young Georgian prince
From Tbilisi arrived and
Fell in love with the beauty
And decided to steal her away.

And once in the lilac mist
He pierced her heart like an arrow.
My mother's a Caucasian captive,
And my father's a dashing prince.

Early one melancholy morning
The cocks crowed the hour,
And on litlle Arn-amour Street
The groom and the bride met.

But then, to others' envy,
In that distant spring
Warm Georgia acquired
One more beauty.

And as the wedding champagne foamed,
The prince danced a lezginka with his wife.
My mother's a Caucasian captive,
And my father's a dashing prince.

So what if Tbilisi has no sea
And Odessa has no mountains;
An Odessan courtyard is
Like a courtyard in Tbilisi.

But then, to others' envy,
In that distant spring

Warm Georgia acquired
One more beauty.

But as long as the Black Sea foams
And the Aragvi is enveloped in mist
My mother's a Caucasian captive,
And my father's a dashing prince.)

NOTES

Affectionate gratitude to Stephanie Sandler for her charitable, transformative reading of this chapter in its original form; to Sasha Prokhorov for assistance with Gaidai; and to Petre Petrov for his recollective 'bib' role in the section pertaining to Dostoevskii.

1. See Susan Layton, *Russian Literature and Empire*, Cambridge University Press, Cambridge, 1994, p. 38.
2. See Layton, op. cit., p. 48 and V.M. Zhirmunskii, *Bairon i Pushkin*, Nauka, Leningrad, 1978, pp. 239-40; for a comparison of various 'captive' narratives spawned by Pushkin's work, see Zhirmunskii, pp. 239-56.
3. See Layton, op. cit., p. 250 and Neia Zorkaia, *Fol'klor. Lubok. Ekran*, 'Iskusstvo', Moscow, 1995, p. 62.
4. As first performed in 1823 at the Bolshoi Theatre in St Petersburg, the ballet had music by C. Cavos; another *Caucasian Captive* was staged at Leningrad's Malyi Theater on 14 April 1938, with music by Boris Asafev; and Khachaturian provided the music for a performance of *The Caucasian Captive* in Paris in 1951.
5. The opera by the nationalistic César Cui (one of the Mighty Five), on which he worked from 1857 to 1882, was produced in 1883. See Lyle K. Neff, 'Story, Style, and Structure in the Operas of César Cui', PhD Dissertation, Indiana University, forthcoming, particularly the analysis in Chapter One of how Cui produced 'musical exoticism'.
6. For definitions of these categories, see Zorkaia, p. 38.
7. The phrase 'bitva s kabardintsami' ('battle with the Kabardians') is a popular idiom in Russian, about which see Zorkaia, op. cit., pp. 62-3.
8. See Zorkaia, op. cit., p. 66.
9. The trend lent credence to Edgar Alan Poe's nauseating dictum that 'The death of a beautiful woman is, unquestionably, the most poetical topic in the world'.
10. As Zorkaia reasons, Zriakhov's name carries no identity, for no traces of it appear in any sources identifying authors, whether they be encyclopedias, dictionaries, or *spravochniki*. For practical purposes, Zriakhov might as well be Mister X: see Zorkaia, op. cit., pp. 62, 70-1.
11. Ibid., pp. 67-8.
12. All three of these titles may equally be rendered into English as *The Caucasian Captive*, although the first two denote a female captive. For the Makanin text, see Vladimir Makanin, *Kavkazskii plennyi*, *Novyi mir*, IV, 1995, pp. 3-19; see also Leonid Gaidai, *Kavkazskaia plennitsa, ili novye prikliucheniia Shurika*, Mosfilm, 1966 and Tamara Gverdtsiteli, *Spasibo, Muzyka, tebe!*, n.d.
13. See Pavel Basinskii, 'Igra v klassiki na chuzhoi krovi', *Literaturnaia gazeta*, XXIII, 7 June 1995, p. 4. and Alla Latynina, 'Ne igra, a prognoz khudozhnika', loc. cit.
14. On this question, see Layton and Stephanie Sandler, *Distant Pleasures: Alexander Pushkin and the Writing of Exile*, Stanford University Press, Stanford, 1989. For insightful commentary on the tale in general, see Luc Beaudoin, *Resetting the Margins: Russian Romantic Verse Tales and the Idealized Woman*, Peter Lang, New York, 1997, also Zhirmunskii, and Sandler, op. cit.
15. Significantly, it is he who summarizes the Caucasus as an 'all-Union smithy'.
16. For the full text of Gverdtsiteli's song, see *Appendix*.
17. The short, compact narrative mimics the plots of fairy tales.

18. Like Sancho Panza, Vovka lives life unthinkingly, in purely physiological terms, at a lower level of possibility than Rubakhin.
19. For explanations of this lexicon, see the notes to the English translation of Makanin's text in *The Loss: A Novella and Two Stories*, translated by Byron Lindsey, Northwestern University Press, Evanston, 1998.
20. The Russian is ambiguous here, leaving uncertain the question of whether the young man dies through strangulation or suffocation.
21. The notion that beauty will save the world appears in Dostoevskii's *The Idiot* (VIII, 1973, p. 317: Ippolit's rather hysterical foreword to his equally manic 'confession': 'Is it true, Prince, that you once said that "beauty" will save the world?'), and, less overtly but more richly, in *The Brothers Karamazov*, in Dmitrii's troubled observation: 'Beauty is a terrible and awful thing! Terrible because it is indefinable, and it is impossible to define because God has only given us puzzles ... another man, even one who is superior in heart and mind, begins with the ideal of the Madonna, and ends with the ideal of Sodom.' (Dostoevskii, XIV, 1976, p. 100). For a discerning examination of beauty as a dualistic entity in Dostoevskii's oeuvre - which, however, does not pursue its argument to its ultimate conclusions - see Robert Louis Jackson, *Dostoevsky's Quest for Form: A Study of His Philosophy of Art*, Yale University Press, New Haven, 1966, chapter entitled 'Two Kinds of Beauty', pp. 40-70.
22. See previous note.
23. See, above all, pp. 3-4 of the Russian text. After his second trip to the Caucasus, for Pushkin the mountains and meditation became inseparable. On this, see G.I. Kusov, ed., *Pushkin i Kavkaz*, Ministerstvo kul'tury i iskusstva Respubliki Severnaia Osetiia-Alaniia, Vladikavkaz, 1999. Throughout his fiction Makanin repeatedly invests vertical spaces with existential value, relying on the standard Romantic associations between mountains and transcendence (see Sermon on the Mount, platonism, Gothic architecture). See especially his *Skhodilos' nebo s kholmami* and *Otstavshii*.
24. On epistemology in Pushkin's work, see Sandler's splendid treatment of the topic.
25. This scene underscores the saliency of perspective to the story and Russians' blind belief in their epistemological supremacy. All events are refracted solely through Russian eyes. Alibekan's insistence that Gurov and his soldiers are prisoners posits other, conflicting viewpoints.
26. Here and elsewhere, the translation has been slightly adjusted for greater accuracy.
27. In this respect, Pushkin's text showcases sexist assumptions.
28. The retrospective story of Gurov's relations with his wife likewise entails her giving him access to food and her body (Makanin, op. cit., p. 8).
29. While the soldiers jeer '"Such ones are loved like a girl!"' (Makanin, op. cit., pp. 11, 12), Rubakhin treats him 'like a woman' (p. 12), staring at the lips that are 'like the lips of a nice young woman' (p. 12), carrying him across a river (p. 12), giving him his own socks (p. 13), adjusting his long hair (p. 14), and so forth.
30. Catherine Clément, 'The Guilty One' in Hélène Cixous and Catherine Clément, *The Newly Born Woman*, translated Betsy Wing, University of Minnesota Press, Minneapolis, 1986, pp. 1-62.
31. Makanin picks up on this moment when subsequently the youth appears to the sexually aroused Rubakhin in his sleep ('son').

Index

Akhmadulina, B. 144, 190, n. 5
Akhmatova, A. 111, 153
Annenkov, P. 3, 54
Auden, W. 158
Austen, J.
   Northanger Abbey 33, n. 4
   Sense and Sensibility 33, n. 4

Bakhtin, M. 51
Batiushkov, K. 45, n. 1, 159
   The Song of Harald the Brave 39, 45, n. 10
Bayley, J. 1, 6
Belinskii, V. 3, 166
Belyi, A. 49, 50
   Silver Dove, The 51
Berdiaev, N. 49, 50-1, 62, n. 19
Bitov, A.
   Pushkin House 136
Blok, A. 1, 50, 62, n. 6, 92, 119, n. 21, 177
   'Oh my Russia, my wife' 49
   On the Field of Kulikovo 49
Bodrov, S. 195, 196-7
Brodsky, J. 7, 10-11, 153-74, 188, 190, n. 5
   1972 161, 166
   Christmas Romance 155
   At the Pushkin Monument in Odessa 167, 169, 175
   Conversation with a Celestial Being 168
   Edification 161
   From the Margin to the Centre 168
   Great Elegy to John Donne 165, 166
   Hundred Years' War 155
   Isaak and Abraham 165
   Lagoon 163
   Letter to General Z., A 164, 168
   Letter to the Academy 169
   Lines on the Winter Campaign 164
   Lithuanian Nocturne 155, 168
   Lullaby of Cape Cod 165
   'Neither country nor parish' 155
   On the Death of a Friend 167
   Performance, A 167
   Petersburg Novel 165
   Polonaise: Variation 169
   Roman Elegies 159
   Sonnet on the Occasion of Lena Valikhan's and Alik Dobrovolskii's Marriage, A 167
   Stop in the Desert, A 154
   To Evgenii 163
   Twenty Sonnets to Mary Queen of Scots 167, 168
Byron, Lord 31, 40, 44, 51, 52, 62, n. 19, 87, n. 14, 114, 118, n. 10, 119, n. 17, 195

Chekhov, A. 139
Chernyshevskii, N. 2, 53-4
   'The Russian Man at a rendezvous' 54
   What Is To Be Done? 54
Conrad, J.
   Heart of Darkness 200

Dante 5, 162, 171, n. 10, 177, 181, 182, 184
   Inferno 177
Derzhavin, G. 162, 195
Diaghilev, S. 196
Dobroliubov, N. 2

Dostoevskii, F. 1, 3, 5, 8, 15, 54, 143, 144, 148, 197, 201
  Bobok 107
  Brothers Karamazov, The 51, 199-200
  Crime and Punishment 53, 65, n. 62, 133, n. 12
  Devils, The 51, 53, 62, n. 19
  Idiot, The 53, 199-201
  Netochka Nezvanova 28-30
  Poor Folk 28-30
Dovlatov, S. 5, 6, 7, 10, 135-51
  Sanctuary, The 5, 6, 135-51
  Zone, The 137, 138, 141
Druzhinin, A. 3

Eikhenbaum, B. 68, 69, 179
Erofeev, V. 143
Esenin, S. 137
Evtushenko, E. 144, 146, 147

Fedotov, G. 49
Fet, A. 67
Flaubert, G.
  Madame Bovary 33, n. 3
folk literature 18, 21, 52-3, 56, 186
Fonvizin, D.
  The Minor 58
Forster, E.
  Passage to India, A 200

Gaidai, L,
  Kavkazskaia plennitsa 197-8, 200
Gan, E. 6, 8, 9, 15, 18, 25-8
  Futile Gift, A 28, 30
  Ideal, The 25-8, 30, 32
  Society's Judgement 25-8
Gverdtsiteli, T.
  Kavkazskaia plennitsa 197-8, 200
Goethe, J. 92, 136
  Werther 52

Gogol, N. 2, 54, 55
  Dead Souls 53, 63, n. 23
  Diary of a Madman 65, n. 62
  Overcoat, The 125, 128, 130-1, 134, n. 32
  Portrait, The 53
  Terrible Vengeance 49
Goncharov, N. 8
  Oblomov 53, 54
  Precipice, The 54
Gordin, Ia. 154, 166, 167
Griboedov, A.
  Woe from Wit 54, 58
Grigorev, A. 3, 5, 6, 79
Gumilev, N. 130

Herzen, A. 55-6
  Who is to Blame? 54
Homer 69

Iskander, F. 143
Ivanov, G. 4-5, 7-8, 121-34
  'All is unchanging . . . ' 122-4
  Disintegration of the Atom 4-5, 10, 121-34
  Petersburg Winters 122
  'You did not catch my words ...' 129
Ivanov, V. 49, 50, 51

Karamzin, N. 23, 37, 45, n. 1, 146
Kheifits, M. 156, 157
Khlebnikov, V. 177
Khodasevich, V. 125-6
Kibirov, T. 11
  To Serezha Gandelevskii 175, 188
Kireevskii, I. 2
Krivulin, V. 154, 162, 171, n. 10
Kruchenykh, A. 7-8, 127-8, 130, 134, n. 21
Kushner, A. 166

Lacan, J. 6, 85, 88, n. 29
Lermontov, M. 8, 62, n. 19, 82, 137, 195-6
 Three Palms 178-9, 181
Limonov, E. 166
Loseff, L. 154, 155, 156, 165
Lotman, Iu. 8, 20, 34, n. 19, 35, n. 44, 51-2, 53, 54, 88, n. 20, 88, n. 21, 105, 107, 138, 144, 147-8, 153, 162, 172, n. 29, 173, n. 46

Maiakovskii, V. 4
Mandelstam, O. 126, 177
Makanin, V. 7, 8, 10
 Kavkazskii plennyi 197-202
Mérimée, P. 186
Mickiewicz, A. 12, n. 11
Milosz, Cz. 165

Nabokov, V. 10, 19, 33, n. 10, 34, n. 18, 105-20
 Death 10, 105-20
 Eye, The 107
Naiman, A. 154, 166
Nekrasov, N. 49, 62, n. 5, 177
Nietzsche, F. 49

Odoevskii, A. 8, 9, 15
 Princess Zizi 24-5, 27, 28, 29-30, 32

Pasternak, B. 6, 8, 91, 92, 96, 98, 99, 101, 102, 188
 Miracle, The 178-9, 181-2
 Doctor Zhivago 179
Pisarev, D. 2, 3
Plato 15
 Republic, The 15
Platonov, A. 3
Prigov, D. 11, 190, n. 3
 Captivating Star of Russian Poetry, The 175

Pushkin, A.
 and Arzamas 37
 and the Decembrists 1, 187
 jubilees 2, 3, 4-5, 77-8, 79, 82, 125, 136
 'Again I have visited ...' 168
 Album Verses 167
 Arion 167
 Battle is familiar to Me 160
 Blizzard, The 8, 15, 17, 21-4, 25, 27, 28, 30, 32
 Black Shawl 43, 184
 Boris Godunov 38, 137
 Bronze Horseman, The 128-9, 131, 153, 163, 172, n.27, 188
 Captain's Daughter, The 95, 141, 144
 Carousing Students, The 158
 Caucasian Captive, The 2, 7, 8, 149, n.6, 195-202, 205, n.4
 Covetous Knight, The 80
 Dubrovskii 140-1
 Egyptian Nights 119, n.17
 Elegy 160, 161
 Epistle to A.M. Gorchakov 158
 Evgenii Onegin 2, 6, 7, 8, 15-25, 27, 28, 29, 31-2, 33, n.9, 33, n.14, 34, 35, n.44, 46, n.12, 51-4, 55, 74, 93-4, 166, 169, 177
 Exegi Monumentum 128
 Feast During the Plague 119, n.17
 Fountain of Bakhchisarai, The 7, 38, 39-41, 43, 44, 46, n.14
 'God, don't let me go mad' 168
 Gypsies, The 79
 Imitation of the Koran 178, 181-2, 184, 188-9
 'In the small square ...' 68
 'It's time my friend, it's time ...' 158, 164
 Kleopatra 119, n.17

'Little Bird' 133, n.11
Little Town, A 161
My Genealogy 160
'My Vision of the Russian Theatre' 37
'On the Hills of Georgia' 10, 121-3, 125-31, 132, n.5, 132, n.7, 133, n.20
Peasant-Lady 9, 16, 69-74
Prophet, The 168
Queen of Spades, The 38, 43, 53
Reminiscences in Tsarskoe Selo 169
Rusalka 119, n.17
Ruslan and Liudmila 7, 38, 39, 45, n.6, 155
Shot, The, 32
'Should I wander ...' 160
Sleep 157, 160
Songs of the Western Slavs 184-9
'Southern Poems, The' 7, 38, 40, 119, n.17
Stone Guest, The 10, 82, 92, 102, 105-20, 172, n.27
Tales of Belkin, The 8, 9, 15, 21-4, 32, 67, 69-74, 144, 146-7, 150, n.16
Tale of the Dead Tsarevna, The 169
'The guests gathered at the dacha' 65
To Baroness M.A. Delvig 160
To Delvig 153
To Her 160
To Iurev 159
To My Aristarkh 157, 158
To Natalia 158
To Prince A.M. Gorchakov 160
To Viazemskii 163
Undertaker, The 32
Wanderer 184

Richardson, S. 16, 19, 34, n. 35, 52
 Clarissa 17, 24-5, 27
Romanticism 8, 15-21, 23-24, 30-2, 38, 52, 58, 63, n. 23, 74, 119, n. 17, 122, 126, 157, 159
Rousseau, J-J. 16, 19, 52
 Julie 17, 20, 21, 22, 23, 25, 33, n. 14, 56
Rozanov, V. 4, 6, 49, 50, 77-89

Sedakova, O. 5, 10, 11, 175-93
 Ballad of Continuation 8, 9, 177-89
 Consolation 184-6
 Dream, A 186
 Elegies 186
 Fifth Stanzas 178
 Iambs 186
 Marching Song 186
 Old Songs 177, 184-7, 190, n.6
 Poems in the Manner of Alexander Pope 186
 Wild Rose, The 177, 186, 188, 190, n. 6
Sentimentalism 15-24, 38
Scott, Sir Walter 41, 44
 Ivanhoe 43
Shakespeare, W. 6, 7, 44, 163
 Hamlet 12, n. 17
 Macbeth 12, n. 17
 Merchant of Venice,The 43
Shakhovskoi, A. 7, 37-47
 Deborah 43
 Fin 38-9, 40, 46, n. 11, 46, n. 12
 Kerim-Girei 39-44, 46, n. 16
 Khrisomania or the Love of Money 43
 Mermaid, The 45, n. 6, 46, n.12
Shestov, L. 12, n. 17
Shishkov, A. 37, 151, n. 33
Shklovskii, V. 68

Silver Age, The 8, 49-51
Siniavskii, A. 4, 11, 144
   Strolls with Pushkin 5, 136, 149, n. 7
society tale 7, 24-8
Sokhanskaia, N. 2, 36, n. 71
Solovev, V. 49, 50, 82
Solzhenitsyn, A. 143, 144, 149, n.7
   Matriona's House 146
de Staël, Mme 17, 26
   Delphine 17, 25
Stendhal
   Le Rouge et le Noir 33, n. 3, 56
Strakhov, N. 67
Sumarokov, A.
   Dimitrii the Impostor 58

Tolstoi, L. 7, 9, 139, 143, 148, 195
   Anna Karenina 9, 67-75, 137
   War and Peace 63, n. 23, 69
Tsvetaeva, M. 2, 4, 5, 6, 78-9, 89, n. 30, 91-104, 158
   Meeting with Pushkin 91
   My Pushkin 4, 89, n. 30, 91, 92-3, 99, 133, n. 20
   Natalia Goncharova 95
   Poem of the End 99
   Poems to Pushkin 91, 96-7, 99-101, 175
   'Pushkin and Pugachev' 95

Turgenev, I. 8, 9, 54, 58, 133, n. 15, 143
   Asia 54
   Fathers and Children 53
   Home of the Gentry 63, n. 23
Tynianov, Iu. 37

Venclova, T. 155, 158, 168
Viazemskii, P. 39, 45, n. 1, 197
village prose 139-41, 146, 147, 201
Virgil 5
   Æneid, The 15
Vladimov, G. 143
Voznesenskii, A. 144, 166-7

Zabolotskii, N. 8, 187
   Lake in the Forest, A 182-4
   Celebration of Agriculture, The 183
Zhukova, M. 8, 15
   Dacha on the Peterhof Road, The 30-3
Zhukovskii, V. 37, 45, n. 1, 55, 177, 195
   Song of an Arab at the Grave of his Steed 178-9, 181
Zoshchenko, M. 143

OHIO UNIVERSITY LIBRARY
Please return this book as soon as you have finished with it. In order to avoid a fine it must be returned by the latest date stamped below. All books are subject to recall after two weeks or immediately if needed for reserve.

CF